DISCARD

An Index to Criticisms
of
British and American Poetry

compiled by

Gloria Stark Cline

and

Jeffrey A. Baker

The Scarecrow Press, Inc.
Metuchen, N.J.   1973

Library of Congress Cataloging in Publication Data

Cline, Gloria Stark.
   An index to criticisms of British and American
poetry.

   Bibliography: p.
   1. English poetry--History and Criticism--Indexes.
2. American poetry--History and criticism--Indexes.
3. English poetry--Indexes. 4. American poetry--
Indexes. I. Baker, Jeffrey A., joint author.
II. Title.
PR89.C5   821'.009   73-15542
ISBN 0-8108-0684-3

In Memory of

JOEL STARK

Apr. 15, 1897 - Oct. 26, 1972

PREFACE

This book was developed to serve as a ready-reference source for criticisms of poems by British and American poets. The entire realm of English language prosody from the earliest period to the twentieth century is encompassed. A total of 2,862 criticisms of 1,510 poems by 285 poets is included.

The books and periodicals indexed were selected primarily on the basis of their availability in college and university libraries. Only collections of criticisms were examined, more than half of which had been listed in Essay and General Literature Index. The periodicals selected for indexing were thought to be common to most college and university libraries. Emphasis was placed upon criticisms suitable for use by undergraduate students. However, because of the scholarly nature of a number of the periodicals indexed, graduate students will also find this book useful. In general, materials indexed were dated during the eleven-year period from 1960 through the end of 1970. Some books copyrighted earlier than 1960, however, were indexed in the original card file from which this book evolved; they were retained in the final listing. A number of the periodicals indexed started publication shortly before 1960 and had not been analyzed for poetry criticisms earlier. Thus the beginning volumes of these periodicals were also examined.

An effort was made to include criticisms of poems by living authors, 105 of whom are listed. Because of the present emphasis on black literature in university curricula, an attempt was made to locate articles on Afro-American poetry. The compilers listed the names of approximately fifty well-known black poets. A thorough search for criticisms of their works was made of the PMLA Bibliography and Essay and General Literature Index for 1960 through 1970, and of Darwin T. Turner's Afro-American Writers (Appleton, 1970). Unfortunately the search resulted in only a very limited number of criticisms, most of which were

v

of a general nature. Since most of the materials on black poetry were written very recently, there is reason to hope that there will soon be an adequate number of serious critical studies in this area.

The text is divided into two parts. Part One is a listing of poets, poem titles, and critic citations. It is alphabetically arranged by poet's surname. Birth and death date and nationality are included for each poet. Articles of a general nature on a poet's work are listed under the heading "General." All other references are listed under poem titles. Cross references are provided in Part One for pseudonyms and variant titles by which poems are known. Emily Dickinson's poems are listed under first line with poem number in parentheses for each. Gerard Manley Hopkins' poems are identified by title and corresponding number is provided for each. Milton's sonnets are listed under sonnet number with cross references from title and, in some cases, first lines. Since Shakespeare's sonnets are known by number, they are listed in this order. First lines are also provided for his sonnets. In Part One, criticism citations provide only the critic's name and page number. Since The Explicator uses item numbers rather than page numbers, item numbers are given for these entries. To locate complete source information, it is necessary to refer to Part Two.

Part Two lists 1, 865 entries under critics' surnames. Complete bibliographical information is given here. Periodical abbreviations are used throughout Part Two. The List of Periodical Abbreviations precedes Part One. Where a critic has written more than one article, entries are assigned numbers in brackets following his name. For example, the entry "Perrine [9]" as it appears in Part One means that the user should refer to Perrine's ninth entry in Part Two for complete information.

An Index to Poem Titles is included at the end of the volume.

Miss Dora Mae Thibodeaux, Reference Librarian, retired, University of Southwestern Louisiana, provided valuable assistance to the compilers when the work first began. She helped to set up the criteria which were used, and she contributed much to the original card file. Her help and encouragement were sincerely appreciated. Robert W. Cline did much of the proof-reading, pointed out inconsistencies, and was very helpful in the final organization of the manuscript. His efforts were appreciated a great deal.

Gloria Stark Cline
Jeffrey A. Baker

TABLE OF CONTENTS

LIST OF PERIODICAL ABBREVIATIONS

AL	American Literature
AR	Antioch Review
ArQ	Arizona Quarterly
BW	Black World
CE	College English
CLAJ	College Language Association Journal
ConL	Contemporary Literature
ConP	Concerning Poetry
CritQ	Critical Quarterly
Criticism	Criticism
Discourse	Discourse
EJ	English Journal
ES	English Studies
Expl	Explicator
Freedomways	Freedomways
HudR	Hudson Review
JEGP	Journal of English and Germanic Philology
JNH	Journal of Negro History
JPC	Journal of Popular Culture
KR	Kenyon Review
LanM	Les Langues Modernes
MLN	Modern Language Notes
MP	Modern Philology
MR	Massachusetts Review
NALF	Negro American Literature Forum
NegroD	Negro Digest
Phylon	Phylon
PLL	Papers on Language and Literature
PMLA	PMLA
Poetry	Poetry
PQ	Philological Quarterly
RES	Review of English Studies
SBL	Studies in Black Literature
SEL	Studies in English Literature 1500-1900
SHR	Southern Humanities Review
SoR	Southern Review
SouthwestR	Southwest Review
SP	Studies in Philology
SR	Sewanee Review
SUS	Susquehanna University Studies
TSLL	Texas Studies in Literature and Language
UR	University Review
VP	Victorian Poetry
VS	Victorian Studies

PART I

POETS, POEMS, CRITIC CITATIONS

AIKEN, CONRAD POTTER (1889-   ), American

    General
        Aldrich, 485-520.

    "Dead Leaf in May"
        Zigerell [1], item 5.

AMMONS, A. R.   (1926-   ), American

    General
        Howard, Richard [1], 1-17.

ANONYMOUS

    "Andreas"
        Clark, George, 654-55.
        Frey, 295-97.

    "Assembly of Ladies"
        Pearsall, Derek, 229-37.

    "Battle of Brunanburh"
        Bolton, 363-72.
        Lipp, 166-77.

    "Battle of Maldon
        Swanton, 441-50.

    "Beowulf"
        Baum, 389-99.
        Blake, 278-87.
        Cherniss [2], 473-86.
        Clark, George, 655-59.

ANONYMOUS   (cont'd)

ANONYMOUS   (cont'd)

"Seafarer"
        Cherniss [1], 146-49.
        Greenfield [2], 212-20.
        Pheifer, 282-84.

"Sir Gawain and the Green Knight"
        Bercovitch [1], 30-37.
        Donner, 306-15.
        Halverson [2], 133-39.
        Hieatt, 339-59.
        Lamba and Lamba [2], item 47.
        McAlindon, 121-39.
        Malarkey and Toelken, 14-20.
        Manning, 165-77.
        Mills, 612-30.

"Soul's Address to the Body"
        Ferguson, Mary Heyward, 72-80.

"Sunset on Calvary"
        Reiss, 375-76.

"Wanderer"
        Dean, 141-43.
        Frey, 294-95.
        Greenfield [2], 212-20.

"Wel, Qwa Sal Thir Hornes Blau"
        Reiss, 377-79.

"Wife's Lament" (Exeter Book)
        Bambas, 303-09.
        Davis, Thomas M., 291-305.
        Fitzgerald, Robert P. [2], 769-77.
        Stevick, 21-25.
        Ward, J. A., 26-33.

"Wynter Wakeneth Al My Care"
        Miller, Lewis H., Jr. [2], 316-17.

"Young Waters"
        Hardy, John Edward, 1-21.

ARENSBERG, WALTER CONRAD (1878-1954),   American

"Portrait"
        Fields, Kenneth [1], 326-27.

"Sleeping Beauty"
        Fields, Kenneth [1], 324-25.

"Voyage a L'Infini"
        Fields, Kenneth [1], 322-24.

ARNOLD, MATTHEW (1822-1888), British

General
        Coursen [2], 569-81.
        Going [3], 387-406.
        Johnson, Wendell Stacy [1], 109-16.
        Reed, John R. [1], 15-24.

"Balder Dead"
        Ryals [1], 67-81.

"Cadmus and Harmonia"
        Ray, Linda Lee, 315-16.

"Dover Beach"
        Askew, 293.
        Cadbury [1], 126-38.
        Feshbach, 271-75.
        Knoepflmacher, 21-24.
        Racin, 49-54.
        Thompson, William I., 34-35.

"Empedocles on Etna"
        Barksdale, 88-95.
        Johnson, Wendell Stacy [1], 115.
        Miller, J. Hillis [2], 215-16.
        Ray, Linda Lee, 309-20.
        Reed, John R. [1], 16.

"Forsaken Merman"
        Fulweiler [1], 208-22.

"Haworth Churchyard"
        Perloff [3], 314-20.

ARNOLD (cont'd)

"In Utrumque Paratus"
      Gordon, 192-96.

"Last Glen"
      Ray, Linda Lee, 312-14.

"New Sirens"
      Allott, 156-58.

"Resignation"
      Knoepflmacher, 18-21.
      Middlebrook, 291-97.
      Sundell [4], 259-64.

"Rugby Chapel"
      Johnson, Wendell Stacy [2], 107-13.
      Middlebrook, 291-97.
      Waller, 633-46.

"Scholar-Gipsy"
      Eggenschwiler [1], 1-9.
      Wilkenfeld [1], 117-28.

"Shakespeare"
      Frierson, 137-40.
      Greenberg [2], 723-33.
      Truss, item 56.

"Sohrab and Rustum"
      Walker, 151-56.

"Stanzas from the Grande Chartreuse"
      Alaya [2], 237-54.
      Boo [2], item 69.
      Reed, John R. [1], 17-19.

"Strayed Reveller"
      Gottfried, Leon A., 403-09.
      Sundell [3], 161-70.

"Thyrsis"
      Delaura [1], 191-202.
      Eggenschwiler [1], 9-11.
      Giannone, 71-80.

"Tristram and Iseult"
    Farrell, John P., 335-38.
    Johnson, Wendell Stacy [1], 113-15.
    Kendall, 140-45.
    Sundell [2], 272-83.

"Typho"
    Ray, Linda Lee, 316-17.

"World and the Quietist"
    Greenberg [1], 284-90.

ASHBERY, JOHN LAWRENCE (1927-   ), American

General
    Howard, Richard [1], 18-37.

"Illustration"
    Howard, Richard [1], 26-27.

"White Paper"
    Stepanchev, 190.

AUDEN, WYSTAN HUGH (1907-   ), British

General
    Replogle, 481-95.

"Bride in the 30's"
    Hardy, Barbara, 666-68.

"Change of Air"
    Ostroff [1], 168-87.
    Ostroff [2], 190-208.

"Christmas 1940"
    Eagleton, 182.

"Dover 1937"
    Eagleton, 185-87.

"Fish in the Unruffled Lakes"
    Bauerle, Ruth H., item 57.

"Healthy Spot"
    Satterwhite, item 57.

AUDEN (cont'd)

"In Memory of Sigmund Freud"
    Callan, 350-51.

"In Memory of W. B. Yeats"
    Callan, 346-50.
    Drew, E. A., 170-75.
    Eagleton, 187-89.
    Rosenheim, 422-25.

"In Praise of Limestone"
    Parkin [3], 295-304.

"In Sickness and in Health"
    Hardy, Barbara, 668-69.

"Lay Your Sleeping Head, My Love"
    Caswell [1], item 44.

"Malverns"
    Hardy, Barbara, 665-66.

"Memorial for the City"
    Hardy, Barbara, 670-71.

"Mundus et Infans"
    Thornburg, item 33.

"Musee des Beaux Arts"
    Bluestone [2], 331-36.
    Eagleton, 179-81.
    Kinney, 529-31.

"1929"
    Hardy, Barbara, 657-62.

"Now the Leaves Are Falling Fast"
    Drew, E. A., 22-26.

"Orators"
    Sellers [1], 455-64.

"Paysage Moralise"
    Drew, E. A., 79-81.

"Petition"
        Drew, E. A., 49-51.

"Questioner Who Sits So Sly"
        Chatman, item 21.

"September 1, 1939"
        Drew, E. A., 107-111.

"Song for St. Cecilia's Day"
        Hough, Ingeborg, item 35.

"Summer Night, 1933"
        Hardy, Barbara, 662-664.

"Surgical Ward"
        Eagleton, 181.

"Two Worlds"
        Hardy, Barbara, 664-665.

"Wanderer"
        Robertson, item 70.

BARAKA, IMAMU
    See Jones, Le Roi

BEAUMONT, JOSEPH (1616-1699), British

    "Psyche"
        Stanwood, 533-50.

BERRYMAN, JOHN (1914-1972), American

    General
        Kostelanetz, 340-47.
        Rosenthal [1], 118-30.

    "Winter Landscape"
        Evans, Arthur and Catherine Evans, 309-18.

BETJEMAN, SIR JOHN (1906-), British

    General
        Wiehe, 37-49.

BISHOP, ELIZABETH (1911-), American

"At the Fishhouses"
     Stepanchev, 78-79.

"Chemin de Fer"
     Stepanchev, 75-76.

"Jeronimo's House"
     Emig, 222-23.

"The Poem as Puzzle"
     Emig, 223-24.

BISHOP, JOHN PEALE (1892-1944), American

"Ballet"
     Moore, S. C., item 12.

"A Recollection"
     Stallman, item 43.

BLAKE, WILLIAM (1757-1827), British

General
          Fisher, 1-18.
          Hirsch, E. D., Jr. [2], 373-90.
          Wimsatt, 147-73.

"Ah, Sun-Flower" (Songs of Experience)
     Simons, 301-02.

"Auguries of Innocence"
     DeSelincourt, 148-49.
     Grant, John E. [1], 489-508.

"Book of Thel"
     Johnson, Mary Lynn, 258-77.
     Raine [1], 420-21.

"Chimney Sweeper" (Songs of Experience)
     Barnes, T. R., 155.

"Chimney Sweeper" (Songs of Innocence)
     Barnes, T. R., 154-55.
     McGlynn, item 20.

"Clod and the Pebble" (Songs of Experience)
        Schulz [2], 217-24.

"Crystal Cabinet"
        Raine [1], 400-01.

"Divine Image" (Songs of Innocence)
        Smith, David J., item 69.

"The Fly" (Songs of Experience)
        Stevenson, 77-82.

"The Four Zoas; Night the Ninth"
        Wenger, item 53.

"The Gates of Paradise"
        Raine [1], 360-61, 364-65.

"Holy Thursday" (Songs of Experience)
        Barnes, T. R., 156-57.

"Holy Thursday" (Songs of Innocence)
        Barnes, T. R., 155-56.

"Imitation of Pope: a Compliment to the Ladies"
        Bacon [1], item 79.

"Jerusalem"
        Kiralis, 193-210.
        Raine [1], 442-49.
        Rose, Edward J. [1], 400-23.
        Rose, Edward J. [2], 47-58.
        Rose, Edward J. [3], 587-606.
        Rose, Edward J. [5], 111-25.

"Little Girl Lost" (Songs of Innocence)
        Drake, 543-45.
        Raine [1], 386-90.
        Wittreich [1], item 61.

"Little Vagabond" (Songs of Experience)
        Baine [1], item 6.

"London" (Songs of Experience)
        Barnes, T. R., 157-58.
        Hill, Archibald A. [1], 1095-1105.

BLAKE (cont'd)

"Marriage of Heaven and Hell"
    Raine [1], 421-23.

"Mental Traveller"
    Enscoe, 400-13.
    Raine [1], 405-19.

"Milton"
    Raine [1], 439-42.

"Poetical Sketches"
    DeSelincourt, 135-37.

"Poison Tree"
    Barnes, T. R., 158-59.

"Pretty Epigram for the Entertainment of Those Who
    Have Paid Great Sums in the Venetian and Flemish
    Ooze"
    Bacon [2], item 79.

"Sick Rose" (Songs of Experience)
    Anshutz and Cummings, item 32.
    Drake, 547.
    Rose, Edgar Smith, 350-52.

"Songs of Experience"
    DeSelincourt, 140-44.

"Songs of Innocence"
    DeSelincourt, 137-44.
    Howard, John [2], 390-99.

"To Autumn"
    Gleckner, 544-46.

"To Spring"
    Gleckner, 541-42.

"To Summer"
    Gleckner, 542-44.

"To the Accuser of This World"
    Rose, Edward J. [4], item 37.

"To Winter"
        Gleckner, 546-48.

"The Tyger" (Songs of Experience)
        Adams, Hazard [2], 18-37.
        Bacon [3], item 35.
        Baine [2], 488-98.
        Brennan, 406-07.
        Drake, 545-46.
        Grant, John E. [2], 38-60.
        Kaplan, Fred [1], 617-27.
        Miner, Paul, 59-73.
        Parsons, Coleman O., 573-92.
        Raine [1], 424-29, 436.
        Robinson, Fred C. [2], 666-69.

"Vala" (or "The Four Zoas")
        Raine [1], 373-79.

BLUNDEN, EDMUND CHARLES (1896-   ), British

"Third Ypres"
        Bergonzi [1], 71-72.

" 'Transport Up' at Ypres"
        Bergonzi [1], 69.

BLUNT, WILFRID SCAWEN (1840-1922), British

"Esther"
        Going [4], 74-77, 83.

"Love Sonnets of Proteus"
        Going [4], 70-74, 82.

"Natalia's Resurrection"
        Going [4], 77-78.

BLY, ROBERT (1926-   ), American

General
        Howard, Richard [1], 38-48.

BOGAN, LOUISE (1897-1970), American

"Come, Break With Time"
        Bader, 126-27.

BOGAN (cont'd)

    "Decoration"
        Bader, 124.

    "Old Countryside"
        Bader, 128-29.
        Roethke, 146.

    "Roman Fountain"
        Bader, 130.

    "Statue and the Birds"
        Bader, 124-26.

BOWERS, EDGAR (1924-), American

    General
        Howard, Richard [1], 49-56.

BRADSTREET, ANNE (1612?-1672), American

    "Contemplations"
        Laughlin, 10-12, 15.
        Lenhart, 43-44.
        Richardson, 323-31.

    "Flesh and the Spirit"
        Richardson, 321.

    "If Ever Two Were One, Then Surely We"
        Richardson, 322-23.

    "Upon a Fit of Sickness, Anno 1632"
        Richardson, 318-19.

    "Upon the Burning of Our House"
        Laughlin, 12-13.
        Richardson, 321-22.

BRANTLINGER, PATRICK (1941?-), American

    "Cavalier and the Nun"
        Jerome [1], 165-66.

    "The Scribes"
        Jerome [1], 164-65.

BRATHWAITE, L. EDWARD (1930-   ), British

    General
        Grant, Damian, 186-92.

BRAWLEY, BENJAMIN (1882-1939), American

    General
        Parker, 50-56.

BRETON, NICHOLAS (1545?-1626), British

    "Passion of a Discontented Mind"
        Shakeshaft, 165-74.

BRIDGES, ROBERT (1844-1930), British

    "Eros and Psyche"
        Altick [1], 253-54, 258-59.

    "Testament of Beauty"
        DeSelincourt, 233-56.

BROME, ALEXANDER (1620-1666), British

    "Leveller's Rant"
        Previte-Orton, 68-70.

BRONK, EDWIN (20th Century), British

    General
        Rosenthal [1], 216-19.

BROOKE, RUPERT (1887-1915), British

    "The Soldier"
        Bergonzi [1], 43-45.

BROOKS, GWENDOLYN (1917-   ), American

    General
        Bigsby, 89-98.
        Bird, 158-66.
        Cutler, 388-89.
        Davis, Arthur P. [1], 90-97.
        Davis, Arthur P. [2], 114-25.
        Emanuel [2], 2-3.
        Stavros, 1-20.

BROWN, STERLING A.   (1901-   ), American

    "Odyssey of Big Boy"
        Collier [1], 79-81.

BROWNING, ELIZABETH BARRETT (1806-1861), British

    "A Curse for a Nation"
        Arinshtein, 33-42.
        Delaura [2], 210-12.
        Gladish, 275-80.

BROWNING, ROBERT (1812-1889), British

    General
        Shmiefsky [2], 701-21.
        Tillotson [1], 389-97.

    "Abt Vogler"
        Plunkett [1], item 14.

    "Andrea del Sarto"
        Bieman, 651-68.
        D'Avanzo [1], 523-36.
        Jones, A. R. [2], 321-22.
        MacEachen [1], 61-64.
        Melchiori, 132-36.
        Mendel [1], item 77.
        Stevens, L. Robert, 23-24.

    "Balaustion's Adventure"
        Friend [1], 179-86.

    "Bishop Blougram's Apology"
        Maurer, Oscar, 177-79.

    "Bishop Orders his Tomb at Saint Praxed's Church"
        Bonner, item 57.
        Chiarenza, item 22.
        Jones, A. R. [2], 325-26.
        Milosevich, item 67.
        Monteiro [1], 209-18.
        Perrine [3], item 12.
        Phipps [1], 199-208.
        Stevens, L. Robert, 20-21.

    "Caliban Upon Setebos"
        Howard, John [1], 249-57.

Perrine [4], 124-27.
Timko [2], 141-51.

"Childe Roland to the Dark Tower Came"
Kintgen, 253-58.
Meyers, Joyce S., 335-38.
Short, 175-77.
Sullivan, Ruth Elizabeth, 296-302.
Thompson, Leslie M. [1], 339-53.
Willoughby [1], 291-99.

"Christmas Eve"
Battenhouse, 126-27.
Guskin, 21-28.

"Cleon"
Lee, 56-62.

"Count Gismond"
Hagopian, 153-55.
Timko [1], 731-42.

"Easter Day"
Battenhouse, 127-28.

"Epistle Containing the Strange Medical Experience of
Karshish, the Arab Physician"
Bennett, 189-91.
Guerin, 132-39.
Irvine, 160-62.

"Evelyn Hope"
Marshall, George O., Jr., 32-34.

"Fra Lippo Lippi"
Jones, A. R. [2], 322-25.
Litzinger [1], 409-10.
Malbone, item 20.
Omans, 129-45.
Shaw [2], 127-32.
Stevens, L. Robert, 22-23.

"The Glove"
Isaacs, Neil D. and Richard M. Kelly, 157-59.

"A Grammarian's Funeral"
Altick [2], 449-60.

BROWNING (cont'd)

"A Grammarian's Funeral" (cont'd)
Foxell, 185-201.
Jones, A. R. [2], 326-28.
Kelly, Robert L., 105-12.
Monteiro [7], 266-70.
Schweik, 411-12.
Svaglic [1], 93-104.

"How It Strikes a Contemporary"
Kvapil, 279-83.

"In a Balcony"
Mudford, 31-40.

"The Italian in England"
Brown, Bernadine, 179-83.

"James Lee's Wife"
Sandstrom, 259-70.

"Johannes Agricola in Meditation"
Wasserman, George R. [3], item 59.
Willoughby [2], item 5.

"The Last Ride Together"
Goldfarb, 255-61.

"Master Hugues of Saxe-Gotha"
Altick [4], 1-7.

"Meeting at Night"
Kroeber, 101-07.
McNally, 219-24.

"Mr. Sludge, 'The Medium' "
Armstrong, Isobel [1], 1-9.
Shapiro, 145-55.

"My Last Duchess"
Cox, Ollie, 70-76.
Fleissner [1], 217-19.
Jones, A. R. [2], 318-20.
Kilburn [2], item 31.
Monteiro [3], 234-37.
Muench, 203-05.

Nathanson, item 68.
Stevens, L. Robert, 20.

"Nationality in Drinks"
McAleer, Edward C., item 34.

"One Word More"
Jones, A. R. [2], 314-15.

"Paracelsus"
Battenhouse, 118-22.

"Parting at Morning"
Kroeber, 101-07.
McNally, 219-24.

"Pauline"
Battenhouse, 117-18.
Collins, Thomas J. [2], 151-60.
Miyoshi, 157-60.

"Pictor Ignotus"
Stevens, L. Robert, 21-22.

"Pied Piper of Hamelin"
Millhauser [1], 163-68.

"Pippa Passes"
Korg, 5-19.
Kramer, Dale [1], 241-49.
Phipps [2], 66-70.

"Porphyria's Lover"
Chandler [2], 273-74.
Eggenschwiler [2], 39-48.
Sutton, Max Keith, 280-89.

"Prince Hohensteil-Schwangau, Saviour of Society"
Previte-Orton, 225-26.

"Rabbi Ben Ezra"
Battenhouse, 130-31.
Fleisher, 46-52.
Slakey [2], 291-94.
Viswanathan [1], 349-52.

"Red Cotton Night-Cap Country or Turf and Towers"
Watkins, Charlotte Crawford, 360-74.

BROWNING (cont'd)

"The Ring and the Book"
Armstrong, Isobel [2], 271-79.
Friedman, Barton R., 693-708.
Gridley [1], 281-95.
Gridley [2], 64-83.
Honan, 215-30.
Loschky, 333-52.
Miller, J. Hillis [2], 218-19.
Nelson, Charles Edwin, 91-98.
Peckham, 243-57.
Raymond, William O., 323-32.
Swingle, 259-69.
Talon, 353-65.
Thompson, Gordon W., 669-86.
Thompson, Leslie M. [2], 80-85.
Thompson, Leslie M. [3], 322-35.

"The Ring and the Book--Book I"
Adams, Laura, 346-47.
Sullivan, Mary Rose, 231-41.

"The Ring and the Book--Book VI"
Boo [1], 179-88.

"The Ring and the Book--Book VII"
Gabbard, 29-31.

"The Ring and the Book--Books VIII and IX"
Drew, Philip, 297-307.
Wyant, 309-21.

"Saul"
Battenhouse, 122-26.
Collins, Thomas J. [1], 121-24.
Shaw [1], 277-82.

"Soliloquy of the Spanish Cloister"
Day, Robert A. [3], item 33.
Fryxwell and Adair, item 24.
Gainer, 158-60.
Malbone [4], 218-21.
Slakey [3], item 42.
Sonstroem [1], 70-73.
Starkman, 399-405.

"Sordello"
     Columbus and Kemper, 251-67.
     Johnson, Alan P., 321-38.

"Too Late"
     Perrine [5], 339-45.

"Two in the Campagna"
     Altick [3], 75-80.

"Up at a Villa--Down in the City"
     Fleck, 345-49.

BRYANT, WILLIAM CULLEN (1794-1878), American

"Thanatopsis"
     McLean, 474-79.

BURNS, ROBERT (1756-1796), British

"Tam O'Shanter"
     MacLaine, 308-16.
     Thomas, W. K. [5], item 33.
     Weston, 537-50.

BUTLER, SAMUEL (1612-1680), British

"Hudibras"
     Previte-Orton, 84-91.

BYRON, (LORD) GEORGE GORDON NOEL (1788-1824),
  British

General
     Bartel, 373-78.

"Age of Bronze"
     Bailey, John Cann, 231-32.
     Previte-Orton, 210-12.

"Childe Harold's Pilgrimage--Canto III"
     Bruffee, 669-78.

"Childe Harold's Pilgrimage--Canto IV"
     Rutherford, 391-97.

"Don Juan"
     Deen, 345-57.

BYRON (cont'd)

        Elledge, 1-13.
        Lauber, 607-19.
        Ridenour, 442-46.

    "Don Juan--Canto III" (Isles of Greece)
        Davidson, Clifford, 194-96.

    "The Giaour"
        Sundell [1], 587-99.

    "Mazeppa"
        Marshall, William H. [2], 120-24.

    "Ode to Napoleon Buonoparte"
        Bailey, John Cann, 230.

    "Vision of Judgment"
        Previte-Orton, 202-08.

CAMPBELL, ROY (1902-1957), British

    "The Zebras"
        Drew, E. A., 66.

CHAPMAN, GEORGE (1559?-1634), British

    "Hero and Leander"
        Alpers [1], 235-50.

    "Hymnus in Noctem" (Shadow of Night, Part I)
        Cannon, Charles Kendrick, 254-62.

    "Ovid's Banquet of Sense"
        Myers, James P., Jr., 192-206.

CHATFIELD, E. HALE (1936?-), American

    General
        Jerome [5], 435-39.

CHAUCER, GEOFFREY (c1340-1400), British

    "An ABC"
        Klinefelter, item 5.

"The Book of the Duchesse"
    DeSelincourt, 28-32.

"The Complaint of Mars"
    North, Pt. I, 137-42.
    Owen [1], 434-35.

"The Complaint Unto Pity"
    Pittock, 160-68.

"The House of Fame"
    David, 333-39.
    DeSelincourt, 36-38.
    Sanders, Barry [2], 3-13.

"Legend of Good Women"
    DeSelincourt, 38-40.
    North, Pt. II, 268-69.

"The Parliament of Fowls"
    North, Pt. II, 270-74.

"Troilus and Criseyde"
    Cook, Robert G. [1], 407-24.
    DeSelincourt, 50-105.
    DiPasquale, 152-63.
    Kelly, Edward Hanford, 28-30.
    Macey, 307-23.
    Mogan, 72-77.
    North, Pt. I, 142-49.
    Owen [1], 439-49.
    Roberts, Robert P. [1], 425-36.
    Roberts, Robert P. [2], 373-85.
    Wenzel, 542-47.

"Troilus and Criseyde--Book III"
    Devereux, 550-52.
    Sturtevant, item 5.

CHURCHILL, CHARLES (1731-1764), British

General
    Golden, Morris, 333-46.

"The Candidate"
    Winters [1], 52-53.

"The Dedication"
    Winters [1], 104-17.

CHURCHILL (cont'd)

"The Ghost"
Golden, Morris, 337-39.
Winters [1], 104-17.

"Gotham"
Golden, Morris, 341-42.

CIARDI, JOHN ANTHONY (1916-   ), American

"Most Like an Arch This Marriage"
Southworth [1], 588.

"Snowy Heron"
Southworth [1], 589.

"Tenzone"
Gallagher, Edward J., item 28.
Perrine [1], item 82.

CLANVOWE, SIR JOHN (14th Century?), British

"The Cuckoo and the Nightingale"
Lampe, 49-62.

CLARE, JOHN (1793-1864), British

"Love and Beauty"
Storey, item 60.

CLEVELAND (or CLIEVELAND), JOHN (1613-1658), British

"Et Caetera"
Previte-Orton, 64.

CLOUGH, ARTHUR HUGH (1819-1861), British

General
Bowers, Frederick, 709-16.
Houghton, Walter E., 35-61.

"Blank Misgivings of a Creature Moving About in
Worlds Not Realised"
McGhee [1], 105-15.

"Dipsychus"
Ryals [2], 182-88.

"Easter Day. Naples, 1849"
Forsyth, 27-28.

"Easter Day, II"
Forsyth, 29-30.

"Epi-Strauss-Ium"
Forsyth, 20-26.

"The Judgement of Brutus"
Greenberger [1], 129-50.

"Sa Majeste Tres Chretienne"
Timko [3], 112-14.

"Salsette and Elephanta"
Greenberger [2], 284-305.

"To the Great Metropolis"
Timko [3], 108-10.

COLERIDGE, SAMUEL TAYLOR (1772-1834), British

General
Sankey, 59-67.

"Christabel"
Alley, 459-60.
Angus, 655-68.
Farrison, 83-94.
Radley, 531-41.
Wain [2], 86-112.

"Dejection: An Ode"
Alley, 454-56.
Thompson, William I., 27-29.

"The Eolian Harp"
Boulger, 693-97.
Gerard [1], 411-22.
Marshall, William H. [3], 229-32.

"The Friend"
Bailey, Dudley, 89-99.

"Frost at Midnight"
Boulger, 705-11.

COLERIDGE (cont 'd)

"Kubla Khan"
  Angus, 655-68.
  Fleissner [2], 45.
  Fogle, 112-16.
  Gerber, 321-41.
  Meier, 15-29.
  Raine [4], 626-42.
  Starr, 117-25.

"Lines Composed in a Concert-Room"
  Werkmeister, 201-05.

"The Nightingale"
  Hopkins, 436-41.

"Rime of the Ancient Mariner"
  Alley, 456-58.
  Angus, 655-68.
  Brett, 78-107.
  Buchan, 669-88.
  Creed, 215-22+.
  Empson [1], 298-319.
  Fulmer, 797-815.
  Gibbons, 257-61.
  Gose [1], 238-44.
  Littmann, 370-89.
  McDonald, 543-54.
  Owen [2], 261-67.
  Pafford, 618-26.
  Rowell, 133-35.
  Tillyard [2], 66-86.
  Ware, 303-04.

"This Lime-Tree Bower"
  Boulger, 702-05.

"Time, Real and Imaginary"
  Byers, item 46.

COLLINS, WILLIAM (1721-1759), British

"Ode on the Poetical Character"
  Lynskey, item 33.
  Spacks [1], 719-28.

"Ode on the Popular Superstitions of the Highlands of
Scotland, Considered as the Subject of Poetry"
Spacks [1], 731-36.

"Ode to Evening"
Askew, 288-91.
Pettit [1], 361-69.

"Ode to Fear"
Crider, John R., 61
Spacks [1], 729-31.

"Ode to Liberty"
Crider, John R., 69-72.

"Ode to Pity"
Crider, John R., 58-61ff.
Spacks [1], 728.

"Ode to Simplicity"
Crider, John R., 62-66.

"Ode Written in the Beginning of the Year 1746"
("How Sleep the Brave")
Spacks [2], 642-45.

"Verses Humbly Address'd to Sir Thomas Hanmer on
His Edition of Shakespeare's Works"
Crider, John R., 57-58.

CORSO, GREGORY NANZIA (1930-   ), American

General
Howard, Richard [1], 57-64.

COWLEY, ABRAHAM (1618-1667), British

"On Hope"
Miller, Clarence H. [2], 64-73.

"To Mr. Hobs"
Korshin, 765-67.

"To Sir William Davenant"
Korshin, 760-61.

"To the Royal Society"
Korshin, 770-73.

COXE, LOUIS OSBORNE (1918-   ), American

    "The Middle Passage"
        Booth, 46-49.

CRABBE, GEORGE (1754-1832), British

    "The Library"
        Chamberlain, 838-52.

    "Widow Goe" (The Parish Register)
        Barnes, T. R., 147-51.

CRANE, HART (1899-1932), American

    General
        Clark, David R. [2], 389-97.
        Slate, 486-511.

    "At Melville's Tomb"
        Lewis, R. W. B., 240-48.

    "Atlantis"
        Langford, Richard E., 22-24.

    "Black Tambourine"
        Dembo [2], 183-84.
        Holton, 220-28.
        Kessler, item 4.

    "The Bridge"
        Grigsby [2], 518-23.
        Metzger, Deena Posy, 36-46.
        Unterecker, 345-48.
        Vogler, 381-408.

    "Cape Hatteras"
        Dembo [3], 77-81.

    "Chaplinesque"
        Dembo [2], 185-86.

    "Emblems of Conduct"
        Dembo [1], 319-21.

    "Lachrymae Christi"
        Yannella, 317-20.

"Legend"
    Yannella, 314-15.

"Passage"
    Lewis, R. W. B., 228-32.

"Pastorale"
    Dembo [2], 184.

"Voyages"
    Kramer, Maurice, 410-23.

"Voyages II"
    Day, Robert A. [2], 224-34.
    Freedman, item 4.
    Poulin, item 15.

"The Wine Menagerie"
    Lewis, R. W. B., 232-39.
    Yannella, 321-22.

CRANE, STEPHEN (1871-1900), American

General
    Nelson, Harland S., 564-82.

"The Blue Battalions" (War Is Kind, 27),
    Nelson, Harland S., 574-77.

"A Man Adrift on a Slim Spar"
    Nelson, Harland S., 577-79.

"A Man Said to the Universe"
    Wegelin [1], item 9.

"War Is Kind"
    Marcus [2], 274-78.

CRASHAW, RICHARD (1612?-1649), British

"On Hope"
    Miller, Clarence H. [2], 64-73.

"On the Bleeding Wound of Our Crucified Lord"
    Jerome [4], 485-86.

"To the Name Above Every Name, the Name of Jesus"
    Strier, 148-51.

CRASHAW (cont'd)

> "To the Noblest and Best of Ladies, the Countess of
>   Denbigh"
>   Strier, 136-48.

> "The Weeper"
>   Bertonasco, 177-88.
>   Chambers, Leland [1], 111-21.

CREELEY, ROBERT WHITE (1926-   ), American

> General
>   Howard, Richard [1], 65-74.
>   Rosenthal [1], 149-59.

> "I Know a Man"
>   Stepanchev, 151-52.

> "Pieces"
>   McGann [1], 201-02.

CROSBY, HARRY HERBERT (1919-   ), American

> General
>   Langford, Richard E., 1-6.

CULLEN, COUNTEE (1903-1946), American

> General
>   Bronz, n.p.
>   Dorsey, 68-77.
>   Reimherr, 65-82.

> "After a Visit"
>   Dorsey, 75-76.

> "From the Dark Tower"
>   Collier [1], 76-78.

> "Icarian Wings"
>   Dorsey, 68-69.

> "The Shroud of Color"
>   Dorsey, 69-70.

CUMMINGS, EDWARD ESTLIN (1894-1962), American

    General
        Friedman, Norman, 114-33.
        Langford, Richard E., 25-27.
        Schroeder, Fred E. H., 469-78.

    "All in Green Went My Love Riding"
        Jumper [1], item 6.
        Robey, item 2.
        Sanders, Barry [1], item 23.

    "Anyone Lived in a Pretty How Town"
        Clark, David R. [1], 36-43.
        Drew, E. A., 59-62.
        Squier [1], item 37.
        Walsh, item 72.

    "The Bigness of Cannon" (LaGuerre, I)
        Osborne [1], item 28.

    "Buffalo Bill's Defunct" (Portraits, VIII)
        Ray, David, 282-90.

    "I"
        White, James E., item 4

    "I Will Be"
        Powers, item 54

    "(IM)C-A-T(MO)"
        Heinrichs, item 59.

    "In Just"
        Turner, C. Steven, item 18.

    "Kind)"
        Williams, Paul O. [1], item 4.

    "Let's, From Some Loud Unworld's Most Rightful
    Wrong"
        Mattfield [1], item 32.

    "Memorabilia"
        Barton, item 26.

CUMMINGS (cont 'd)

    "The Noster Was a Ship of Swank"
        Luedtke, item 59.

    "Pity This Busy Monster, Manunkind"
        Gargano [1], item 21.
        Henry [6], item 68.

    "Poem"
        Clark, David R. [3], item 48.

    "Sonnet Entitled How to Run the World"
        Lasser, item 44.

    "262"
        Henry [2], item 72.

    "275"
        Henry [3], item 63.

    "303" (Nor Woman)
        Henry [4], item 2.

    "305"
        Henry [5], item 49.
        Wagener, item 18.

    "What If a Much of a Which of a Wind"
        Clagget, 353-54.
        Drew, E. A., 75-76.

DANA, RICHARD HENRY, SR. (1787-1879), American

    "The Little Beach Bird"
        Lenhart, 88-89.

DANIEL, SAMUEL (c1562-1619), British

    "Delia"
        Goldman, Lloyd, 49-63.
        Williamson, C. F., 251-60.

DAVIDSON, DONALD GRADY (1893-1968), American

    "A Touch of Snow"
        Bradford, 516-23.

DAVIE, DONALD ALFRED (1922-   ), British

> General
>> Bergonzi [3], 293-304.
>
> "The Fountain"
>> Swinden, 353-55.

DAVIES, SIR JOHN (1569-1626), British

> "Nosce Teipsum"
>> Alpers [1], 321-26.
>> Colie, 154-56.
>
> "Orchestra"
>> Tillyard [2], 30-48.

DE LA MARE, WALTER (1873-1956), British

> "The Listeners"
>> Dyson [2], 150-54.
>> Pierson, 373-81.

DENHAM, SIR JOHN (1615-1669), British

> "Cooper's Hill"
>> Previte-Orton, 77.

DICKEY, JAMES (1923-   ), American

> General
>> Howard, Richard [1], 75-98.
>> Nemerov, 99-104.
>
> "Approaching Prayer"
>> Weatherby [2], 672-73.
>
> "Armor"
>> Howard, Richard [1], 86-87.
>
> "Chenille"
>> Weatherby [2], 674.
>
> "Cherrylog Road"
>> Howard, Richard [1], 89-90.
>> Weatherby [2], 674-75.

DICKEY (cont 'd)

"A Dog Sleeping on My Feet"
Weatherby [2], 669-71.

"Drinking from a Helmet"
Weatherby [2], 675-76.

"The Driver"
Weatherby [2], 675.

"Falling"
Baker, Donald W., 401

"The Fiend"
Weatherby [2], 677-78.

"The Firebombing"
Howard, Richard [1], 93-94.
Weatherby [2], 677.

"Orpheus Before Hades"
Howard, Richard [1], 77.

"Performance"
Howard, Richard [1], 79-80.

"Slave Quarters"
Howard, Richard [1], 94-95.

"Springer Mountain"
Weatherby [2], 673.

DICKEY, WILLIAM (1928-   ), American

General
Jerome [2], 50-53.

DICKINSON, EMILY (1830-1886), American

General
Cunningham, 436-56.
Ford, Thomas W., 199-203.
Griffith [1], 93-100.
Martz, 90-104.
Parsons, Thornton H. [1], 19-25.
Patterson, 441-57.
Porter, David T., 559-69.

"After Great Pain, a Formal Feeling Comes" (No. 341)
    Stein, William Bysshe [2], 54-55.

"As By the Dead We Love to Sit" (No. 88)
    Lair, item 58.

"Aurora Is the Effort" (No. 1002)
    Newell [1], item 5.

"Because I Could Not Stop for Death" (No. 712)
    Manierre [3], 5-11.
    Wheatcroft, 144-45.

"Bustle in a House" (No. 1078)
    Jordan, Raymond J. [1], item 49.

"Butterfly Obtains" (No. 1685)
    Houghton, Donald E., item 5.

"A Clock Stopped" (No. 287)
    Bolin, item 27.
    Rossky, item 3.

"Crickets Sang" (No. 1104)
    Tugwell [1], item 46.

"Death Is a Dialogue Between" (No. 976)
    Adair, item 52.

"Elysium Is as Far as To" (No. 1760)
    Whicher, item 45.

" 'Faith' Is a Fine Invention" (No. 185)
    Witherington, item 62.

"Feet of People Walking Home" (No. 7)
    Pebworth and Summers, item 76.

"Further in Summer Than the Birds" (No. 1068)
    Lind, 163-69.

"Go Make Thee Fair" (No. 318)
    Wilson, Suzanne M. [2], 56-57.

"I Felt a Funeral in My Brain" (No. 280)
    Monteiro [8], 656-63.
    Stein, William Bysshe [2], 52-54.

DICKINSON (cont'd)

"I Had Not Minded Walls" (No. 398)
        Merideth, item 25.

"I Heard a Fly Buzz When I Died" (No. 465)
        Beck, Ronald, item 31.
        Connelly [1], item 34.
        Hogue, Caroline, item 26.
        Hollahan [1], item 6.
        Manierre [3], 11-14.
        Spencer, 141-43.

"I Like to See It Lap the Miles" (No. 585)
        Lowrey, 54-58.

"I Never Saw a Moor" (No. 1052)
        Howard, William, item 13.

"I Started Early, Took My Dog" (No. 520)
        Carlson [2], item 72.

"I Taste a Liquor Never Brewed" (No. 214)
        Davis, Lloyd M., item 53.
        Eby, 516-18.
        Garrow, 366.
        Malbone [2], item 14.
        Stein, William Bysshe [2], 49-52.

"If You Were Coming in the Fall" (No. 511)
        Keefer and Vlahos, item 23.

"It Don't Sound So Terrible--Quite--As It Did" (No. 426)
        Ford, Thomas W., 201-02.

"The Lamp Burns Sure Within" (No. 233)
        Lewis, Stuart, item 4.

"My Life Had Stood--A Loaded Gun" (No. 754)
        Perrine [12], item 21.

"No Brigadier Throughout the Year" (No. 1561)
        Forde, item 41.

"Not With a Club the Heart Is Broken" (No. 1304)
        Marcus [1], item 54.

"Of Bronze and Blaze" (No. 290)
Hiatt [3], item 6.

"One Day Is There of the Series" (No. 814)
Williams, Paul O. [2], item 28.

"One Dignity Delays for All" (No. 98)
Essig [1], item 16.
Michel, 98-100.

"Poets Light But Lamps" (No. 883)
Lewis, Stuart, item 4.

"Praise It--'Tis Dead" (No. 1384)
Mullican [1], item 62.

"Reverse Cannot Befall" (No. 395)
Anderson, Charles R. [2], item 46.

"The Soul Selects Her Own Society" (No. 303)
Bowman, item 13.
Faris, item 65.
Jumper [2], item 5.
Manierre [3], 14-16.
Tugwell [2], item 37.

"The Soul's Superior Instants" (No. 306)
Wilson, Suzanne M. [1], 351-52.

"There Came a Day at Summer's Fall" (No. 322)
Anthony [1], 557-61.

"Tint I Cannot Take Is Best" (No. 627)
Fitzgerald, Sister Ellen, item 29.

"Two Butterflies Went Out at Noon" (No. 533)
Matchett [1], 436-41.
Perrine [9], 389-90.

"Water Makes Many Beds" (No. 1428)
Mullican [2], item 23.

"We Should Not Mind So Small a Flower" (No. 81)
Newell [2], item 65.

"What Soft Cherubic Creatures" (No. 401)
Harvey, item 17.

DICKINSON (cont'd)

"When Roses Cease to Bloom, Sir" (No. 32)
Griffith [1], 93-94.

"Wild Nights" (No. 249)
Connelly [2], item 44.
Wegelin [2], item 25.
Wilson, Suzanne M. [1], 353-54.

DONNE, JOHN (1572-1631), British

General
Martz, 1-32.
Sackton, 67-82.
Simpson, Evelyn M., 140-50.

"Aire and Angels"
Prosky, item 27.

"Anniversaries"
Colie, 159-70.
Mahony [2], 407-13.
Quinn, 97-105.
Williamson, George [2], 183-91.

"Apparition"
Guss, 18-22.

"Batter My Heart, Three Person'd God" (Holy Sonnet 14)
Clements [1], 484-89.
Cornelius [1], item 25.
Mueller, 312-14.
Parish [1], 299-302.
Schwartz [1], item 27.
Wanninger, item 37.

"Bracelet" (Elegy 11)
Bryan [2], 310-11.
Thumboo, item 14.

"Broken Heart"
Wilson, G. R., Jr., 116-17.

"Canonization"
Chambers, A. B. [1], 252-59.

Clair, 300-02.
Corin, 89-93.
Guss, 22-28.
Matchett [2], 290-92.
Wilson, G. R., Jr., 113-15.

"La Corona"
Chambers, A. B. [2], 212-17.

"The Curse"
Bryan [2], 310.

"Death Be Not Proud" (Holy Sonnet 10)
Barnes, T. R., 72-73.
Jerome [4], 488-90.

"The Dreame"
Schwartz [2], item 67.

"Elegie" (Elegy 7)
Daniels and Dean, item 34.

"Expostulation"
Bryan [2], 311-12.

"Extasie"
Carey [2], 51-53.
Cirrillo [1], 90-92.
Graziani, 121-36.
McCanles, 59-75.
Mitchell [1], 91-101.
Paffard, item 13.
Wilson, G. R., Jr., 111-13.

"First Anniversary"
Love, Harold [1], 125-31.

"Funerall Elegie"
Barnes, T. R., 66-67.

"Going to Bed" (Elegy 19)
Empson [2], 258-59.
Gregory, 51-54.

"Good Friday, 1613. Riding Westward"
Barnes, T. R., 70-72.
Beck, Rosalie, 166-69.

DONNE (cont 'd)

"Good-Morrow"
    Wilson, G. R., Jr., 109-11.

"Heroicall Epistle: Sapho to Philaenis"
    Wilson, G. R., Jr., 118-19.

"His Picture" (Elegy 5)
    Barnes, T. R., 60-61.

"Hymn to God My God, In My Sickness"
    Martz, 40-43.

"A Lecture Upon a Shadow"
    Henry [7], item 60.
    Moody, item 60.
    Perrine [10], item 40.

"Legacie"
    Cowan, S. A. [2], item 58.

"Loves Growth"
    Alphonse, item 43.

"Metaphysical Conceit"
    Sloan, 42.

"A Nocturnall Upon St. Lucies Day, Being the
    Shortest Day"
    Miller, Clarence H. [1], 77-86.
    Shawcross [2], item 56.
    Wain [2], 31-58.

"Primrose"
    Durr [1], 218-22.

"Relique"
    Harrington [3], item 22.
    Rickey [2], item 58.

"Satyre III" (Kinde Pity Chokes My Spleene)
    Daniels [3], item 52.
    Moore, Thomas V., 41-49.
    Roberts, John R. [1], 105-15.

"Satyres" (All Five)
    Andreasen, 59-75.

Zivley, 87-95.

"Second Anniversary"
Mahoney, 205-08.

"Sun Rising"
Morris, William E., item 45.
Pomeroy, item 4.

"To His Mistress Going to Bed"
Love, Harold [2], item 33.

"To the Contesse of Huntingdon"
Harrison, Robert [2], item 33.

"Undertaking"
Sloan, 39-41.

"A Valediction: Forbidding Mourning"
Barnes, T. R., 61-64.
Foxell, 1-12.

"A Valediction: Of My Name, in the Window"
Wilson, G. R., Jr., 117-18.

"A Valediction: Of Weeping"
Barnes, T. R., 64-65.
Carey [2], 50-51.
Wilson, G. R., Jr., 119-20.

"What If This Present Were the World's Last Night?"
(Holy Sonnet 13)
Parish [4], item 19.

"Why Are We by All Creatures Waited On?" (Holy
Sonnet 12)
Simpson, Arthur L., Jr. [2], item 75.

"Witchcraft by a Picture"
Wilson, G. R., Jr., 115-16.

DOUGLAS, KEITH (1920-1944), American

"Deceased"
Hughes, Ted, 45-46.

"Encounter with a God"
Hughes, Ted, 43-44.

DOWSON, ERNEST CHRISTOPHER (1867-1900), British

General
        Baker, Houston A. [1], 21-28.

DRAKE, JOSEPH RODMAN (1795-1820), American

"The Culprit Fay"
        Lenhart, 93-94.

DRAYTON, MICHAEL (1563-1631), British

"The Barons Warres"
        LaBranche [1], 82-95.
        LaBranche [2], 1-19.

"Muses Elizium"
        Hiller, 1-13.

"The Shepheard's Garland"
        Ackerman, Catherine A., 106-13.
        Bristol, 42-48.

DRYDEN, JOHN (1631-1700), British

General
        Blair, 379-93.
        Emslie, 51-57.
        Hughes, R. E. [2], 458-63.
        Miner, Earl [3], 120-29.

"Absalom and Achitophel"
        Ball, Albert, 25-35.
        Brodwin [1], 24-44.
        Crider, J. R., item 63.
        French, A. L., 397-413.
        Guilhamet, 395-413.
        King, Bruce [1], item 28.
        King, Bruce [2], 332-33.
        Maurer, A. E. Wallace [1], item 6.
        Miner, Earl [6], 312-16.
        Peterson, 236-44.
        Previte-Orton, 97-100.
        Thomas, W. K. [1], item 66.
        Thomas, W. K. [3], 92-99.

"Alexander's Feast, or The Power of Music"
        Foxell, 23-40.

Proffitt, 1307-16.

"Anne Killigrew"
See "To the Pious Memory ... Anne Killigrew"

"Annus Mirabilis"
Miner, Earl [1], item 75.
Rosenberg [1], 254-58.

"Astraea Redux"
Leed, 127-30.
Maurer, A. E. Wallace [3], 13-20.

"The Hind and the Panther"
Anselment, 256-67.
Barnes, T. R., 110-13.
Benson [1], 406-12.
Hamm, 400-15.
Miller, Clarence H. [3], 511-27.
Previte-Orton, 103-05.
Wasserman, George [1], item 71.

"Mac Flecknoe"
Alssid, 387-402.
Eleanor, 47-54.
French, David P., item 39.
McFadden [1], 55-72.
Miner, Earl [6], 316-19.
Towers, 323-34.

"The Medall"
Maurer, A. E. Wallace [2], 293-304.

"Religio Laici"
Barnes, T. R., 107-10.
Benson [1], 395-406.
Benson [2], 238-51.
Corder, 245-49.
Fujimura, 205-17.
Hamm, 190-98.
Welcher, 391-96.

"Song for St. Cecilia's Day, 1687"
Levine [1], 38-50.

"To My Honored Friend, Dr. Charleton"
Colden, Samuel A., item 53.

DRYDEN (cont'd)

"To the Memory of Mr. Oldham"
    Bache, 237-43.

"To the Pious Memory of the Accomplisht Young Lady,
    Mrs. Anne Killigrew"
        Eleanor, 47-54.
        Jerome [4], 486-87.
        Tillyard [2], 49-65.
        Vieth [2], 91-100.

DUGAN, ALAN (1923-), American

    General
        Howard, Richard [1], 99-106.

DUNCAN, ROBERT EDWARD (1919-), American
    General
        Rosenthal [1], 174-84.

"Often I Am Permitted to Return to a Meadow"
    Rosenthal [1], 174-76.

DURRELL, LAWRENCE (1912-), British

"Song for Zarathustra"
    Silverstein and Lewis, item 10.

DYER, JOHN (1699-1757), British

"Grongar Hill"
    Reichert, 123-29.

EBERHART, RICHARD (1904-), American

"Am I My Neighbor's Keeper"
    Ostroff [1], 142-66.

"The Fury of Aerial Bombardment"
    Bader, 91-98.
    Bradham [2], item 71.

"The Horse Chestnut Tree"
    Drew, E. A., 66-68.

"Throwing the Apple"
    Bauerle, Richard F., item 21.

EDWARDS, JONATHAN (1703-1758), American

> General
>> Davidson, Clifford, 149-56.

EIGNER, LAURENCE NOEL (1927-), American

> "Keep Me Still, I Do Not Want to Dream"
>> Kinnell, 402-03.

ELIOT, GEORGE (1819-1880), British

> General
>> Paris, 539-58.

> "A College Breakfast-Party"
>> Paris, 554-58.

> "I Grant You Ample Leave"
>> Paris, 551-58.

> "In a London Drawingroom"
>> Paris, 549-51.

ELIOT, THOMAS STEARNS (1888-1965), American

> General
>> Austin [2], 309-12.
>> Leavis, 9-34.
>> LeBrun, Pt. I, 149-61; Pt. II, 274-86.
>> Martz, 105-24.
>> Nitchie, 403-06.
>> Tate, Allen [2], entire issue.
>> Unger [2], 197-224.
>> Weatherby [1], 330-47.
>> Woodbery, 53-66.
>> Yeomans, 267-75.

> "Animula"
>> Askew, 294-96.
>> Stroud, item 14.

> "Ash-Wednesday"
>> Drew, E. A., 148-62.
>> Rajan [2], 368-70.
>> Wooton [1], 31-42.

ELIOT (cont'd)

    "Burnt Norton"
        Anthony [2], 81-89.
        Bogan, 58-61.
        Brett, 122-27.
        Cox, C. B. [3], 326-35.
        Gardner, Helen, 325-26.
        Porter, M. Gilbert, 57-61.

    "Cape Ann"
        Hansen, 374-76.

    "Coriolan"
        Bollier, 625-33.

    "The Dry Salvages"
        Bogan, 58-61.
        Brett, 123-27.
        Gardner, Helen, 327-28.
        Porter, M. Gilbert, 62-64.

    "East Coker"
        Bogan, 58-61.
        Brett, 122-27.
        Gardner, Helen, 326-27.
        Kligerman, 101-12.
        Porter, M. Gilbert, 61-62.

    "Four Quartets"
        Brett, 108-35.
        Clubb, Merrel D., Jr., 19-33.
        Gardner, Helen, 325-29.
        Musacchio, 238.
        Rajan [2], 370-73.

    "Gerontion"
        Dye, item 39.
        Griffith [2], item 46.
        Halverson [1], 580-86.
        Kaplan, Robert B. and Richard J. Wall [1],
            item 36.
        Monteiro [4], item 30.
        Rajan [2], 365-67.
        Ransom [1], 398-414.

    "The Hollow Men"
        Krause, 368-77.

ELIOT (cont'd)

"Preludes"
Drew, E. A., 26-31.

"Rannoch, by Glencoe"
Hansen, 373-74.

"The Readers of the Boston Evening Transcript"
Barnes, T. R., 280-82.

"Rhapsody on a Windy Night"
Woodbery, 64.

"A Song for Simeon"
Langford, Richard E., 42-45.

"Sweeney Among the Nightingales"
Battenhouse, 155-56.
Davidson, James, 400-03.
Gillis, 55-63.

"Sweeney Erect"
Cook, Robert G. [2], 221-26.

"Usk"
Hansen, 370-73.

"Virginia"
Hansen, 367-70.

"The Waste Land"
Andreach, 296-309.
Battenhouse, 156-59.
Cargill, 275-96.
Cox, C. B. [3], 308-19.
Craig, 241-52.
Day, Robert A. [1], 285-91.
Fortin, item 32.
Foster [2], 77-95.
Jones, Florence, 285-302.
Kermode, 232-37.
Knust, item 74.
Kramer, Dale [2], item 74.
Lees, 339-48.
Lorch, 123-33.
Merritt, item 31.

"The Waste Land--I, Burial of the Dead"
Barnes, T. R., 292-95.

"The Waste Land--IV, Death by Water"
Barnes, T. R., 295-96.

ELLIOTT, GEORGE P. (1918-), American

"Fever and Chills"
Van Duyn, 390-92.

EMERSON, RALPH WALDO (1803-1882), American

General
Bloom, Harold, 23-33.

"Brahma"
Stein, William Bysshe, et. al., item 29.
White, Robert L. [1], item 63.

"Ever the Rock of Ages Melts"
Keller [2], 94-98.

"Give All to Love"
Cowan, Michael H., item 49.

"Hamatreya"
Sharma, Mohan Lal, item 63.

"Ode Inscribed to W. H. Channing"
Arms, 407-09.

"The Snow-Storm"
Reiten, item 39.

"Uriel"
Witemeyer, 98-103.

EMMONS, RICHARD (1788-1831?), American

"The Fredoniad"
Rothwell, 373-78.
Squier [2], 446-54.

EMPSON, WILLIAM (1906-), American

"Invitation to Juno"
Ormerod [2], item 13.

EMPSON (cont'd)

    "Missing Dates"
        Drew, E. A., 78-79.

ENGLISH, THOMAS DUNN (1819-1902), American

    "Caesar Rowan"
        Moore, Rayburn S., 74-75.

    "Momma Phoebe"
        Moore, Rayburn S., 75.

EVANS, DONALD (1882-1921), American

    "En Monocle"
        Fields, Kenneth [1], 336-37.

EVANS, NATHANIEL (1742-1767), American

    "Aeolian Harp"
        Lenhart, 76-77.

    "Daphnis and Menalcas"
        Lenhart, 72-73.

    "Occasioned by Hearing Him Play on the Harmonica"
        Lenhart, 75-76.

FELDMAN, IRVING (1928-), American

    General
        Howard, Richard [1], 107-15.

FINKEL, DONALD (1929-), American

    General
        Howard, Richard [1], 131-44.

    "Hunting Song"
        Howard, Richard [1], 134-35.

    "In Gratitude"
        Wright, James, 374-75.

    "Simeon"
        Howard, Richard [1], 136-37.

FRENEAU, PHILIP (1752-1832), American

"The Indian Burying Ground"
Wasserman, George R. [2], item 43.

FROST, ROBERT (1874-1963), American

General
Francis, Cole and Cook, 237-49.
Robson, 735-51.
Ryan, 5-23.
Sheffey, 51-59.
Sinyavsky, 431-41.

"Acquainted with the Night"
Friend [2], 363-65.
Martin, Wallace, item 64.
Perrine [1], item 50.

"After Apple-Picking"
Drew, E. A., 69-72.
Ferguson, Joe M., Jr., item 54.
Stein, William Bysshe [1], 301-05.

"The Armful"
Brenner, 24.

"A-Wishing Well"
Ferguson, A. R., 370-73.

"Birches"
Berger [3], 18-22.
Monteiro [2], 129-33.
Sheffey, 53-54.

"Build Soil"
Robson, 755-56.

"The Census-Taker"
Love, Glen A., 198-200.

"Come In"
Drew, E. A., 16-18.

"The Death of the Hired Man"
Bowen, James K., 155-57.
Robson, 751-53.
Sinyavsky, 436-37.

FROST (cont'd)

"Desert Places"
        Berger [3], 12-15.
        Miller, Lewis H., Jr. [2], 314-16.

"Design"
        Drew, E. A., 72-73.
        Eberhart, 769-70.
        Hiatt [1], item 41.
        Lynen, 814-15.
        Unger [1], 23-24.

"Directive"
        Blum, 524-25.
        Briggs, item 71.
        Drew, E. A., 113-17.
        Eberhart, 773-76.
        Juhnke, 163-64.
        Peters, Robert, 29-32.

"The Draft Horse"
        Burrell, item 60.
        Gwynn, 223-25.
        Hoetker, 485.
        Perrine and Blum, item 79.

"Dust of Snow"
        Berger [3], 2-4.
        Knapp, Edgar H., item 9.

"The Fear"
        Bowen, James K., 157-58.

"For Once, Then, Something"
        Unger [1], 20-21.

"From Sight to Insight"
        Berger [3], 16-18.

"Good-Bye and Keep Cold"
        Brenner, 21-23.

"The Hill Wife"
        Swennes, 365-66.

"Home Burial"
    Allen, D. C. [4], 99-132.
    Bowen, James K., 158-60.
    Brown, Terence, 114-15.
    Swennes, 366-67.

"I Will Sing You One-O"
    Juhnke, 154-55.

"In the Clearing" (Collection of Poems)
    Brown, Terence, 110-18.

"In White"
    Hiatt [2], item 41.

"Iris by Night"
    Berger [3], 54-57.

"Kitty Hawk"
    Juhnke, 159-60.

"Lesson for Today"
    Lynen, 802-05, 806-08.

"Masque of Mercy"
    Irwin [2], 302-12.
    Juhnke, 161-63.

"Masque of Reason"
    Irwin [1]. 305-06.
    Irwin [2], 302-12.
    Juhnke, 160-61.
    Todasco, 227-30.

"Mending Wall"
    Dragland, item 39.
    Gibb, item 48.
    Ward, William S., 428-29.

"Neither Out Far Nor In Deep"
    Eberhart, 776.
    Lynen, 808-13.

"Nothing Gold Can Stay"
    Anderson, Charles R. [1], item 63.

"An Old Man's Winter Night"
    Davis, Charles G., item 19.

FROST (cont'd)

"Once By the Pacific"
Parsons, D. S. J., 205-10.

"The Onset"
Eberhart, 777.

"Out, Out"
Thornton, item 71.

"The Oven Bird"
Burgess [2], item 59.
Combellack [1], item 17.
Herndon, item 64.
Osborne [3], item 47.

"Range-Finding"
Mansell, item 63.

"The Road Not Taken"
Malbone [3], item 27.
Perrine [15], item 28.

"The Rose Family"
Perrine [16], item 43.

"A Servant to Servants"
Jones, Donald, 150-61.

"The Silken Tent"
Eberhart, 768-69.

"Snow"
Brenner, 20.

"Span of Life"
Bader, 86-87.

"Spring Pools"
Toor, item 28.

"Stopping By Woods on a Snowy Evening"
Armstrong, James, 440-45.
Brooks, 495-96.
Coursen [1], 236-38.
Dendinger, 822-29.

Drew, E. A., 68-69.
Faulkner, 560-61.
Knieger [4], 344-45.
Rosenberry, 526-28.
Wilcox, item 7.

"Two Tramps in Mud Time"
Braverman and Einbond, item 25.

"West-Running Brook"
Swennes, 369-71.

"Witch of Coos"
Brenner, 20.
Slights and Slights, item 40.

"The Wood-Pile"
Bishop, item 58.
Kern, item 49.
Narveson, 39-40.
Sinyavsky, 434-35.

GARDNER, ISABELLA (1895-   ), American

"Mea Culpa"
Logan, 251.

"The Widow's Yard"
Carroll, 215-16.

GARRIGUE, JEAN (1914-   ), American

"A Dream"
Lieberman, 122.

"The Little Pony"
Stepanchev, 88.

"Proem"
Bock, 229-30.

"A Water Walk by Villa D'Este"
Holmes, Theodore [2], 119-20.

GARTH, SIR SAMUEL (1661-1719), British

"The Dispensary"
Cook, Richard I., 107-16.

GASCOYNE, DAVID (1916-   ), British

General
    Raine [2], 193-229.

"Phantasmagoria"
    Raine [2], 214-15.

GINSBERG, ALLEN (1926-   ), American

General
    Howard, Richard [1], 145-52.
    Rosenthal [1], 89-112.

"Ankor Wat"
    Lehman, 403-05.

"Kaddish"
    Stepanchev, 171-72.

"A White Paper"
    Stepanchev, 169-70.

GOODMAN, PAUL (1911-   ), American

General
    Howard, Richard [1], 153-63.

GRAVES, ROBERT (1895-   ), British

"Certain Mercies"
    Gaskell, 217-18.

"Goliath and David"
    Bergonzi [1], 65-66.

"It's a Queer Time"
    Bergonzi [1], 66-67.

"Saint"
    Lacerva, item 31.

"To Juan at the Winter Solstice"
    Rosenberg [3], item 3.

GRAY, THOMAS (1716-1771), British

    "Elegy Written in a Country Churchyard"
        Bailey, John Cann, 267-70.
        Greene, Richard Leighton, item 47.

    "Ode on a Distant Prospect of Eton College"
        Ellis, 130-38.
        Foxell, 103-21.
        Spacks [3], 527-32.
        Wilkins, item 66.

    "Ode on the Spring"
        Spacks [3], 520-24.

    "Sonnet on the Death of Richard West"
        Mell, 131-43.
        Spacks [3], 524-25.

GRENFELL, JULIAN (1888-1915), British

    "Into Battle"
        Bergonzi [1], 49-51.

    "Prayes for Those on the Staff"
        Bergonzi [1], 48-49.

GREVILLE, FULKE (1554-1628), British

    "The Treatie of Humane Learning"
        Farmer, 660-70.
        Mahoney, 209-12.

GUNN, THOM (1929-), British

    "Helen's Rape"
        Fraser [1], 361-62.

    "In Santa Maria Del Popolo"
        Swinden, 352.

    "On the Move"
        Fraser [1], 364-66.

    "Waking in a Newly-Built House"
        Swinden, 356.

HALLAM, ARTHUR HENRY (1811-1833), British

> "Long Hast Thou Wandered on the Happy Mountain"
> Antippas [2], 294-96.

> "The Palace of Art"
> Antippas [2], 294-96.

HARDY, THOMAS (1840-1928), British

> General
> Guerard, 363-88.
> Holmes, Theodore [1], 285-300.

> "Afterwards"
> Mitchell [2], 68-70.
> Wain [3], 169-71.

> "At Castle Botrel"
> Barnes, T. R., 263-65.

> "Beeny Cliff"
> Friedman, Alan Warren, 224-28.

> "The Blinded Bird"
> Allen, D. C. [1], 95-96.

> "The Burghers"
> Allen, D. C. [1], 97.

> "Channel Firing"
> Alexis, item 61.
> Pitts, Arthur W., Jr. [1], item 24.
> Ransom [4], 170-73.

> "The Chapel-Organist"
> Allen, D. C. [1], 103.

> "The Cheval-Glass"
> Allen, D. C. [1], 101-02.

> "Contretemps"
> May, Charles E., 72.

> "The Convergence of the Twain"
> Thatcher, item 34.

> "The Dance of the Phoenix"
> Allen, D. C. [1], 98.

"The Darkling Thrush"
  Allen, D. C. [1], 96.
  Knieger [4], 345.

"Doom and She"
  May, Charles E., 68.

"A Dream or No"
  Guerard, 386-88.

"Drinking Song"
  Zietlow, 117-18.

"During Wind and Rain"
  Marcus and Marcus, item 14.

"The Dynasts"
  Bailey, John Cann, 234-37.

"The Face at the Casement"
  Zietlow, 122-23.

"Former Beauties"
  Neumeyer, 263-66.

"God-Forgotten"
  Perrine [8], 187-88.

"The Head Above the Fog"
  Allen, D. C. [1], 92-93.

"Her Death and After"
  Allen, D. C. [1], 97-98.

"The House of Hospitalities"
  Hyde, 266-67.

"I Found Her Out There"
  Guerard, 383-86.

"If You Had Known"
  Guerard, 369-72.

"Last Week in October"
  Hyde, 267-68.

"A Man"
  Barnes, T. R., 259-63.

HARDY (cont'd)

"The Moth-Signal"
Allen, D. C. [1], 99.

"My Cicely"
Holmes, Theodore [1], 296-97.

"Nature's Questioning"
Allen, D. C. [1], 89-99.

"Neutral Tones"
Guerard, 369-71.

"The Noble Lady's Tale"
Allen, D. C. [1], 98-99.

"The Rift"
Hyde, 267.

"The Sacrilege"
Allen, D. C. [1], 99.

"She Did Not Turn"
Holmes, Theodore [1], 285-86.

"The Sign-Seeker"
May, Charles E., 69.

"The Subalterns"
Ransom [4], 173-78.

"The Sun on the Letter"
Allen, D. C. [1], 91-92.

"A Sunday Morning Tragedy"
Allen, D. C. [1], 98.

"A Trampwoman's Tragedy"
Allen, D. C [1], 98.

"The Two Wives"
May, Charles E., 72.

"Under the Waterfall"
Friedman, Alan Warren, 224-28.

"A Wasted Illness"
     Hyde, 268.

"Wessex Heights"
     Miller, J. Hillis [3], 339-59.

HAYDEN, ROBERT E. (1913-   ), American

General
     Galler, 268.
     Pool, 39-43.

HECHT, ANTHONY (1923-   ), American

General
     Howard, Richard [1], 164-73.

HEMINGWAY, ERNEST (1899-1961), American

General
     San Juan [2], 51-58.

HENLEY, WILLIAM ERNEST (1849-1903), British

"Space and Dread and the Dark"
     Herman, item 14.

HENRYSON, ROBERT (1430?-1506), British

"The Testament of Cresseid"
     Aswell, 471-87.
     Tillyard [2], 5-29.

HERBERT, GEORGE (1593-1633), British)

General
     Hanley [2], 121-35.
     Knieger [5], 111-24.
     Knieger [7], 138-47.
     Rickey [1], 745-60.

"The Agony"
     Hughes, R. E. [1], 90.
     Lamba and Lamba [1], item 51.

"Anagram of the Virgin Mary"
     Leiter [2], 543-44.
     Reiter [1], 59-60.

HERBERT (cont'd)

"Assurance"
    Wolfe, Jane E., 213-22.

"The Bag"
    El-Gabalawy, 417-18.

"The Bunch of Grapes"
    McGrath, item 15.
    Montgomery, 463-65.

"Christmas"
    Hughes, R. E. [1], 92.

"The Church"
    Stewart, Stanley, 103-05.

"The Church Militant"
    Stewart, Stanley, 105-10.

"The Collar"
    Levitt and Johnston, 329-30.

"Easter"
    Hughes, R. E. [1], 93-94.

"Employment (II)"
    Knieger [5], 120-22.

"The Flower"
    Stewart, Stanley, 100-03.

"Frailtie"
    Hanley [1], item 18.

"Jordan"
    Barnes, T. R., 74-76.

"Love"
    Montgomery, 469-71.

"Love (III)"
    Thorpe, item 16.

"Love-Joy"
    Montgomery, 462-63.

"Love Unknown"
       Montgomery, 465-69.

"Paradise"
       Williams, R. Darby, 182-86.

"Peace"
       El-Gabalawy, 413-14.

"The Pilgrimage"
       El-Gabalawy, 410-13.

"Prayer"
       Hughes, R. E. [1], item 89.

"Providence"
       Mollenkott, 34-41.

"The Quip"
       Daniels [2], item 7.

"Redemption"
       El-Gabalawy, 414-16.
       Hughes, R. E. [1], 91-92.
       Knieger [7], 143-44.

"The Rose"
       Allen, D. C. [2], 102-14.

"The Temper"
       Bowers, Fredson [2], 202-13.

"Vertue"
       Collins, Dan S., item 50.
       French, Roberts W. [2], item 4.

"The Windows"
       Barnes, T. R., 73-74.
       Forsyth, 21-25.

HERRICK, ROBERT (1591-1674), British

"The Carkanet"
       Huttar, item 35.
       Sanders, Charles, item 24.

HERRICK (cont'd)

"Corinna's Going 'A-Maying' "
      Hughes, Richard E., 420-21.
      Rea, 544-46.

"Delight in Disorder"
      Spitzer, 209-14.

"A Dirge Upon the Death of the Right Valiant Lord,
   Bernard Stuart"
      Deming, 163-65.

"The Faerie Temple"
      Woodward, 276-79.

"The Funerall Rites of the Rose"
      Deming, 154-58.

"Good Friday: Rex Tragicus, or Christ Going to
   His Crosse"
      Allen, D. C. [2], 138-51.

"The Hock-Cart, or Harvest Home"
      Clark, Paul O., item 70.
      Hughes, Richard E., 420-22.
      Lougy, item 13.

"How Roses Came Red"
      Rose, Edgar Smith, 350.

"Oberons Feast"
      Woodward, 279-81.

"Oberons Palace"
      Woodward, 281-84.

"To M. Denham, on his Prospective Poem"
      Tyner, item 72.

"To Perilla"
      Deming, 158-60.

"To the Reverend Shade of his Religious Father"
      Deming, 160-62.

"Upon Julia's Clothes"
>   Harris, William O. [2], item 29.
>   Leiter [4], item 41.
>   Shuchter, item 27.
>   Weinberg, item 12.

HINE, DARYL (1936-   ), British

General
>   Howard, Richard [1], 174-86.

HOFFMAN, DANIEL (1923-   ), American

General
>   Howard, Richard [1], 187-99.

"A Little Geste"
>   Howard, Richard [1], 196.

HOLLANDER, JOHN (1929-   ), American

General
>   Howard, Richard [1], 200-31.

"Icarus Before Knossos"
>   Howard, Richard [1], 206-07.

HOLMES, JOHN (1926-   ), American

"Herself"
>   Holmes, Doris, item 77.

HOLMES, OLIVER WENDELL, SR. (1809-1894), American

"The Deacon's Masterpiece"
>   Webb, Howard, item 17.

HOPKINS, GERARD MANLEY (1844-1889), British

General
>   Hafley, 215-22.
>   Murphy [2], 1-16.
>   Nist [2], 497-500.
>   Wooton [2], 367-75.

"As Kingfishers Catch Fire" (No. 57)
>   Litzinger [3], 45.

HOPKINS (cont'd)

"The Caged Skylark" (No. 39).
  Jordan, Frank, Jr., item 80.

"The Candle Indoors" (No. 46.)
  Chevigny, 149-50.
  Gavin, item 50.

"Carrion Comfort" (No. 64)
  Carson, J. Angela, 547-57.
  Chevigny, 152-53.
  Wolfe, Patricia, 91-93.

"Felix Randal" (No. 53)
  Chevigny, 149.

"God's Grandeur" (No. 31)
  Bender, item 55.
  Chevigny, 145-46.
  Gafford, item 21.
  Giovannini, item 36.
  Montag [1], 302-03.
  Pendexter, item 2.
  Reiman [1], 39-42.
  Slakey [1], 159-63.
  Taylor, Michael, item 68.
  Watson, Thomas L., item 47.
  White, Gertrude M., 284-87.

"The Habit of Perfection" (No. 22)
  Greiner, item 19.

"Harry Ploughman" (No. 71)
  Fike, 328-29.

"Heaven-Haven" (No. 9)
  Mellown, 263-65.

"Henry Purcell" (No. 45)
  Barnes, T. R., 255-57.

"Hurrahing the Harvest" (No. 38)
  Chevigny, 147-48.
  Donoghue, 235-37.

"I Must Hunt Down the Prize" (No. 88)
  Mellown, 263-65.

"I Wake and Feel the Fell of Dark, Not Day" (No. 67)
    Wolfe, Patricia, 98-100.

"Inversnaid" (No. 56)
    Barnes, T. R., 251-53.

"The Loss of the Eurydice" (No. 41)
    O'Dea, 291-93.

"My Own Heart Let Me More Have Pity On" (No. 69)
    Wolfe, Patricia, 101-03.

"No Worst, There Is None" (No. 65)
    Wolfe, Patricia, 93-96.

"Patience, Hard Thing! The Hard Thing But to Pray"
    (No. 68)
    Wolfe, Patricia, 100-01.

"Pied Beauty" (No. 37)
    Drew, E. A., 75.
    Litzinger [3], 45.

"Ribblesdale" (No. 58)
    Barnes, T. R., 253-55.

"St. Thecla" (No. 136)
    Sharples, 204-09.

"The Shepherd's Brow" (No. 75)
    Mariani, 63-68.

"Spelt from Sibyl's Leaves" (No. 61)
    White, Norman E., 546-47.

"Spring" (No. 33)
    Hallgarth, 87.

"Spring and Fall: To a Young Child" (No. 55)
    Doherty, 140-43.
    Drew, E. A., 52-54.
    Fike, 329-32.
    Louise, item 65.
    Smith, Julian, item 36.

"That Nature Is a Heraclitean Fire and of the Comfort
    of the Resurrection" (No. 72)
    Litzinger [3], 46.

HOPKINS (cont'd)

"That Nature Is a Heraclitean Fire and of the Comfort
of the Resurrection" (No. 72) (cont'd)
Stevens, Sister Mary Dominic, item 18.

"Thou Art Indeed Just, Lord" (No. 74)
Drew, E. A., 48-51.

"To R. B. [Robert Bridges]" (No. 76)
Bremer, 144-48.

"To Seem the Stranger" (No. 66)
Wolfe, Patricia, 96-98.

"A Vision of the Mermaids" (No. 2)
Hallgarth, 81-82.

"The Windhover" (No. 36)
August [1], 465-68.
August [2], 72-74.
Baxter, 71-75.
Brophy [1], 673-74.
Chevigny, 146-47.
Haskell, 75-77.
Hill, Archibald A. [2], 349-59.
Litzinger [2], 228-30.
Miller, Bruce E. [2], 115-19.
Montag [2], 109-18.
Schneider [1], item 22.
Shea, 219-39.
Stempel, 305-07.
Templeman [2], 103-06.
Thomas, J. D., item 31.
Wain [2], 138-52.
Winter, 212-13.

"The Woodlark" (No. 138)
Fike, 326-28.

"The Wreck of the Deutschland" (No. 28)
Cotter [1], 73-79.
Foxell, 203-54.
Hallgarth, 84-85.
Litzinger [5], item 7.
McNamee [2], 267-76.
Miller, J. Hillis [1], 509-14.
Pitts, Arthur W., Jr. [2], item 7.

Schneider [2], 110-22.
Wooton [2], 369-71.

HOPKINSON, FRANCIS (1737-1791), American

"Ode Sacred to the Memory of his Late Gracious
Majesty George II"
Lenhart, 65-67.

"Prologue in Praise of Music: Ode on Music"
Lenhart, 58-60.

HOUSMAN, ALFRED EDWARD (1859-1936), British

General
Brashear [3], 81-90.
Haber, 57-67.
Reedy, 51-61.

"Be Still, My Soul"
Pitts, Gordon, 137-38.

"The Carpenter's Son"
Andrews, item 3.

"Epitaph on an Army of Mercenaries"
Allen, D. C. [4], 78-92.

"He, Standing Hushed"
Pearsall, Robert Brainard [2], 62-64.

"Is My Team Plowing?"
Brenner, 183-86.
Pearsall, Robert Brainard [1], 42-44.

"The Land of Biscay"
Wight, 341-44.

"On Wenlock Edge the Wood's in Trouble"
Reese, 371-72.

"The Oracles"
Spivey, item 44.

"The Recruit"
Leggett, item 25.

HOUSMAN (cont'd)

        "A Shropshire Lad"
                Kowalczyk, 223-35.

HUGHES, JAMES LANGSTON (1902-1967), American

        General
                Bigsby, 77-87.
                Bontemps, 140-43.
                Cartey, 22-25. 83-92.
                Davis, Arthur P. [3], 280-96.
                Emanuel [1]. 335-44.
                Emanuel [3], 25-30, 74-92.
                Gross, Seymour Lee and John Edward Hard,
                        194-203.
                Holmes, Eugene, 144-51.
                Hudson, 345-48.
                Isaacs, Harold R., 247-54.
                Jones, Harry L., 331-34.
                King, Woodie, Jr., 27-32, 95-96.
                Kramer, Aaron, 159-66.
                Mayfield, 34-35.
                Presley [1], 380-86.
                Presley [2], 79-84.

HUGHES, TED (1930-   ), British

        General
                Rosenthal [1], 224-33.

        "Childbirth"
                John [2], 9-10.

        "The Hawk in the Rain"
                John [2], 6-8.

        "Lupercalia"
                John [2], 13.

HUGO, RICHARD FRANKLIN (1923-   ), American

        General
                Howard, Richard [1], 232-46.

HUXLEY, ALDOUS (1894-1963), British

        General
                Holmes, Charles M., 391-406.

"Beauty"
>Holmes, Charles M. , 401-02.

"Leda"
>Holmes, Charles M. , 405.

"Soles Occidere et Redire Possunt"
>Holmes, Charles M. , 405.

IGNATOW, DAVID (1914-), American

General
>Contoski, 211-13.

JAMES I (1566-1625), British

"Kingis Quair"
>MacQueen, 117-31.

JARRELL, RANDALL (1914-1965), American

"Cinderella"
>Ransom [3], 276-78.

"A Front"
>Hill, H. Russell, 162-68, 178.

"Losses"
>Jackson, James L. [1], item 49.

"The Lost World"
>Ransom [3], 278-80.

"Thinking of the Lost World"
>Ransom [3], 280-81.

JEFFERS, ROBINSON (1887-1962), American

General
>Langford, Richard E. , 14-17.

"The Cruel Falcon"
>Boyers, 500-03.

"Rearmament"
>Boyers, 505-07.

JEFFERS (cont'd)

> "Return"
>> Boyers, 498-99.

> "Roan Stallion"
>> Boyers, 490-91.
>> Keller [1], 111-20.

JOHNSON, JAMES WELDON (1871-1938), American

> General
>> Adelman, 128-45.
>> Collier [2], 351-59.
>> Jackson, Miles, Jr., 32-34.
>> Levy, Eugene, 357-70.

JOHNSON, LIONEL PIGOT (1867-1902), British

> "The Dark Angel"
>> Wain [2], 153-78.

JOHNSON, SAMUEL (1709-1784), British

> "On the Death of Mr. Robert Levett"
>> Barnes, T. R., 132-33.

> "Vanity of Human Wishes"
>> Aden [1], 295-303.
>> Barnes, T. R., 130-32.

JONES, LE ROI (1934-), American

> General
>> Collins, Douglas, 336-38.
>> Major, Clarence, 54-56.
>> Otten, 5-11.
>> Rosenthal [1], 189-91.

JONSON, BEN (1572?-1637), British

> General
>> Parfitt, 123-34.
>> Spanos [1], 1-23.

> "An Elegy"
>> Allen, D. C. [1], 62-65.

"Epitaph on Elizabeth, L. H."
     Babb, 738-44.

"Epitaph on Solomon Pavy"
     May, Louis F., item 16.

"A Fit of Rime Against Rime"
     Clubb, Roger L., 145-47.

"The Ghyrlond"
     Cubeta [1], 98-100.

"A Hymne on the Nativitie of my Saviour"
     Cubeta [1], 107-10.

"Queene and Huntresse (or Hymne)"
     Rackin [1], 186-96.

"The Reverse"
     Cubeta [1], 100-01.

"The Sinners Sacrifice"
     Cubeta [1], 103-07.

"A Song"
     Steese, item 31.

"To Heaven"
     Allen, D. C., 65-69.
     Cubeta [1], 101-03.

"To John Donne"
     Wiersma, item 4.

"To Penshurst"
     Cubeta [2], 14-24.
     McCutcheon, item 52.
     Parfitt, 123-26.
     Wilson, Gayle Edward, 77-89.

JUSTICE, DONALD RODNEY (1925-   ), American

General
     Howard, Richard [1], 247-57.

"The Metamorphosis"
     Howard, Richard [1], 250-51.

KEATS, JOHN (1795-1821), British

    General
            Haworth [1], 371-94.
            Heinen, 382-88.
            Reid [2], 472-95.
            Yost, 555-66.

    "La Belle Dame Sans Merci"
            Slote [1], 22-30.

    "Endymion"
            Harrison, Robert [1], 538-54.

    "The Eve of St. Agnes"
            Barnes, T. R., 219-22.
            Bloom, Edward A., item 3.
            Chandler [2], 273-74.
            Scholl, item 33.
            Stillinger [2], 533-55.

    "The Fall of Hyperion: A Dream"
            Chayes, 499-515.
            Haworth [2], 637-49.
            Manierre [2], 264-79.
            Miller, Bruce E. [1], 234-39.
            Sperry, 77-84.

    "Isabella"
            Stillinger [3], 593-605.

    "Ode on a Grecian Urn"
            Austin [1], 434-36.
            Burgess [1], item 30.
            Cornelius [2], item 57.
            Halpern, 284-88.
            Hutton, item 40.
            Kenney [1], item 69.
            Swanson, Roy Arthur, 302-05.
            Teich, 496-502.

    "Ode on Melancholy"
            Little, item 46.
            Smith, Barbara Harrnstein, 679-91.

    "Ode to a Nightingale"
            Harrison, Thomas P., 353-59.

        Hecht, 50-71.
        Matthey, 303-17.
        Mayerson, item 29.

    "Ode to Psyche"
        Schulz [1], 55-65.

    "On First Looking into Chapman's Homer"
        Slote [2], 256-60.

    "On Sitting Down to Read King Lear Once Again"
        Williams, Porter, Jr., item 26.

    "Sleep and Poetry"
        Haworth [1], 371-73, 380.

    "To Autumn"
        Barnes, T. R., 222-24.
        Haworth [1], 375-76.
        Lindenberger, 123-34.

    "To Sleep"
        Thomas, W. K. [4], item 55.

KENNEDY, JOSEPH CHARLES (1929-   ), American

    "Poets"
        McGann [1], 198-99.

KENNEDY, X. J., pseud.
    See Kennedy, Joseph Charles

KILMER, ALFRED JOYCE (1886-1918), American

    "Trees"
        Garlitz [2], 299-301.
        Kenney [2], 431-33.
        Nims, 322-31.

KINGSLEY, HENRY (1830-1876), British

    "Magdalen at Michael's Gate"
        Scheuerle, 144-46.

KINNELL, GALWAY (1927-   ), American

    General
        Cambon, 30-33.

KINNELL (cont'd)

>   General (cont'd)
>   Howard, Richard [1], 258-71.
>
>   "Easter"
>   Cambon, 33-36.
>
>   "First Song"
>   Hurt, item 23.

KIZER, CAROLYN (1925-   ), American

>   General
>   Howard, Richard [1], 272-80.

KOCH, KENNETH (1925-   ), American

>   General
>   Howard, Richard [1], 281-91.
>
>   "When the Sun Tries to Go On"
>   Lehman, 401-03.

KUNITZ, STANLEY (1905-   ), American

>   "Father and Son"
>   Ostroff [1], 56-80.

LANDOR, WALTER SAVAGE (1775-1864), British

>   "Yes, I Write Verses"
>   Perrine [9], 393-95.

LANGLAND (or LANGLEY), WILLIAM (c1332-c1400), British

>   "Piers the Plowman"
>   Adams, John F., 23-41.
>   Kaske, R. E., 32-60.
>   Kean [1], 349-63.
>   Kean [2], 241-61.
>   Martin, Jay, 535-48.
>   Previte-Orton, 18-30.
>   Schroeder, Mary C., 8-18.
>   Spearing [1], 241-53.
>   Spearing [3], 722-37.
>   Vasta [2], 17-29.
>   Wesling, 277-89.

LANIER, SIDNEY (1842-1881), American

"Betrayal"
Lenhart, 243-44.

"Corn"
Lenhart, 247-52.

"In Absence"
Lenhart, 252-53.

"June Dreams, in January"
Lenhart, 244-46.

"Life and Song"
Lenhart, 242-43.

"The Marshes of Glynn"
Lenhart, 272-76.
Ross, 403-16.

"Song of the Chattahoochee"
Lenhart, 269-71.

"Sunrise"
Lenhart, 277-81.

"The Symphony"
Lenhart, 255-60.

LARKIN, PHILIP ARTHUR (1922-), British

General
Rosenthal [1], 233-44.

"Maiden Name"
Swinden, 347-48.

"Naturally the Foundation Will Bear Your Expenses"
Wain [1], 171-72.

LATTIMORE, RICHARD ALEXANDER (1906-), American

"Witness to Death"
Swetnam, item 59.

LAUGHLIN, JAMES (1914-   ), American

> "Go West Young Man"
>> Perrine [7], item 61.

LAWRENCE, DAVID HERBERT (1885-1930), British.

> General
>> Rich, 218-25.

> "A Doe at Evening"
>> Pinto, 11-12.

> "Love on the Farm"
>> Pinto, 8-9.

> "Piano"
>> Pinto, 9-10.

> "Snake"
>> Pinto, 13-14.

> "Song of a Man Who Has Come Through"
>> Levy, Raphael, item 44.

LEE-HAMILTON, EUGENE

> "The New Medusa"
>> MacBeth, 144-45.

LEVERTOV, DENISE (1923-   ), American

> General
>> Howard, Richard [1], 292-305.
>> Hunt, Jean M. [2], 149-53.
>> Rosenthal [1], 184-88.

> "At the Edge"
>> Duddy, 142-43.

> "The Coming Fall"
>> Duddy, 148-49.

> "The Disclosure"
>> Duddy, 148.

> "The Garden Wall"
>> Duddy, 147-48.

"The Goddess"
    Duddy, 139-40.

"Olga Poems"
    Hunt, Jean M. [1], 171-75.

"The Third Dimension"
    Duddy, 140-41.

LEWIS, JAMES FRANKLIN (20th Century), American

"In Memoriam"
    Lund, item 23.

LISTER, RICHARD PERCIVAL (1914-   ), British

"Target"
    Perrine [9], 390-92.

LOGAN, JOHN BURTON (1923-   ), American

General
    Cambon, 36-42.
    Howard, Richard [1], 306-17.

LONGFELLOW, HENRY WADSWORTH (1807-1882), American

General
    Bewley, 297-304.
    Ruland, 661-68.

"Chaucer"
    Tenfelde, item 55.

"The Cross of Snow"
    Cox, James M. [1], 97-100.

"The Occultation of Orion"
    Zimmerman [2], 540-46.

"Serenade"
    Tanselle, item 48.

LOVELACE, RICHARD (1618-1658), British

General
    King, Bruce [3], 511-15.

LOVELACE (cont'd)

    "Advice to My Best Brother"
        King, Bruce [3], 513-14.
        Wadsworth, 637-39.

    "The Grasse-Hopper"
        Allen, D. C. [2], 152-64.
        King, Bruce [3], 514-15.

    "The Snayl"
        Wadsworth, 639.

LOWBURY, EDWARD (1913-   ), British

    General
        Press [1], 302-16.

LOWELL, AMY (1874-1925), American

    "A Fairy Tale"
        Brenner, 37-38.

    "The Hammers"
        Brenner, 57.

    "The Overgrown Pasture"
        Brenner, 55.

    "Patterns"
        Brenner, 53-54.

LOWELL, JAMES RUSSELL (1819-1891), American

    "A Fable for Critics"
        Oggel, item 60.

LOWELL, ROBERT (1917-   ), American

    General
        Carruth, 429-47.
        Jones, A. R. [1], 17-21.
        Powell, 180-85.
        Rosenthal [1], 25-78.

    "Christmas Eve Under Hooker's Statue"
        Fein, 823-26.

"The Dead in Europe"
Fein, 832-33.

"The Death of the Sheriff"
Weatherhead, 192-96.

"The Exile's Return"
Brumleve, 144-45.
Fein, 833-34.

"The First Sunday of Lent"
Brumleve, 145-46.

"For the Union Dead"
Brumleve, 150-51.
Stepanchev, 34-35.

"Mary Winslow"
McAleer, John J., item 29.

"The Mills of the Kavanaughs"
Bowen, Roger, 81-89.
Stepanchev, 28-29.

"My Last Afternoon with Uncle Devereux Winslow"
Brumleve, 147-48.

"The Quaker Graveyard in Nantucket"
Fein, 826-32.
Stepanchev, 24-27.

"Skunk Hour"
Ostroff [1], 82-110.
Stepanchev, 31-32.

"Waking Early Sunday Morning"
Howard, Richard [2], 413-15.

"Washers of the Shroud"
Anderson, John Q., 361-63.

LOWENFELS, WALTER (1897-), American

General
Guttmann, 843-50.

LOY, MINA (1882-1966), Anglo-American

"Apology of Genius"
Fields, Kenneth [2], 602-05.

"Der Blinde Junge"
Fields, Kenneth [2], 605-07.

MACBETH, GEORGE (1932-), British

General
Rosenthal [1], 260-62.

MCKAY, CLAUDE (1890-1948), American

General
Bigsby, 53-63, 69-70.
Cooper, 297-306.

"The Harlem Dancer"
Collier [1], 81-83.

MACLEISH, ARCHIBALD (1892-), American

"Ars Poetica"
Sullivan, Harry R., 1280-83.

"The Hamlet of A. MacLeish"
Gottesman, 157-62.

"Songs for Eve"
Sickels, 205-09.

MACNEICE, LOUIS (1907-1963), British

"Perseus"
Cope, John I., item 48.

"The Riddle"
Dorrill, item 7.

MALLOCK, WILLIAM HURRELL (1849-1923), British

"Chorus from a Tragedy"
Nickerson, 172-74.

"Melancholy"
Nickerson, 174-75.

MARKHAM, EDWIN (1852-1940), American

> General
> > Filler, 447-59.

MARLOWE, CHRISTOPHER (1564-1593), British

> "Hero and Leander"
> > Cubeta [3], 500-05.

> "Hero and Leander--Part I"
> > Marsh, item 30.

> "The Passionate Shepherd to his Love"
> > Leiter [1], 444-49.

MARVELL, ANDREW (1621-1678), British

> General
> > Lord, 207-24.
> > Toliver [1], 83-97.

> "Antipodes in Shoes"
> > Alvarez, 421-24.

> "Bermudas"
> > Cummings, R. M., 331-40.

> "The Coronet"
> > Carpenter [1], 50-62.
> > Hardy, John Edward, 45-60.

> "Damon the Mower"
> > Nevo, 18-20.
> > Toliver [1], 92-95.

> "Daphnis and Cloe"
> > Nevo, 15-17.

> "The Definition of Love"
> > Alvarez, 424-28.
> > Berthoff [1], 16-29.
> > Legouis, 49-54.
> > Zwicky, item 52.

> "A Dialogue Between the Resolved Soul and Created Pleasure"
> > Toliver [2], 58-69.

MARVELL (cont'd)

"A Dialogue Between the Soul and Body"
        Barnes, T. R., 86-88.
        Warnke, 28-30.

"A Dialogue Between the Two Horses"
        Sutherland, 51-53.

"The Gallery"
        Warnke, 23-26.

"The Garden"
        Carpenter [2], 155-69.
        Godshalk [1], 639-53.
        Hecht, 50-71.
        Holditch, item 5.
        Salerno [1], 103-20.
        Walcutt, item 48.
        Williamson, George [1], 590-98.

"An Horatian Ode Upon Cromwell's Return from
   Ireland"
        Coolidge, 111-20.
        French, A. L. 397-413.
        Gerard [2], item 22.
        Syfret, 160-72.
        Wain [2], 59-74.
        Wallace, 33-45.
        Wilson, A. J. N., 325-41.
        Wimsatt, 99-130.

"Hortus"
        Williamson, George [1], 590-98.

"The Last Instructions to a Painter"
        Miner, Earl [5], 288-94.

"The Mower Against Gardens"
        Cinquemani, item 77.

"The Mower to the Glo-Worms"
        Godshalk [2], item 12.
        Mitchell [4], item 50.

"The Mower's Song"
        Everett [1], 219-24.

"The Nymph Complaining for the Death of her Faun"
    Allen, D. C. [2], 165-86.
    Jones, Evan, item 73.
    Miner, Earl [2], 9-16.
    Nevo, 5-15.
    Rapin [1], item 71.

"The Picture of Little T. C. in a Prospect of Flowers"
    Cullen, 1559-70.
    Simmons, item 62.
    Warnke, 26-28.

"To His Coy Mistress"
    Hartwig, 572-75.
    Hogan, 1-11.
    Hyman, Lawrence W. [1], 8-10.
    Keogh [1], item 13.
    King, Bruce [4], 689-703.
    Low and Pival, 414-21.
    Moldenhauer, 189-206.

"The Unfortunate Lover"
    Patrick, item 65.
    Salerno [2], item 42.

"Upon Appleton House"
    Allen, D. C. [2], 187-225.
    Evett, 504-13.
    Lord, 211-16.
    Rostvig [2], 337-51.

MASEFIELD, JOHN (1878-1967), British

"Cargoes"
    Brenner, 245-46.

"Dauber"
    Brenner, 238-40.

"The Everlasting Mercy"
    Brenner, 236-38.

MELVILLE, HERMAN (1819-1891), American

"Billy in the Darbies"
    Warren, Robert Penn, 840-55.

MELVILLE (cont'd)

"Clarel"
        Warren, Robert Penn, 826-35.

"The Little Good Fellows"
        Stein, William Bysshe [3], 142.

"The Loiterer"
        Stein, William Bysshe [3], 139-41.

"The March into Virginia"
        Warren, Robert Penn, 807-10.

"Naples in the time of Bomba"
        Bridgman [1], 236-39.

"The Rose Farmer"
        Bridgman [1], 242-44.

"Rose Window"
        Bridgman [1], 242.

"Stockings in the Farm-House Chimney"
        Stein, William Bysshe [3], 144-45.

"Time's Betrayal"
        Stein, William Bysshe [3], 139.

"Trophies of Peace"
        Stein, William Bysshe [3], 143-44.

"When Forth the Shepherd Leads the Flock"
        Stein, William Bysshe [3], 141-42.

MENCKEN, HENRY LOUIS (1880-1956), American

    General
        Martin, Edward A., 346-53.

MEREDITH, GEORGE (1828-1909), British

    "Daphne"
        Bogner, 113-14.

    "Earth and a Wedded Woman"
        Bogner, 110-11.

"Lucifer in Starlight"
    Morris, John W., 76-80.

"Margaret's Bridal Eve"
    Bogner, 118-19.

"Modern Love"
    Plunkett [2], item 42.
    Simpson, Arthur L., Jr. [1], 341-56.

"Modern Love--Sonnet 23"
    Kwinn, 151-53.

"The Nuptials of Atilla"
    Bogner, 116-17.

"Ode to the Spirit of Earth in Autumn"
    Bogner, 108-09.

"Odes in Contribution to the Song of French History"
    Bailey, John Cann, 237-38.

"The Old Chartist"
    Bartlett, item 56.

"Pass We to Another Land"
    Perkus, 268-72.

"Periander"
    Tompkins, 286-95.

"Phantasy"
    Ketcham, 241-48.

"The Rape of Aurora"
    Bogner, 112-13.

"The Teaching of the Nude"
    Bogner, 117-18.

"The Test of Manhood"
    Bogner, 111-12.

"The Woods of Westermain"
    Crunden, 265-82.

MEREDITH, WILLIAM (1919-   ), American

    General
        Howard, Richard [1], 318-26.

MERRILL, JAMES (1926-   ), American

    General
        Howard, Richard [1], 327-48.

    "From the Cupola"
        Howard, Richard [3], 329-32.

    "The Thousand and Second Night"
        Howard, Richard [3], 332-33.

MERWIN, WILLIAM STANLEY (1927-   ), American

    General
        Cambon, 16-22.
        Howard, Richard [1], 349-81.

    "Dictum: For a Masque of Deluge"
        Howard, Richard [1], 356-58.

    "The Drunk in the Furnace"
        Howard, Richard [1], 370-71.

    "Leviathan"
        Wild, 954-57.

    "You, Genoese Mariner"
        Howard, Richard [1], 363-64.

MIDDLETON, CHRISTOPHER (1926-   ), British

    General
        Rosenthal [1], 257-60.

MILLAY, EDNA ST. VINCENT (1892-1950), American

    "Justice Denied in Massachusetts"
        Brenner, 79-80.

MILTON, JOHN (1608-1674), British

    General
        Allain, 379-84.

Allen, D. C. [3], 614-30.
Berry, Francis, 83-113.
Boswell, 83-94.
French, J. Milton, 376-89.
Roscelli, 463-84.
Wheeler [1], 359-68.
Wimsatt, 131-45.

"Ad Patrem"
Carey [1], 180-84.

"L'Allegro"
Battenhouse, 50-51.
Geckle, 455-73.
Howard, H. Wendell, item 3.
Riggs, item 44.
Stringer, 221-29.
Tate, Eleanor, 585-90.

"Elegy Five: 'In Adventum Veris' " (On the Coming
of Spring)
Allen, D. C. [2], 115-37.

"Epitaphium Damonis" (On the Death of Damon)
Condee, 577-94.

"How Soon Hath Time the Suttle Theef of Youth"
See "Sonnet VII"

"I Did But Prompt"
See "Sonnet XII"

"Lycidas"
Adams, Robert Martin, 293-304.
Battenhouse, 51-52.
Brett, 39-50.
Daniels [1], item 43.
Fletcher, 250-57.
French, Roberts W. [3], 15-25.
Hardy, John Edward, 22-44.
Lawry [1], 27-32.
Madsen, 1-7.
Rajan [1], 51-64.
Schweitzer, item 18.
Wittreich [2], 60-70.

"On his Blindness"
See "Sonnet XIX"

MILTON (cont'd)

"On his Deceased Wife"
    See "Sonnet XXIII"

"On the Death of a Fair Infant"
    Cope, Jackson I., 660-74.
    Roscelli, 472-74.

"On the Late Massacher in Piemont"
    See "Sonnet XVIII"

"On the Morning of Christ's Nativity"
    Barnes, T. R., 92-93.
    Battenhouse, 49-50.
    Cullen, 1559-70.
    Roscelli, 477-83.

"On Time"
    Hardison, 107-22.
    Williams, R. Darby, 186-92.

"Paradise Lost"
    Aryanpur, 151-66.
    Barnes, T. R., 98-106.
    Battenhouse, 44-47.
    Bowers, Fredson [1], 264-73.
    Bryan [1], 197-214.
    Bush, 631-40.
    Chambers, A. B. [4], 693-95.
    Chambers, A. B. [5], 186-93.
    Champion, 384-94.
    Clark, Ira, 426-31.
    Collett, 88-96.
    Fenderson, 255-64.
    Fields, Albert W., 392-99.
    Fish [1], 162-82.
    Fish [2], 162-78.
    Fox [1], 30-39.
    Gross, Barry Edward, 95-106.
    Hart, 576-82.
    Hughes, Merritt Y., 1-33.
    Knott [1], 487-95.
    Lawry [2], 582-86.
    Low [1], 171-81.
    Low [3], 30-35.
    Marshall, William H. [1], 15-20.

MILTON (cont'd)

"Paradise Lost--Book X"
    Muldrow [1], 194-206.
    Steadman [2], 35-40.
    Tillyard [1], 808-16.

"Paradise Lost--Book XI"
    Lewalski [1], 25-35.
    Miner, Earl [4], 43-53.

"Paradise Lost--Book XII"
    Greenfield [1], item 57.
    Lewalski [1], 25-35.
    Miner, Earl [4], 43-53.
    Reiter [2], item 2.

"Paradise Regained"
    Battenhouse, 44-47.
    Dyson [1], 197-211.
    Langford, Thomas, 37-46.
    Lewalski [2], 186-220.
    Muldrow [2], 377-80.
    Ricks, 701-04.
    Seaman, 97-107.
    Steadman [3], 384-91.

"Paradise Regained--Books I and II"
    Nieman, 133-39.

"The Passion"
    Roscelli, 474-75.

"Il Penseroso"
    Battenhouse, 50-51.
    Stringer, 221-29.
    Tate, Eleanor, 585-90.

"Sonnet VII" (On his Having Arrived at the Age of
  Twenty-Three)
    Stoehr, 292-93.

"Sonnet XII" (I Did But Prompt)
    Maresca, 491-94.
    Rauber, 561-64.

"Sonnet XVI" (To the Lord General Cromwell, May, 1652)
    Stoehr, 296-99.

"Sonnet XVIII" (On the Late Massacher in Piemont)
        Stoehr, 299-300.

"Sonnet XIX" (On his Blindness)
        Foxell, 13-22.
        Gossman and Whiting, 364-72.
        Monteiro [5], item 67.
        Pequigney, 485-98.
        Stoehr, 293-94.

"Sonnet XXIII" (On his Deceased Wife)
        Stoehr, 294-96.
        Wheeler [2], 510-15.

"To the Lord General Cromwell, May, 1652"
        See "Sonnet XVI"

"When I Consider How My Light Is Spent"
        See "Sonnet XIX"

MOFFITT, JOHN (1908-   ), American

"Along the Curb"
        Jerome [3], 220-21.

"Nightmare's Nest"
        Jerome [3], 219-20.

"The Signals"
        Jerome [3], 218-19.

"The Well"
        Jerome [3], 222.

MONTGOMERIE, ALEXANDER (1556?-1610?), British

General
        Jack, 168-81.

MOORE, MARIANNE (1887-1972), American

"Apparition of Splendor"
        Parkin [1], 167-72.
        Parkin [4], 406-07.

"Bird-Witted"
        Kenner [3], 111-13.

MOORE (cont'd)

"Dream"
Going [2], 145-53.

"The Fish"
Kenner [2], 761-63.
Renick, item 7.

"No Swan So Fine"
Parkin [4], 407.

"O to Be a Dragon"
Parkin [4], 406.

"An Octopus"
Kenner [2], 765-66.

"The Pangolin"
Parkin [4], 403-06.

"St. Nicholas"
Weatherhead, 197-98.

"Tell Me, Tell Me"
Parkin [4], 407.

"Then the Ermine"
Parkin [4], 407.

"To a Snail"
Warlow, item 51.

"What Are Years?"
Drew, E. A., 84-89.

MOORE, THOMAS STURGE (1870-1944), British

"From Titian's 'Bacchanal' in the Prado at Madrid"
Winters [2], 13-15.

"Silence (I)"
Winters [2], 12-13.

"To Silence"
Winters [2], 10-12.

MORRIS, WILLIAM (1834-1896), British

> "The Chapel in Lyoness"
> Raymond, Meredith B. [1], 215-18.
>
> "The Defence of Guenevere"
> Perrine [11], 234-41.
> Raymond, Meredith B. [1], 214-15.
> Silver, 695-702.
>
> "The Earthly Paradise"
> Fleissner [3], 171-77.
>
> "The Haystack in the Floods"
> Hollow, 353-55.
> MacEachen [2], 73-75.
>
> "King Arthur's Tomb"
> Raymond, Meredith B. [1], 214-15.
>
> "Sir Galahad"
> Raymond, Meredith B. [1], 215-17.

MOSS, HOWARD (1922-), American

> General
> Howard, Richard [1], 382-95.
>
> "Persistence of Song"
> Howard, Richard [4], 334.

MUIR, EDWIN (1887-1959), British

> General
> Scholten, 322-26.
> Summers [1], 240-60.
> Watson, J. R., 237-49.
>
> "The Annunciation"
> Holloway [2], 566-67.
>
> "Ballad of Hector in Hades"
> Allen, D. C. [1], 34-36.
>
> "The Enchanted Knight"
> Allen, D. C. [1], 36-37.
>
> "The Island"
> Allen, D. C. [1], 37-38.

MUIR (cont'd)

"Milton"
Holloway [2], 552-54, 565.

"The Return"
Allen, D. C. [1], 30-31, 41-42.
Holloway [2], 554-59.

"Telemachos Remembers"
Holloway [2], 554-59, 565.

"The Toy Horse"
Goodwin, item 6.
Scott-Craig [2], item 62.

"Troy"
Holloway [2], 561-65.

"Variations on a Time Theme"
Watson, J. R., 234-37.

NASHE, THOMAS (1567-1601), British

"Adieu, Farewell Earth's Bliss"
Robinson, Fred C. [1], 89-92.

O'HARA, FRANK (1922?-1966), American

General
Howard, Richard [1], 396-412.

OLDHAM, JOHN (1653-1683), British

"Satyrs Upon the Jesuits"
Mackin, 78-90.

OLSON, CHARLES (1910-   ), American

General
Rosenthal [1], 160-73.

"The Kingfishers"
Rosenthal [1], 160-66.

ORLOVITZ, GIL (1918-   ), American

"The Rooster"
Ignatow, 247-48.

OWEN, WILFRED (1893-1918), British

    General
        Stallworthy [1], 199-214.

    "Futility"
        Barnes, T. R., 276.
        Bergonzi [1], 129-30.

    "Hospital Barge at Cerisy"
        Barnes, T. R., 276-77.

    "Strange Meeting"
        Bergonzi [1], 132-34.
        Gose [2], 417-19.

PATCHEN, KENNETH (1911-   ), American

    General
        See, 136-46.

PATMORE, COVENTRY (1823-1896), British

    "Angel in the House"
        Dunn, John J., 203-05.

    "Eros and Psyche"
        Dunn, John J., 211-14.

    "King Cophetua the First"
        Dunn, John J., 210-11.

    "Love at Large"
        Cadbury [2], 239-51.

    "Pain"
        Dunn, John J., 215-18.

    "Psyche's Discontent"
        Dunn, John J., 214-15.

    "The Rod, the Root and the Flower"
        Dunn, John J., 205-07, 210.

    "Sponsa Dei"
        Dunn, John J., 208

PATMORE (cont'd)

    "To the Body"
        Dunn, John J., 208-09.

    "To the Unknown Eros"
        Dunn, John J., 209.

PINDAR, PETER, pseud.
    See Wolcot, John.

PLATH, SYLVIA (1932-1963), American

    General
        Claire, 552-60.
        Howard, Richard [1], 413-22.
        Rosenthal [2], 79-89.

    "Daddy"
        Cox, C. B. and A. R. Jones, 108-12.

    "In Plaster"
        Jones, A. R. [1], 22-23.

POE, EDGAR ALLAN (1809-1849), American

    "Al Aaraaf"
        Lenhart, 152-54.

    "The Bells"
        Lenhart, 145-47, 156.

    "The City in the Sea"
        Amacher, item 60.
        Keefer, 436-39.
        Tate, Allen [1], 224-25.

    "The Conqueror Worm"
        Lubbers, 375-79.
        Swanson, Donald R., item 52.

    "Eldorado"
        Carlson [1], 232-33.

    "An Enigma"
        Brandy, item 35.

"Evening Star"
        Kilburn [1], item 76.

"Hymn"
        Lenhart, 144.

"Introduction"
        Rein, item 8.

"Israfel"
        Lenhart, 147-48.

"Lenore"
        Broderick, 504-10.

"The Raven"
        Burch, 81-83.
        Tate, Allen [1], 225.

"To Helen"
        Gargano [2], 652-53.
        Lenhart, 144-45.
        Tate, Allen [1], 221-22.

"Ulalume"
        Carlson [3], 22-37.
        Connolly, item 4.

POPE, ALEXANDER (1688-1744), British

General
        Miller, John H., 185-92.
        Moskovit, 445-62.
        Wellington, 225-35.

"Brutus"
        Torchiana, 853-67.

"Dunciad"
        Edwards, Thomas R., Jr., 447-63.
        Howard, William J., 463-74.
        Johnson, Carol, 108-16.
        Kernan, 256-66.
        Piper [1], 522-24.
        Tanner, 145-60.

"Dunciad--Book I"
        Vieth [3], 71-73.

POPE (cont'd)

"Dunciad--Book IV"
    Bluestone [1], item 40.
    Chambers, Jessie Rhodes, 185-92.
    Hauser [1], 224-29.
    Vieth [1], item 36.

"Elegy to the Memory of an Unfortunate Lady"
    Wain [2], 75-85.

"Eloisa to Abelard"
    Kalmey, 164-78.
    Mandel, 57-68.

"Epilogue to the Satires"
    Boyette, item 46.
    Piper [1], 519-22.

"Epistle to Augustus"
    Aden [2], item 70.
    Levine [2], 427-51.
    Schonhorn, 431-43.

"Epistle to Dr. Arbuthnot"
    Bradham [1], item 50.
    Dixon [2], 191-97.
    Dodd, item 17.
    Foxell, 41-101.
    Hunter, J. Paul, 625-47.
    Piper [1], 515-18.

"Essay on Criticism"
    Cruttwell, 396-97, 400.
    Fenner, 435-46.

"Essay on Man"
    Brett, 51-77.
    Kallich [1], 21-37.
    Kallich [3], 109-24.
    Mack, 105-07.
    Piper [1], 510-15.

"Essay on Man--Epistle II"
    Dixon [1], item 21.
    Goldgar, 730-43.
    Kallich [2], item 17.

"Moral Essays--Epistle II" (Of the Characters of
   Women)
         Barnes, T. R., 126-28.

"Moral Essays--Epistle III" (Of Avarice and Allied
   Vices)
         Mack, 104-05.

"Moral Essays--Epistle IV" (Of the Use of Riches)
         Korte, item 34.

"The Rape of the Lock"
         Barnes, T. R., 120-25.
         Cook, Richard I., 107-16.
         Hoffman, Arthur W., 530-46.
         Hyman, Stanley Edgar, 406-12.
         Wasserman, Earl R., 425-44.
         Williams, Aubrey, 412-25.

"Windsor Forest"
         Hauser [2], 465-82.
         Mack, 100-03.

POUND, EZRA (1885-1972), American

General
         Cambon [2], 387-89.
         Smith, Richard Eugene, 522-27.

"Canto XCI"
         Baumann, 265-76.

"The Cantos"
         Bader, 39-45.
         Langford, Richard E., 7-13.

"Fan Piece, for Her Imperial Lord"
         Smith, Richard Eugene, 522-26.

"Homage to Sextus Propertius"
         Drew-Bear, 204-10.

"Hugh Selwyn Mauberley"
         Bader, 45-51.
         Drew, E. A., 31-34.

"In a Station of the Metro"
         Friend [2], 362-63.

POUND (cont'd)

    "In a Station of the Metro" (cont'd)
        Lasser and Iwamoto, item 30.

    "A Pact"
        D'Avanzo [2], item 51.

PRIOR, MATTHEW (1664-1721), British

    "To the Honourable Charles Montague, Esq."
        Held, item 75.

RAINE, KATHLEEN (1908-   ), British

    General
        Russell, Peter, 723-28.

    "The Crystal Skull"
        Foltinek, 17-18.

    "The Pythoness"
        Foltinek, 16.

RALEIGH (or RALEGH), SIR WALTER (1552?-1618),
 British

    "The Last Booke of the Ocean to Scinthia"
        Duncan-Jones, 143-58.

RANSOM, JOHN CROWE (1888-   ), American

    General
        Hough, Graham [1], 8-21.
        Langford, Richard E., 46-52.

    "Blue Girls"
        Osborn, item 22.
        Osborne [2], item 53.

    "Captain Carpenter"
        Drew, E. A., 81-84.
        Hall, Vernon, item 28.
        Kelly, Richard, item 57.

    "The Equilibrists"
        Bergonzi [2], 127-37.

"Janet Waking"
     Drew, E. A., 54-56.

"Little Boy Blue"
     Mitchell [3], item 5.

"Master's in the Garden Again"
     Ostroff [1], 112-40.

"Philomela"
     Woods, 408-13.

"Prelude to an Evening"
     Parsons, Thornton H. [2], 460-63.
     Peck [2], item 41.
     Ransom [2], 70-80.

"Two in August"
     Snipes, item 15.

READ, SIR HERBERT (1893-1968), British

"The End of War"
     Bergonzi [1], 75-79.

"Execution of Cornelius Vane"
     Bergonzi [1], 75.

"Fear"
     Bergonzi [1], 74.

REDGROVE, PETER (1932-   ), British

General
     Rosenthal [1], 211-16.

RICH, ADRIENNE (1929-   ), American

General
     Howard, Richard [1], 423-41.

ROBINSON, EDWIN ARLINGTON (1869-1935), American

General
     Donaldson, 219-29.

"Battle After War"
     Sherman, item 64.

ROBINSON (cont'd)

"Ben Jonson Entertains a Man from Stratford"
Brenner, 101-03.

"Captain Craig"
Hepburn, 267-69.

"Conrad in Twilight"
Crupi, item 20.

"Firelight"
Barry, item 21.

"The Garden"
Davis, Charles T. [1], 383.

"The Glory of the Nightingales"
Davis, Charles T. [1], 385-86.

"King Jasper"
Davis, Charles T. [1], 384.

"Lost Anchors"
Cowan, S. A. [3], item 68.
Jenkins, item 64.

"Mr. Flood's Party"
Parish [3], 696-99.

"Richard Cory"
Brenner, 97-98.
Burkhart, item 9.
Morris, Charles R., item 52.
Turner, Steven, item 73.

"The Tree in Pamela's Garden"
Klotz, item 42.
Wright, Elizabeth, item 47.

"Tristram"
Davis, Charles T. [1], 383-85.

"Veteran Sirens"
Barbour, item 20.
Stanford, Donald E., 490-92.

ROCHESTER, EARL OF (John Wilmot) (1647-1680), British

> "Tunbridge-Wells"
>   Berman, 365-66.

ROETHKE, THEODORE (1908-1963), American

> General
>   Martz, 162-82.
>   Powell, 180-85.
>   Rosenthal [1], 112-18.
>   Southworth [4], 326-38.
>   Wain [4], 322-38.
>
> "The Abyss"
>   Heyen, 1052-68.
>
> "The Far Field"
>   Southworth [5], 413-18.
>   Staples, 201-02.
>
> "The Gentle"
>   Colussi, item 73.
>
> "I Knew a Woman"
>   Buttel [2], item 78.
>   Henry [1], item 31.
>   Peck [1], item 66.
>
> "In a Dark Time"
>   Ostroff [1], 24-53.
>
> "The Long Waters"
>   Staples, 199-201.
>
> "The Longing"
>   Staples, 193-95.
>
> "Luke Havergal"
>   Hepburn, 271-72.
>
> "Meditation at Oyster River"
>   Staples, 196-98.
>
> "My Papa's Waltz"
>   Bader, 98-100.

ROETHKE (cont'd)

"Open House"
Garmon, item 27.

"Praise to the End"
Southworth [4], 328-29.

"The Rose"
Staples, 202-03.

"Unfold, Unfold"
Southworth [4], 337.

"Where Knock Is Wide Open"
Reichertz, item 34.
Southworth [4], 328.

ROSENBERG, ISAAC (1890-1918), British

"August 1914"
Bergonzi [1], 112.

"Break of Day in the Trenches"
Bergonzi [1], 115-16.

"Dead Man's Dump"
Bergonzi [1], 116-19.

"Marching"
Bergonzi [1], 113-15.

ROSSETTI, CHRISTINA GEORGINA (1830-1894), British

"A Birthday"
Lynde, 261-63.

"Goblin Market"
Weathers, 82-84.

"A Triad"
Weathers, 84-85.

ROSSETTI, DANTE GABRIEL (1828-1882), British

"The Blessed Damozel"
Holberg, 311-14.
McGann [2], 48-54.

"Bridal Birth"
   Buttel [1], item 22.
   Stein, Richard L., 786-87.

"The Bride's Prelude"
   Holberg, 304-08.

"The Card Dealer"
   Holberg, 309-10.

"Chimes"
   Harris, Wendell V., 306.

"The Dark Glass"
   Eldredge, 302-03.

"Death's Songsters"
   Vogel [1], item 64.

"Heart's Hope"
   Stein, Richard L., 788-90.

"The House of Life"
   Baker, Houston A., Jr. [2], 1-14.
   Harris, Wendell V., 300-05.
   Hume, Robert D., 282-95.
   Ryals [3], 241-57.

"Jenny"
   Seigel, 677-93.

"A Last Confession"
   Howard, Ronnalie Roper, 21-29.

"Memorial Thresholds"
   Vogel [2], item 29.

"My Sister's Sleep"
   Holberg, 302-04.
   McGann [2], 42-45.
   Nelson, James G., 154-59.

"On Mary's Portrait Which I Painted Six Years Ago"
   Holberg, 308-09.

"The Paris Railway-Station"
   McGann [2], 46-47.

ROSSETTI (cont'd)

  "Rose Mary"
      Hyder, 197-207.

  "St. Luke the Painter"
      Stein, Richard L., 777-79.

  "The Vase of Life"
      Stein, Richard L., 785-86.

  "Woodspurge"
      Harris, Wendell V., 305.
      Holberg, 301-02.
      McGann [2], 45-46.

RUSKIN, JOHN (1819-1900), British

  "A Walk in Chamouni"
      Levin, Gerald, 283-90.

SACKVILLE, SIR THOMAS (1537-1608), British

  "The Complaint of Henry, Duke of Buckingham"
      Hogue, L. Lynn, item 8.

SANDBURG, CARL (1878-1967), American

  "A Fence"
      Wagner, Selma, item 42.

SASSOON, SIEGFRIED (1886-   ), British

  "Counter-Attack"
      Bergonzi [1], 102-03.

  "Died of Wounds"
      Bergonzi [1], 96-97.

  "The Kiss"
      Bergonzi [1], 94-95.

SCHWARTZ, DELMORE (1913-1966), American

  "Cupid's Chant"
      Knapp, James F., 515-16.

"Father and Son"
   Deutsch, 918-19.
   Knapp, James F., 510-11.

"Genesis: Book One"
   Knapp, James F., 512-14.

"The Heavy Bear Who Goes With Me"
   Halio [1], 805-07.
   Knapp, James F., 511-12.

"In the Naked Bed, in Plato's Cave"
   Halio [1], 808-09.

"The Masters of the Heart Touched the Unknown"
   Knapp, James F., 508-09.

"Starlight Life Intuition Pierced the Twelve"
   Deutsch, 922-24.

SEXTON, ANNE (1928-   ), American

General
   Howard, Richard [1], 442-50.

"The Operation"
   Jones, A. R. [1], 27-28.

"With Mercy for the Greedy"
   Jones, A. R. [1], 29.

SHAKESPEARE, WILLIAM (1564-1616), British

"The Phoenix and the Turtle"
   Wain [2], 1-16.

"The Rape of Lucrece"
   Allen, D. C. [2], 58-76.
   Griffin [3], 52-54.
   Sylvester, 505-11.

"Sonnets--General"
   Alpers [1], 274-320.
   Barber, 648-72.

"Sonnet XII" (When I Doe Count the Clock)
   Berry, J. Wilkes, item 13.

SHAKESPEARE (cont'd)

"Sonnet XIX" (Devouring Time Blunt Thou the Lyons
    Pawes)
        Allen, D. C. [1], 55-56.

"Sonnet XXIX" (When in Disgrace with Fortune and
    Mens Eyes)
        Allen, D. C. [1], 56-57.

"Sonnet XXX" (When to the Sessions of Sweet Silent
    Thought)
        Kaula, 53-54.

"Sonnet XXXIII" (Full Many a Glorious Morning Have
    I Seen)
        Kaula, 53.

"Sonnet XXXIV" (Why Didst Thou Promise Such a
    Beautious Day)
        Combellack [2], item 30.
        Kallsen, item 63.

"Sonnet XLIX" (Against That Time [If Ever That Time
    Come])
        Kaula, 54.

"Sonnet LX" (Like as the Waves Make Towards the
    Pibbled Shore)
        Kaula, 51-52.

"Sonnet LXIV" (When I Have Seene by Times Fell
    Hand Defaced)
        Levin, Richard [2], item 39.

"Sonnet LXVI" (Tyr'd with All These for Restfull
    Death I Cry)
        Allen, D. C. [1], 48-49.
        Levin, Richard [3], item 36.

"Sonnet LXXI" (Noe Longer Mourne for Me When I
    Am Dead)
        Davis,   Jack M. and J. E. Grant, 214-32.

"Sonnet LXXIII" (That Time of Yeare Thou Maist in
    Me Behold)
        Askew, 285-88.
        Hovey, 672-73.

Keogh [2], item 6.
Schroeter, 250-55.
White, Robert L. [2], 125-32.

"Sonnet LXXVII" (Thy Glasse Will Shew Thee How
Thy Beauties Were)
Allen, D. C. [1], 58-60.

"Sonnet LXXX" (O How I Faint When I of You Do
Write)
Schaar, 253-55.

"Sonnet XCVII" (How Like a Winter Hath My Absence
Beene)
Reese, 372-73.

"Sonnet CVII" (Not Mine Owne Feares, Nor the
Prophetick Soule)
Allen, D. C. [1], 52-55.

"Sonnet CXVI" (Let Me Not to the Marriage of True
Mindes)
Allen, D. C. [1], 50-52.

"Sonnet CXXIV" (If My Deare Love Were But the
Childe of State)
Bercovitch [2], item 22.

"Sonnet CXXVIII" (How Oft When Thou My Musike
Musike Playst)
Barnes, T. R., 20-22.
Purdum, 235-39.

"Sonnet CXXX" (My Mistres' Eyes Are Nothing. Like
the Sunne)
Friend [2], 365-66.

"Sonnet CXXXVIII" (When My Love Sweares That She
Is Made of Truth]
Helgerson, item 48.
Hux, item 45.

"Sonnet CXLVI" (Poore Soule the Center of My Sinfull
Earth)
Gerard [3], 157-59.

"Venus and Adonis"
Allen, D. C. [2], 42-57.

SHAKESPEARE (cont'd)

> "Venus and Adonis" (cont'd)
>> Griffin [3], 43-52.
>> Hamilton, 1-15.

SHAPIRO, KARL JAY (1913-   ), American

> General
>> Smith, Hammett W., 97-100.
>> Southworth [2], 161-66.

> "Auto Wreck"
>> Coleman, Alice, 631-33.

> "The Bourgeois Poet"
>> Ostroff [1], 190-216.

SHELLEY, PERCY BYSSHE (1792-1822), British

> General
>> Berry, Francis, 66-82.
>> Bostetter, 203-13.
>> Delasanta, 173-79.
>> Ford, Newell F., 1-22.
>> Norman, 223-37.
>> Raine [3], 856-63, 868-73.

> "Adonis"
>> French, Roberts W. [1], item 16.
>> Mahony [1] 555-68.
>> Riddel [1], 124-29.

> "Alastor"
>> Benoit, 139-41.
>> Raben [2], 278-92.
>> Webb, Timothy [1], 402-11.

> "The Boat on the Serchio"
>> Raben [3], 58-68.

> "The Cloud"
>> Hunter, Parks C., Jr., 687-92.

> "Drinking"
>> Hunter, Parks C., Jr., 687-92.

"Hymn to Venus"
   Webb, Timothy [2], 315-24.

"Indian Serenade"
   Levin, Richard [1], 305-07.

"Invocation to Misery"
   Raben [2], 65-74.

"Lines Written Among the Euganean Hills"
   Reiman [2], 404-13.

"Lines Written in the Bay of Lerici"
   Matthews, 40-48.

"Lines Written on Hearing the News of the Death of
   Napoleon"
   Bailey, John Cann, 232-33.

"The Mask of Anarchy"
   Previte-Orton, 213-15.

"Mont Blanc"
   Rees, 185-86.

"Music, When Soft Voices Die"
   Hirsch, E. D., Jr. [1], 296-98.
   Massey, 430-38.

"Ode to the West Wind"
   Askew, 292-93.
   Barnes, T. R., 207-11.
   Bass [1], 327-38.
   Thompson, William I., 32-33.

"The Revolt of Islam" (Laon and Cythna)
   Murray, 570-85.

"The Sensitive Plant"
   St. George, 479-88.

"Stanzas Written in Dejection: Near Naples"
   Waters, Leonard A., item 54.

"To a Skylark"
   Foxell, 143-63.
   Hunter, Parks C., Jr., 681-87.
   Raine [3], 863-67.

SHELLEY (cont'd)

"To the Cicada"
    Hunter, Parks C., Jr., 681-87.

"The Triumph of Life"
    Butter, 40-51.
    Reiman [3], 536-50.

SIDNEY, PHILIP (1554-1586), British

"And Have I Heard Her Say? O Cruel Pain!"
    Dempsey, item 51.

"Arcadia"
    Challis, 561-76.
    Isler, 171-91.
    Lindheim, 159-86.

"Astrophel and Stella"
    Alpers [1], 187-209.
    Barnes, T. R., 19-20.
    Brodwin [2], 25-40.
    Cotter [4], 381-403.
    Cowan, Stanley A. and Fred A. Dudley, item 76.
    Harfst, 397-414.
    Ryken [1], 648-54.
    Stillinger [1], 617-39.

"Astrophel and Stella--Sonnet 1"
    Kalstone, 30-31.

"Astrophel and Stella--Sonnet 2"
    Ryken [1], 649.

"Astrophel and Stella--Sonnet 4"
    Ryken [1], 649-50.

"Astrophel and Stella--Sonnet 9"
    Putzel, item 25.

"Astrophel and Stella--Sonnet 10"
    Ryken [1], 650-51.

"Astrophel and Stella--Sonnet 14"
    Ryken [1], 651.

"Astrophel and Stella--Sonnet 40"
  Cotter [2], item 51.

"Astrophel and Stella--Sonnet 71"
  Kalstone, 26-29.

"Astrophel and Stella--Sonnet 75"
  Cotter [3], item 70.

"Leave Me, O Love Which Reachest But to Dust"
  Ryken [2], item 9.
  Thomas, W.K. [2], item 45.

"With How Sad Steps, O Moon"
  Burhans, item 26.
  Essig [2], item 25.

SILL, EDWARD ROWLAND (1841-1887), American

"Field Notes"
  Ferguson, A. R., 370-73.

SIMPSON, LOUIS (1923-   ), American

General
  Howard, Richard [1], 451-70.

"Carentan, O Carentan"
  Cox, C. B. [2], 73.

"A Farm in Minnesota"
  Stepanchev, 199-200.

"Moving the Walls"
  Cox, C. B. [2], 78-83.

"My Father in the Night Commanding No"
  Cox, C. B. [2], 75-76.

SITWELL, EDITH (1887-1964), British

"Metamorphosis"
  Harrington [2], 83-91.

"Still Falls the Rain"
  Brophy [2], item 36.
  Drew, E. A., 101-03.

SKELTON, JOHN (c1460-1529), British

    "The Bowge of Courte"
        Larson, 288-95.
        Phillips, Norma, 19-23.

    "Magnificence"
        Phillips, Norma, 23-29.

    "Manerly Margery Milk and Ale"
        Harrington [1], item 42.

    "Philip Sparrow"
        Targan, 74-80.

    "The Tunning of Elinour Rumming"
        Hawkins, 199-203.

SMART, CHRISTOPHER (1722-1771), British

    "Jubilate Agno"
        Adams, Francis D., 195-209.
        Christensen, Allan C., 366-73.
        Fitzgerald, Robert P. [1], 487-99.
        Parkin [2], 1191-96.

    "Song to David"
        Adams, Francis D., 125-32.

SMITH, STEVIE (1902-   ), British

    "The Frog Prince"
        McGann [1], 195-96.

SMITH, WILLIAM JAY (1918- .), American

    "American Primitive"
        Burgess [3], 71-75.

SNODGRASS, WILLIAM DEWITT (1926-   ), American

    General
        Howard, Richard [1], 471-84.

    "Heart's Needle"
        Cambon, 25-29.

SNYDER, GARY (1930-   ), American

> General
>> Howard, Richard [1], 485-98.
>> Parkinson, 616-32.

> "A Stone Garden"
>> Parkinson, 620-22.

SORLEY, CHARLES HAMILTON (1895-1915), British

> "All the Hills and Vales Along"
>> Bergonzi [1], 57-59.

SOUTHWELL, ROBERT (1561-1595), British

> General
>> Roberts, John R. [2], 450-56.

> "New Heaven, New Warre"
>> Roberts, John R. [2], 454-55.

> "The Visitation"
>> McKay, item 15.

SPENDER, STEPHEN (1909-   ), British

> General
>> Sellers [2], 646-50.

> "The Express"
>> Blakeslee, 556-58.
>> Potter, 426-28.

> "He Will Watch the Hawk with an Indifferent Eye"
>> Cowan, S. A. [1], item 67.

> "The Juggler"
>> Allen, D. C. [4], 25.

SPENSER, EDMUND (1552?-1599), British

> "Amoretti"
>> Cummings, Peter M., 163-79.
>> Stewart, Jack F., item 74.

> "April"
>> Cullen, 1559-70.

SPENSER (cont'd)

"April" (cont'd)
Staton [3], 111-18.

"Colin Clouts Come Home Againe"
Meyer, 206-18.

"Epithalamion"
Cirillo [3], 19-34.

"The Faerie Queene"
Alpers [1], 329-524.
Alpers [2], 27-46.
Anderson, Judith H. [2], 65-77.
Barnes, T. R., 14-17.
Berger [1], 135-54.
Berger [2], 234-61.
Berger [4], 93-120.
Berger [5], 1-18.
Blissett, 87-104.
Cirillo, [1], 81-90.
Cosman, 85-107.
Dallett, 639-43.
DeSelincourt, 106-30.
Dundas, 59-75.
English, 417-29.
Evans, Maurice, 132-43.
Gottfried, Rudolf, 1362-77.
Guth, 474-79.
Huston [2], 212-17.
Kaske, Carol V., 609-38.
Koller, 128-39.
Marotti, 69-86.
Williams, J. M.   481-84.

"The Faerie Queene--Book I"
Anderson, Judith H. [1], 17-32.
MacIntyre [2], 473-82.
Major, John W., Jr., 269-74.
Orange, 555-61.
Rusche, 29-39.
Viswanathan [2], item 44.
Waters, D. Douglas [1], 258-75.
Waters, D. Douglas [2], 53-62.

"The Faerie Queene--Book II"
    Fowler, 143-49.
    Fox [2], 1-6.
    Miller, Lewis H., Jr. [1], 33-44.
    Sonn, 17-30.

"The Faerie Queene--Book III"
    Baybak, Delany and Hieatt, 227-34.
    Berger [6], 39-51.
    Grellner, 35-43.
    MacIntyre [1], item 69.

"The Faerie Queene--Book IV"
    Staton [2], 105-14.

"The Faerie Queene--Book V"
    Iredale, 373-81.
    Knight, 267-94.

"The Faerie Queene--Book VI"
    Staton [1], 35-42.
    Williams, Kathleen, 337-46.

"Lyke as a Huntsman" (Sonnet 67)
    Piper [2], 405.

"Mother Hubbard's Tale"
    Barnes, T. R. 17-19.
    Previte-Orton, 49-52.

"Muiopotmos, or the Fate of the Butterflie"
    Allen, D. C. [2], 20-41.
    Court, 1-15.

"Prothalamion"
    Halio [2], 390-92.
    Wine, 111-17.

"The Shepheardes Calender"
    Alpers [1], 169-86.
    Bristol, 33-42.
    Previte-Orton, 48-49.
    Reamer, 504-27.

"The Shepheardes Calender--The March Eclogue"
    Allen, D. C. [2], 1-19.

SPENSER (cont'd)

    "The Shepheardes Calender--The Aprill Eclogue"
        Cain, 45-58.

    "The Shepheardes Calender--The May Eclogue"
        Hume, Anthea, 155-67.

    "The Shepheardes Calender--The June Eclogue"
        Barnes, T. R., 11-14.

    "The Shepheardes Calender--The July Eclogue"
        Anderson, Judith H. [1], 17-32.

STAFFORD, WILLIAM (1914-   ),   American

    General
        Howard, Richard [1], 499-506.

    "The Rescued Year"
        Adams, Hazard [1], 43.

STEVENS, WALLACE (1879-1955), American

    General
        Doggett [2], 373-80.
        Hough, Graham [2], 201-18.
        King, Montgomery W., 141-48.
        Langford, Richard E., 36-41.
        Martz, 183-223.
        Morse, 431-46.
        Sheehan, 57-66.

    "Anecdote on the Jar"
        Merivale, 527-32.

    "Arcades of Philadelphia the Past"
        Ackerman, R. D., item 80.

    "The Auroras of Autumn"
        Bloom, Harold, 36-41.
        Brown, Merle E., 263.

    "The Auroras of Autumn--II"
        Doggett [2], 378-80.

    "The Auroras of Autumn--VIII"
        Doggett [2], 380.

"Bantams in Pine-Woods"
    Hartsock, item 33.

"The Bird with the Coppery, Keen Claws"
    Leiter [3], 551-54.

"The Comedian as the Letter C"
    Brown, Merle E., 246.
    Hough, Graham [2], 209-10.
    Langford, Richard E., 39-40.

"Credences of Summer"
    Huston [1], 263-72.

"Earthy Anecdote"
    Betar, item 43.
    Smith, Hugh L., [1], item 37.

"Emperor of Ice-Cream"
    Culbert and Violette, 38-47.
    McFadden [2], 188-89.

"Esthetique du Mal"
    Doggett [2], 376-77.

"Flyer's Fall"
    Whitbread, 469-70.

"The Glass of Water"
    French, Warren G., item 23.
    Therese, item 56.

"The Green Plant"
    Perloff [2], 335-36.

"The Hermitage at the Center"
    Perloff [2], 338-39.

"Holiday in Reality"
    Doggett [1], 35-36.

"The Idea of Order at Key West"
    Drew, E. A., 164-66.
    Hough, Graham [2], 204-05.
    Perloff [2], 329-30.

"Life is Motion"
    Smith, Hugh L., Jr. [2], item 48.

STEVENS (cont'd)

"Like Decorations in a Nigger Cemetery"
    Brown, Merle E., 246-47.
    Vendler, 136-46.

"Lions in Sweden"
    Guthrie, item 32.

"Looking Across the Fields and Watching the Birds
    Fly"
    Perloff [2], 334-35.

"The Man with the Blue Guitar"
    Brown, Merle E., 246-69.
    Cavitch, item 30.
    Hough, Graham [2], 210-12.

"Martial Cadenza"
    Perloff [2], 331-32.

"The Men That Are Falling"
    Griffith [3], item 41.

"Metaphors of a Magnifico"
    King, Bruce [5], 450-52.
    Liddle, item 15.

"No Possum, No Sop, No Taters"
    Brown, Merle E., 247-49.

"Not Ideas About the Thing But the Thing Itself"
    Perloff [2], 339.

"Notes Toward a Supreme Fiction"
    Brown, Merle E., 246-69.
    Clough, item 24.

"On the Road Home"
    Hough, Graham [2], 215-16.

"One of the Inhabitants of the West"
    Perloff [2], 331-32.

"An Ordinary Evening in New Haven"
    Brown, Merle E., 246-69.

"The Owl in the Sarcophagus"
        Whitbread, 470-80.

"Peter Quince at the Clavier"
        Nassar, 549-51.
        Nelson, Phyllis E., item 52.
        Perrine [13], 430.
        Riddel [2], 307-09.

"Prologues to What Is Possible"
        Perloff [2], 332-34.

"Sea Surface Fall of Clouds"
        Rosenthal [2], item 38.

"The Sense of the Sleight-of-Hand Man"
        Drew, E. A., 73-74.

"The Snow Man"
        Hough, Graham [2], 205-06.
        Morse, 430-31.

"Sunday Morning"
        Allen, D. C. [1], 72-75.
        Drew, E. A., 117-23.
        Hough, Graham [2], 201-04.
        Zimmerman [1], 113-23.

"Theory"
        Grube, item 26.

"Thirteen Ways of Looking at a Blackbird"
        McFadden [2], 187-88.
        McNamara, 446-48.

"Two Figures in Dense Violet Night"
        Hough, Graham [2], 214-15.

"Two Illustrations That the World Is What You Make
    of It"
        Perloff [2], 337-38.

"Visibility of Thought"
        Riddel [3], 482-98.

"The Well Dressed Man with a Beard"
        Doggett [2], 377-78.

STEVENS (cont'd)

"Woman Looking at a Vase of Flowers"
Doggett [3], item 7.

"World as Meditation"
Perloff [2], 330-31.

STICKNEY, JOSEPH TRUMBELL (1874-1904), American

General
Whittle, 899-914.

"In Ampezzo"
Whittle, 904-05.

"Oneiropolos"
Whittle, 908.

STRAND, MARK (1934-), American

General
Howard, Richard [1], 507-16.

SUCKLING, SIR JOHN (1609-1642), British

"Why So Pale and Wan"
Beaurline, 553-63.

SURREY, EARL OF (Henry Howard) (1517?-1547), British

"Love That Doth Reign and Live Without My Thought"
Harris, William O. [1], 298-305.

"Prisoned in Windsor, He Recounteth His Pleasure
There Passed"
Mathew, item 11.

SWENSON, MAY (1919-), American

General
Howard, Richard [1], 517-32.
Stanford, Ann, 58-75.

SWIFT, JONATHAN (1667-1745), British

General
San Juan [1], 387-96.

"Cadenus and Vanessa"
    Ohlin, 485-96.

"Cassinus and Peter"
    Greene, Donald, 674-76.

"The Day of Judgment"
    Smith, T. Henry, item 6.

"The Lady's Dressing Room"
    Greene, Donald, 676-80.

"Strephon and Chloe"
    Greene, Donald, 680-86.

"Verses on the Death of Dr. Swift"
    Fischer, 422-41.
    Waingrow, 513-18.

"Verses Wrote in a Lady's Ivory Table-Book"
    Schakel, item 83.

"The Windsor Prophecy"
    Roberts, Philip, 254-58.

SWINBURNE, ALGERNON CHARLES (1837-1909), British

"Hertha"
    Tillyard [2], 87-105.

"Lancelot and Elaine"
    Peters, Robert L. [1], 292-93

"A New-Year Ode: To Victor Hugo"
    Altick [1], 257-58, 259.

"On the Cliffs"
    Raymond, Meredith B. [2], 125-41.

"Thalassius"
    McGhee [2], 127-36.

"Tristram of Lyonesse"
    Reed, John R. [2], 99-120.

"The Triumph of Time"
    Bass [2], 56-61.

SYMONDS, JOHN ADDINGTON (1840-1893), British

> General
>> Going [1], 25-38.

SYMONS, ARTHUR (1865-1945), British

> "Studies in Strange Sins: After the Designs of
> Aubrey Beardsley"
>> Peters, Robert L. [2], 150-63.

TAFT, ROBERT W. (1938?-), American

> "Attack on Barbados at Sandy Point"
>> Humphries, item 44.

TATE, ALLEN (1899-), American

> "The Buried Lake"
>> Squires, 554-59.

> "The Death of Little Boys"
>> Harrington and Schneider, item 16.
>> Pearce, 213-14.
>> Uhlman, item 58.

> "The Maimed Man"
>> Squires, 549-53.

> "The Meaning of Life"
>> Meiners [3], item 62.

> "The Mediterranean"
>> Meiners [1], 155-59.

> "Seasons of the Soul"
>> Meiners [2], 34-80.

> "The Swimmers"
>> Squires, 547-49, 553-54.

TAYLOR, EDWARD (c1642-1729), American

> General
>> Manierre [1], 296-99.

> "The Ebb and Flow"
>> Jordan, Raymond J. [2], item 67.

"An Ecstacy of Joy Let In By This Reply Return'd
in Admiration"
Lenhart, 46.

"God's Determinations"
Thomas, J. L., 452-62.

"Huswifery"
Davis, Charles T. [2], 5-6.
Grabo [1], 554-60.

"Preparatory Meditations--General"
Martz, 54-81.

"Preparatory Meditation One [First Series]" (What
Love Is This of Thine, That Cannot Bee)
Penner, 193-99.

"Preparatory Meditation Six [First Series]" (Am Id
Thy Gold?)
Grabo [2], item 40.

"Preparatory Meditation Eight [First Series]" (I Ken-
ning Through Astronomy Divine)
Alexis [2], item 77.
Monteiro [6], item 45.

"Preparatory Meditation Twenty-Seven [Second
Series]" (My Mentall Eye)
Rowe, 370-74.

"Preparatory Meditation Twenty-Nine [First Series]"
(My Shattred Phancy Stole Away from Mee)
Halbert, 25-27.

"Preparatory Meditation Thirty [First Series]" (The
Daintiest Draught Thy Pensill Ever Drew)
Halbert, 31-32.

"Preparatory Meditation Thirty-Three [First Series]"
(My Lord, My Life, Can Envy Ever Bee)
Halbert, 30-31.

"Preparatory Meditation Forty-Three [Second Series]"
(When, Lord, I Seeke to Shew Thy Praises, Then)
Benton, Robert M., 39-40.

TAYLOR (cont'd)

"Preparatory Meditation Sixty-Two [Second Series]"
(Oh! Thou My Lord)
Clare, item 16.

"Preparatory Meditation One Hundred and Ten [Second
Series]" (The Angells Sung a Caroll at Thy Birth)
Lenhart, 50-53.

"The Reflextion"
Garrison, 492-94.

"The Soul's Admiration Hereupon"
Lenhart, 47-49.

"Upon a Spider Catching a Fly"
Secor, item 42.

"Upon Wedlock, and Death of Children"
Combellack [3], item 12.
Halbert, 23-25.
Russell, Gene, item 71.

TENNYSON, ALFRED, LORD (1809-1892), British

General
Berry, Francis, 47-65.
Preyer, 325-52.
Walton, 733-50.

"The Ancient Sage"
Shaw [4], 84-89.

"Break, Break, Break"
Rackin [2], 217-28.

"Cambridge"
Golffing, 278.

"The Coming of Arthur"
Gray [2], 339-41.

"Crossing the Bar"
Kincaid [1], 57-61.
Millhauser [2], 34-39.
Perrine [18], 127-31.
Sonstroem [2], 55-60.

"The Dreamer"
Golffing, 282-84.

"Geraint and Enid"
Gray [3], 131-32.

"Idylls of the King"
Adicks, 65-71.
Battenhouse, 99-105.
Brashear [2], 29-49.
Gray [1], 68-69.
Kozicki, 15-20.
Poston [1], 269-75.
Poston [3], 372-82.
Shaw [3], 41-53.
Solomon, 258-71.

"In Memoriam"
Adey, 261-63.
Ball, Patricia M., 10-13.
Barksdale, 96-101.
Battenhouse, 90-99.
Drew, E. A., 26-31.
Grant, Stephen Allen, 481-95.
Hirsch, Gordon D., 93-106.
Hunt, John Dixon, 187-98.
Metzger, Lore, 189-96.
Moore, Carlisle, 155-69.
Shaw [4], 89-93.
Shmiefsky [1], 721-39.
Svaglic [2], 810-25.
Taaffe, 123-31.

"In Memoriam--Prologue"
Moews, 185-87.

"In Memoriam, XLI"
Elliott, item 66.

"In Memoriam, XCV"
Preyer, 343-44.

"The Kraken"
Preyer, 345-46.

"Lady Clara Vere de Vere"
Chandler [1], 55-57.

TENNYSON (cont'd)

"The Palace of Art"
    Ball, Patricia M., 13-14.
    Britton, item 17.
    Cadbury [3], 23-44.
    Sendry, 149-62.
    Shaw and Gertlein, 215-16.

"Pelleas and Ettarre"
    Poston [2], 199-204.

"The Poet"
    Pipes, 74-76.

"The Princess"
    Danzig, 83-89.
    Ryals [4], 268-75.
    Walton, 748-49.

"Recollections of the Arabian Nights"
    John [3], 275-79.

"Saint Agnes' Eve"
    Shaw and Gertlein, 214-15.

"Sea Dreams"
    Shaw and Gertlein, 217-19.

"Tears, Idle Tears"
    Vandiver, item 53.

"The Two Voices"
    Brashear [1], 283-86.
    Shaw [4], 80-84.
    Wilkenfeld [2], 163-73.

"Ulysses"
    Halio [2], 392-94.
    Mitchell [5], 87-95.
    Pettigrew, 27-45.

THOMAS, DYLAN (1914-1953), British

General
    Moynihan, 313-26.
    Nist [1], 101-06.

THOMAS (cont'd)

"Altarwise by Owl-Light"
Beardsley and Hynes, 315-22.
Knieger [1], 623-28.

"Ballad of the Long-Legged Bait"
Leach, 724-28.

"The Conversation of Prayer"
Moynihan, 324-25.

"Do Not Go Gentle Into That Good Night"
Murphy [1], item 55.

"Especially When the October Wind"
Perrine [6], item 1.

"Fern Hill"
Cox, C. B. [1], 134-38.
Davidow, 78-81.
Drew, E. A., 56-60.

"How Shall My Animal"
Montague [1], 420-34.

"How Soon the Harvest Sun"
Halperen [1], item 65.

"I, In My Intricate Image"
Morton, 160-62.

"If I Were Tickled by the Rub of Love"
Halperen [2], item 25.

"In Country Sleep"
Moynihan, 325-26.

"In the White Giant's Thigh"
Chambers, Marlene [1], item 1.
Chambers, Marlene [2], item 39.

"It Rains"
Tolley, 390-91.

"Light Breaks Where No Sun Shines"
Morton, 159-60.

"Love in the Asylum"
        Knieger [2], item 13.

"O Make Me a Mask"
        Harvill, item 12.

"On the Marriage of a Virgin"
        Knieger [3], item 61.

"Our Eunuch Dreams"
        Smith, A. J., 68-74.

"Over Sir John's Hill"
        Ormerod [1], 449-50.

"Poem in October"
        Daiches, 127-28.
        Perrine [14], item 43.

"A Refusal to Mourn the Death, by Fire, of a Child
    in London"
        Daiches, 125-26.
        Drew, E. A., 103-05.

"Sonnet III"
        Knieger [6], item 25.

"To-Day, This Insect"
        Montague [2], item 15.

"Twenty-Four Years"
        Knieger [8], item 4.
        Ormerod [3], item 76.

"Unluckily for a Death"
        Morton, 156-58.

"Vision and Prayer"
        Daiches, 127.
        Nist [1], 104-06.

"When All My Five and Country Senses See"
        Zigerell [2], item 11.

"A Winter's Tale"
        Tritschler, 422-30.

THOMAS, EDWARD (1878-1917), British

   "Liberty"
            Danby, 310-11.

   "Manor Farm"
            Danby, 311-12.

   "Old Man"
            Danby, 313-15.

   "The Owl"
            Barnes, T. R., 272-73.

   "The Sign-Post"
            Danby, 308-09.

THOMAS, RONALD STUART (1913-   ), British

   General
            Merchant, 341-51.

THOMPSON, FRANCIS (1859-1907), British

   "The Hound of Heaven"
            Buchen, 111-15.

THOMSON, JAMES (1834-1882), British

   "The Castle of Indolence"
            Griffin [1], item 33.

   "Spring"
            Cohen, 1107-82.

TOMLINSON, CHARLES (1927-   ), British

   General
            Donoghue, 238-46.
            Rosenthal [1], 244-57.

   "Antecedents"
            Donoghue, 238.

   "Cezanne at Aix"
            Donoghue, 238-39.

TOOMER, JEAN (1894-1967), American

    "Song of the Son"
        Lieber, 37.

TRAHERNE, THOMAS (1637-1674), British

    General
        Goldknopf, 48-59.

    "An Infant-Ey"
        Ridlon, 627-39.

    "The Preparative"
        Clements [2], 500-21.

TREVELYAN, GEORGE (1876-1962), British

    "Ladies in Parliament"
        Previte-Orton, 184-86.

TURBERVILLE, GEORGE (1540?-1610?), British

    General
        Sheidley, 631-49.

VAUGHAN, HENRY (1622-1695), British

    General
        Rudrum, 469-80.
        Sandband, 141-52.

    "Cock-Crowing"
        Allen, D. C. [2], 226-41.

    "The Morning-Watch"
        Low [2], item 13.

    "The Night"
        Durr [2], 34-40.

    "To His Learned Friend and Loyal Fellow-Prisoner"
        Simmonds [1], 454-57.

    "The Water-Fall"
        Pebworth, 258-59.

VAUGHAN (cont'd)

    "The World"
        Chambers, Leland H. [2], 137-50.
        Daniels [4], item 70.
        Rostvig [1], 415-22.
        Simmonds [2], 77-93.

VIERECK, PETER (1916-　), American

    "Don't Look Now But Mary Is Everybody"
        Benton, Richard P., item 30.

WAGONER, DAVID (1926-　), American

    General
        Howard, Richard [1], 533-51.

WALKER, TED (1934-　), British

    General
        Press [2], 676-81.

WALLER, EDMUND (1606-1687), British

    "Panegyric to My Lord Protector"
        Chernaik, 113-24.

WARREN, ROBERT PENN (1905-　), American

    General
        Strandberg, 26-37.

WEISS, THEODORE (1916-　), American

    General
        Howard, Richard [1], 552-74.

WHEATLEY, PHILLIS (1753?-1784), American

    General
        Robinson, William H., 25-38.

WHITE, KENNETH (1936-　), British

    General
        Press [2], 685-88.

WHITMAN, WALT (1819-1892), American

> General
>> Allen, Gay Wilson, 7-17.
>> Brown, Clarence A., 33-45.
>> Martz, 82-90.
>
> "As I Ebb'd With the Ocean of Life"
>> Bloom, Harold, 33-36.
>> Carlisle, 265.
>
> "Calamus Poems"
>> Griffith [4], 18-38.
>
> "Chants Democratic"
>> Hoople, 181-96.
>
> "Children of Adam"
>> Carlisle, 267.
>
> "A Child's Reminiscence"
>> see "Out of the Cradle Endlessly Rocking"
>
> "Crossing Brooklyn Ferry"
>> Carlisle, 268-70.
>> Cox, James M. [2], 189.
>> Gargano [3], 262-69.
>
> "From Paumanok Starting"
>> Lenhart, 183-85.
>
> "Leaves of Grass"
>> Waldhorn, 368-73.
>
> "A Noiseless Patient Spider"
>> Eckley, item 20.
>
> "Of the Terrible Doubt of Appearances"
>> Griffith [4], 24-27.
>
> "Out of the Cradle Endlessly Rocking"
>> Carlisle, 270-71.
>> Cox, James M. [2], 189-90.
>> Griffith [4], 31-37.
>
> "Passage to India"
>> Sharma, Som P., 394-99.

WHITMAN (cont'd)

"The World Below the Brine"
Fasel, item 7.
Freedman, item 39.

WHITTIER, JOHN GREENLEAF (1807-1892), American

"Ichabod"
Kime, item 59.
Maddox, item 38.

"Snow-Bound"
Pickard, 338-43.
Ringe, 139-44.

WILBUR, RICHARD (1921-), American

General
Cambon, 12-16.
Southworth [3], 24-29.

"Altitudes"
McGuinness, 314-15.

"A Baroque Wall-Fountain in the Villa Sciarra"
McGuinness, 315-16.

"The Beacon"
McGuinness, 322-24.

"For the New Railway Station in Rome"
McGuinness, 325-26.

"Love Calls Us to the Things of This World"
McGuinness, 319-20.
Ostroff [1], 2-21.

"Objects"
Cambon, 9-11.

"The Puritans"
Mattfield [2], item 53.

"Statues"
McGuinness, 316-17.

"Water Walker"
Cambon, 11-12.

WILLIAMS, OSCAR (1900-1964), American

> "The Leg in the Subway"
> > Russell, Robert, item 18.

WILLIAMS, WILLIAM CARLOS (1883-1963), American

> General
> > Cambon [2], 387-89.
> > Kenner [2], 328-30.
> > Langford, Richard E., 28-35.
> > Martz, 125-46.
> > Slate, 486-511.
> > Solt, 304-18.
> > Wagner, Linda Welshimer [2], 43-49.
> > Wagner, Linda Welshimer [3], 425-30.

> "Asphodel, That Greeny Flower"
> > Nilsen, 279-83.
> > Wagner, Linda Welshimer [1], 362-65.

> "The Attic Which Is Desire"
> > Jacobs [1], item 61.

> "Between Walls"
> > Jacobs [2], item 68.

> "Choral: The Pink Church"
> > Payne, 158-60.

> "The Desert Music"
> > Myers, Neil, 38-50.

> "Great Mullen"
> > Jacobs [3], item 63.

> "The Locust Tree in Flower"
> > Phillips, Linus L. and Mrs. William W. Deaton,
> > > item 26.

> "The Orchestra"
> > Wagner, Linda Welshimer [1], 365-67.

> "Paterson"
> > Conarroe [1], 547-58.
> > Grigsby [1], 277-81.
> > Gustafson, 532-39.

Martz, 147-61.
Sutton, Walter, 242-59.

"The Red Wheelbarrow"
Tolley, 386-87.

"Song"
Nilsen, 277.

"The Term"
Jacobs [4], item 73.

"To a Solitary Disciple"
Langford, Richard E., 31-32.

"To Waken an Old Lady"
Jacobs [5], item 6.

"Without Invention Nothing Is Well Spaced"
Conarroe [2], item 26.

"The Yachts"
Schneider [3], item 40.

"The Young Housewife"
Jacobs [6], item 81.

WILMOT, JOHN
see Rochester, Earl of

WINTERS, YVOR (1900-1968), American

General
Hefferman, 605-15.
Holloway [1], 54-68.
Ramsey, 451-64.

"At the San Francisco Airport"
Stanford, Donald E., 493-94.

"The California Oaks"
Stanford, Donald E., 493.

"Sir Gawaine and the Green Knight"
Ramsey, 458-59.

"A Summer Commentary"
Ramsey, 459-60.

WITHER, GEORGE (1588-1667), British

> "A Christmas Carol"
> Oetgen, item 6.

WOLCOT, JOHN (1738-1819), British

> "Ode Upon Ode"
> Previte-Orton, 148-51.

WORDSWORTH, WILLIAM (1770-1850), British

> General
> Warren, Leland E., 155-62.

> "Anecdote for Fathers"
> Donoghue, 234-35.

> "The Barberry-Tree"
> Reed, Mark L., 60-61.
> Wordsworth, 455-65.

> "Daffodils"
> Schelp, 307-09.

> "Descriptive Sketches"
> Hartman [2], 519-27.

> "Elegiac Stanzas" (Peele Castle)
> Bernhardt-Kabisch, item 71.
> O'Hara, 69-82.
> Tillotson [2], 426-28.

> "The Excursion"
> Lainoff, 64-68.
> Sellers [2], 644-46.

> "I Wandered Lonely as a Cloud"
> Drew, E. A., 21-26.

> "Idiot Boy"
> Turner, Paul [1], 369-75.

> "Inscription for the House (an Outhouse) on the Island
> of Grasmere"
> Nabholtz, 265-68.

"Lines Composed a Few Miles Above Tintern Abbey"
     see "Tintern Abbey"

"Nutting"
     Grob, 826-32.

"October, 1803"
     Rapin [2], item 10.

"Ode: Intimations of Immortality"
     Cox, Roger L., item 34.
     Garlitz [1], 639-49.
     Meyers, Robert, item 3.
     Wimsatt, 175-202.

"On the Power of Sound"
     Lainoff, 71-73.

"Personal Talk"
     Battenhouse, 63-64.

"Peter Bell"
     Jordan, John E., 559-603.
     Watson, Melvin R., 519-30.

"Prelude"
     Battenhouse, 70-73.
     Christensen, Francis, 69-75.
     Davidson, Clifford, 198-201.
     Everett [2], 338-50.
     Goldman, Michael, item 41.
     Hartman [1], 214-24.
     Ruotolo, 546-49.
     Satterfield, item 15.
     Sellers [2], 643-44.

"Resolution and Independence"
     Conran, 66-74.
     Tillotson [2], 428.
     Wain [2], 113-28.

"The Ruined Cottage"
     Finch, 179-99.

"She Dwelt Among the Untrodden Ways"
     Brooks, 490-91.

WORDSWORTH (cont'd)

    "Simplon Pass"
        Wildi, 368-77.

    "A Slumber Did My Spirit Seal"
        Brooks, 491-92.

    "The Solitary Reaper"
        Hardy, John Edward, 61-81.

    "The Tables Turned"
        Barnes, T. R., 170-71.

    "Tintern Abbey"
        Battenhouse, 73-76.
        Foxell, 123-42.
        Maniquis, 358-82.
        Sellers [2], 642-43.
        Thompson, William I., 29-32.

    "To Lucy"
        Battenhouse, 64-65.

WRIGHT, JAMES (1927-), American

    General
        Cambon, 29-30.
        Howard, Richard [1], 575-86.

    "At the Slackening of the Tide"
        Toole, item 29.

WRIGHT, RICHARD (1908-1960): American

    General
        Fabre, 10-22.
        Kinnamon, 39-50.

WYATT, SIR THOMAS (1503-1542), British

    General
        Friedman, Donald M. [2], 32-48.
        Maynard, 245-57.

    "The Long Love That in My Thought Doth Harbor"
        Harris, William O. [1], 298-305.

"My Galy Charged with Forgetfulness"
        Barnes, T. R., 2-3.

"My Lute Awake"
        Barnes, T. R., 7.

"My Poynz, I Cannot Frame Me Tune to Fayne"
        Barnes, T. R., 3-4.

"Penitential Psalms"
        Twombly [2], 345-80.

"They Fle From Me"
        Berthoff [2], 477-94.
        Friedman, Donald M. [1], 1-13.
        Twombly [1], 489-503.

YEATS, WILLIAM BUTLER (1865-1939), British

General
        Beum [1], 338-50.
        Beum [2], 89-96.
        Henn, 57-75.
        Holloway [3], 58-66.
        Loftus, 168-77.
        Saul [1], 63-68.
        Saul [2], 101-16.
        Shmiefsky [2], 701-21.
        Spanos [2], 214-27.
        Stallworthy [2], 199-214.
        Watkins, Vernon, 475-98.

"An Acre of Grass"
        Perrine [2], item 64.
        Taube, item 40.

"Among School Children"
        Barnes, T. R., 310-14.
        Gallagher, Michael P., 9-16.
        Thompson, William I., 35-39.
        Wain [2], 194-210.

"Among School Children--V"
        Rosenbaum, item 14.
        Walcutt [1], item 72.

"The Black Tower"
        Keith, 119-23.

YEATS (cont'd)

"A Bronze Head"
    Denham, item 14.

"Byzantium"
    Barnes, T. R., 306-10.
    Fraser [2], 253-61.

"The Cap and Bells"
    Natterstad, item 75.

"The Chambermaid's First Song"
    Garab [1], 245-46.

"The Chambermaid's Second Song"
    Garab [1], 246-47.

"Coole Park and Ballylee, 1931"
    Barnes, T. R., 314-17.
    Perloff [1], 223-40.

"Crazy Jane Grown Old Looks at the Dancers"
    Antippas [2], 558-59.

"Crazy Jane Talks with the Bishop"
    Drew, E. A., 123-26.

"A Dialogue of Self and Soul"
    Drew, E. A., 139-41.

"Easter 1916"
    Malins, 271-84.
    Perloff [3], 308-28.

"The Gyres"
    Bierman, item 44.

"Her Vision in the Wood"
    Allen, James L., Jr. [1], item 45.

"High Talk"
    John [1], item 22.
    Reed, Victor, item 52.

"His Confidence"
    Bader, 36-38.

"King and No King"
    Allen, D. C. [4], 92-95.

"The Lady's First Song"
    Garab [1], 239-40.

"The Lady's Second Song"
    Garab [1], 240-41.

"The Lady's Third Song"
    Garab [1], 241-43.

"The Lake Isle of Innisfree"
    Drew, E. A., 65-66.

"Lapis Lazuli"
    Mendel [2], item 64.

"Leda and the Swan"
    Berdelman, 229-30.
    Ellmann, 31-33.

"Long-Legged Fly"
    Allen, James L., Jr. [2], item 51.
    Southam, item 73.

"The Lover Asks Forgiveness Because of his Many
    Moods"
    Spivak, 884-85.

"The Lover's Song"
    Garab [1], 243-45.

"The Magi"
    Sanders, Paul, item 53.

"Michael Robartes Asks Forgiveness Because of his
    Many Moods"
    See "The Lover Asks Forgiveness..."

"The Municipal Gallery Revisited"
    Garab [2], 243-54.
    Reid [1], 343-44.

"News for the Delphic Oracle"
    Ower, item 7.

"Nineteen Hundred and Nineteen"
    Drew, E. A., 94-101.

YEATS (cont'd)

"Parnell's Funeral"
     Wilson, F. A. C., item 72.

"A Prayer for My Daughter"
     Hardy, John E., 116-50.

"The Rose Tree"
     Loftus, 173-75.

"Sailing to Byzantium"
     Barnes, T. R., 303-06.
     Drew, E. A., 166-70.
     Lesser, 291-310.
     Phillips, Robert S., item 11.

"The Second Coming"
     Drew, E. A., 129-32.

"The Song of the Wandering Aengus"
     Rosenberg [2], 527-35.

"The Stolen Child"
     Caswell [2], item 64.

"That the Night Come"
     Unger [3], 698-709.

"The Three Bushes"
     Garab [1], 235-39.

"The Tower"
     Drew, E. A., 132-39.

"Under Ben Bulben"
     Stallworthy [2], 30-53.

"The Wild Swans at Coole"
     Hahn, 419-21.

YOUNG, EDWARD (1683-1765), British

"Night Thoughts"
     Hall, Mary S., 452-63.
     Pettit [2], xi-xx.

PART II

SOURCES OF CRITICISMS

ACKERMAN, Catherine A. "Drayton's Revision of 'The Shepheard's Garland'," CLAJ 3 (Dec., 1959).

ACKERMAN, R. D. "Arcades of Philadelphia the Past," Expl 24 (May, 1966).

ADAIR, Virginia H. "Death Is a Dialogue Between," Expl 27 (Mar., 1969).

ADAMS, Francis D. [1]. "Jubilate Agno and the 'Theme of Gratitude'," PLL 3 (Sum., 1967).

_____ [2]. "The Seven Pillars of Christopher Smart," PLL 1 (Spr., 1965).

ADAMS, Hazard [1]. "Place and Movement," Poetry 110 (Apr., 1967).

_____ [2]. "Reading Blake's Lyrics: 'The Tyger'," TSLL 2 (Spr., 1960).

ADAMS, John F. "Piers Plowman and The Three Ages of Man," JEGP 61 (Jan., 1962).

ADAMS, Laura. "Browning's Rings and Posies," VP 8 (Wint., 1970).

ADAMS, Robert Martin. "Bounding 'Lycidas'," HudR 23 (Sum., 1970).

ADELMAN, Lynn. "A Study of James Weldon Johnson,"

*An asterisk before an item in this section means that it was not examined.

149

JNH 52 (Apr., 1967).

ADEN, John M. [1]. " 'Rasselas' and 'The Vanity of Human Wishes'," Criticism 3 (Fall, 1961).

_____ [2]. "To Augustus," Expl 26 (May, 1968).

ADEY, Lionel. "Tennyson's Sorrow and Her Lying Lip," VP 8 (Aut., 1970).

ADICKS, Richard. "The Lily Maid and the Scarlet Sleeve, White and Red in Tennyson's Idylls," UR 34 (Oct., 1967).

ADLER, Thomas P. "The Uses of Knowledge in Tennyson's Merlin and Vivien," TSLL 11 (Wint., 1970).

ALAYA, Flavia M. [1]. "Tennyson's 'The Lady of Shalott'," VP 8 (Wint., 1970).

_____ [2]. " 'Two World' Revisited: Arnold, Renan, The Monastic Life, and the 'Stanzas from the Grande Chartreuse'," VP 5 (Wint., 1967).

ALDRICH, Jennifer. "The Deciphered Heart, Conrad Aiken's Poetry and Prose Fiction," SR 75 (Sum., 1967).

ALEXIS, Gerhard T. [1]. "Channel Firing," Expl 24 (Mar., 1966).

_____ [2]. "Meditation Eight," Expl 24 (Mar., 1966).

ALLAIN, Mathe. "The Humanist's Dilemma; Milton, God, and Reason," CE 27 (Feb., 1966).

ALLEN, D. C. [1]. Four Poets on Poetry. Baltimore: Johns Hopkins Press, 1967.

_____ [2]. Image and Meaning: Metaphoric Traditions in Renaissance Poetry. New enl. ed. Baltimore: Johns Hopkins Press, 1968.

_____ [3]. "Milton and the Descent to Light," JEGP 60 (Oct., 1961).

_____ [4]. The Moment of Poetry. Baltimore: Johns Hopkins Press, 1962.

ALLEN, Gay Wilson. "Walt Whitman's Inner Space," <u>PLL</u>
5 (Suppl., Sum., 1969).

ALLEN, James L., Jr. [1]. "Her Vision in the Wood,"
<u>Expl</u> 18 (May, 1960).

_____ [2]. "Long-Legged Fly," <u>Expl</u> 21 (Feb., 1963).

ALLEY, Alvin D. "Coleridge and Existentialism," <u>SHR</u> 2
(Fall, 1968).

ALLOTT, Kenneth. "Matthew Arnold's 'The New Sirens'
and George Sand," <u>VP</u> 1 (Apr., 1963).

ALPERS, Paul J. (comp.) [1]. <u>Elizabethan Poetry; Modern
Essays in Criticism.</u> New York: Oxford University
Press, 1967.

_____ [2]. "Narrative and Rhetoric in <u>The Faerie Queene</u>,"
<u>SEL</u> 2 (Wint., 1962).

ALPHONSE, Mary. "Love's Growth," <u>Expl</u> 25 (Jan., 1967).

ALSSID, Michael W. "Shadwell's <u>MacFlecknoe</u>," <u>SEL</u> 7
(Sum., 1967).

ALTICK, Richard D. [1]. "Four Victorian Poets and an
Exploding Island," <u>VS</u> 3 (Mar., 1960).

_____ [2]. " 'A Grammarian's Funeral': Browning's
Praise of Folly?" <u>SEL</u> 3 (Aut., 1963).

_____ [3]. "Lovers' Finiteness: Browning's 'Two in the
Campagna'," <u>PLL</u> 3 (Wint., 1967).

_____ [4]. "The Symbolism of Browning's 'Master Hugues
of Saxe-Gotha'," <u>VP</u> 3 (Wint., 1965).

ALVAREZ, A. "Marvell and the Poetry of Judgment," <u>HudR</u>
13 (Aut., 1960).

AMACHER, Richard E. "The City in the Sea," <u>Expl</u> 19
(May, 1961).

ANDERSON, Charles R. [1]. "Nothing Gold Can Stay,"
<u>Expl</u> 22 (Apr., 1964).

_____ [2]. "Reverse Cannot Befall," <u>Expl</u> 18 (May, 1960).

ANDERSON, J. J.   "The Prologue of 'Patience'," MP 63
     (May, 1966).

ANDERSON, John Q.   "Lowell's 'The Washers of the Shroud'
     and the Celtic Legend of the Washer of the Ford,"
     AL 35 (Nov., 1963).

ANDERSON, Judith H. [1].   "The July Eclogue and the
     House of Holiness: Perspective in Spenser," SEL 10
     (Wint., 1970).

_____ [2].   " 'Nor Man It Is': The Knight of Justice in
     Book V of Spenser's Faerie Queene," PMLA 85 (Jan.,
     1970).

ANDREACH, Robert J.   "Paradise Lost and the Christian
     Configuration of The Waste Land," PLL 5 (Sum.,
     1969).

ANDREASEN, N. J. C.   "Theme and Structure in Donne's
     'Satyres'," SEL 3 (Wint., 1963).

ANDREWS, S. G.   "The Carpenter's Son," Expl 19 (Oct.,
     1960).

ANGUS, Douglas.   "The Theme of Love and Guilt in
     Coleridge's Three Major Poems," JEGP 59 (Oct.,
     1960).

ANSELMENT, Raymond A.   "Martin Marprelate: A New
     Source for Dryden's Fable of the Martin and the Swal-
     lows," RES 17 (Aug., 1966).

ANSHUTZ, H. L. and D. W. CUMMINGS.   "The Sick Rose,"
     Expl 29 (Dec., 1970).

ANTHONY, Mother Mary [1].   "Emily Dickinson's Scriptural
     Echoes," MR 2 (Spr., 1961).

_____ [2].   "Verbal Pattern in 'Burnt Norton I',"
     Criticism 2 (Wint., 1960).

ANTIPPAS, Andy P. [1].   "A Note on Yeats' 'Crazy Jane'
     Poems," ES 49 (Dec., 1968).

_____ [2].   "Tennyson, Hallam, and The Palace of Art,"
     VP 5 (Wint., 1967).

ARINSHTEIN, Leonid M.   " 'A Curse for a Nation': A
    Controversial Episode in Elizabeth Barrett Browning's
    Political Poetry," RES 20 (Feb., 1969).

ARMS, George.   "Emerson's 'Ode Inscribed to W. H.
    Channing'," CE 22 (Mar., 1961).

ARMSTRONG, Isobel [1].   "Browning's 'Mr. Sludge, "The
    Medium" '," VP 2 (Wint., 1964).

_____ [2].   "A Note on the Conversion of Caponsacchi,"
    VP 6 (Aut.-Wint., 1968).

ARMSTRONG, James.   "The 'Death Wish' in 'Stopping by
    Wood'," CE 25 (Mar., 1964).

ARYANPUR, Manoocher.   "Paradise Lost and The Odyssey,"
    TSLL 9 (Sum., 1967).

ASKEW, Melvin W.   "Form and Process in Lyric Poetry,"
    SR 72 (Spr., 1964).

ASPIZ, Harold.   "Spirit That Form'd This Scene," Expl 28
    (Nov., 1969).

ASWELL, E. Duncan.   "The Role of Fortune in The Testa-
    ment of Cresseid," PQ 46 (Oct., 1967).

AUGUST, Eugene R. [1].   "The Growth of 'The Windhover',"
    PMLA 82 (Oct., 1967).

_____ [2].   "Hopkins' Dangerous Fire," VP 1 (Jan.,
    1963).

AUSTIN, Allen [1].   "Keats's Grecian Urn and the Truth of
    Eternity," CE 25 (Mar., 1964).

_____ [2].   "T. S. Eliot's Theory of Dissociation,"
    CE 23 (Jan., 1962).

BABB, Howard S.   "The 'Epitaph on Elizabeth, L. H.,'
    and Ben Jonson's Style," JEGP 62 (Oct., 1963).

BACHE, William B.   "Dryden and Oldham: Hail and Fare-
    well," CLAJ 12 (Mar., 1969).

BACON, M. E. [1].   "Imitation of Pope: A Compliment to

the Ladies," Expl 28 (May, 1970).

_____ [2]. "A Pretty Epigram for the Entertainment of Those Who Have Paid Great Sums in the Venetian and Flemish Ooze," Expl 28 (May, 1970).

_____ [3]. "The Tyger," Expl 26 (Dec., 1967).

BADER, Arno Lehman. (ed.) To the Young Writer. Ann Arbor: University of Michigan Press, 1965.

BAILEY, Dudley. "Coleridge's Revision of 'The Friend'," MP 59 (Nov., 1961).

BAILEY, John Cann. Continuity of Letters. Freeport, New York: Books for Libraries, 1967.

BAINE, Rodney M. [1]. "The Little Vagabond," Expl 27 (Sept., 1968).

_____ [2]. "Blake's 'Tyger': The Nature of the Beast," PQ 46 (Oct., 1967).

BAKER, Donald W. "The Poetry of James Dickey," Poetry 111 (Mar., 1968).

BAKER, Houston A., Jr. [1]. "A Decadent's Nature: The Poetry of Ernest Dowson," VP 6 (Spr., 1968).

_____ [2]. "The Poet's Progress: Rossetti's The House of Life," VP 8 (Spr., 1970).

BALDWIN, Anne W. "Henry II and The Owl and The Nightingale," JEGP 66 (Apr., 1967).

BALL, Albert. "Charles II: Dryden's Christian Hero," MP 59 (Aug., 1961).

BALL, Patricia M. "Tennyson and the Romantics," VP 1 (Jan., 1963).

BAMBAS, Rudolph C. "Another View of the Old English Wife's Lament," JEGP 62 (Apr., 1963).

BARBER, C. L. "Shakespeare in His Sonnets," MR 1 (Sum., 1960).

BARBOUR, Brian M. "Veteran Sirens," Expl 28 (Nov., 1969).

BARKSDALE, Richard K. "Arnold and Tennyson on Etna,"
    CLAJ 2 (Dec., 1958).

BARNES, T. R. English Verse; Voice and Movement from
    Wyatt to Yeats. Cambridge: Cambridge University
    Press, 1967.

BARNES, W. J. "T. S. Eliot's 'Marina'," UR 29 (June,
    1963).

BARRY, James D. "Firelight," Expl 22 (Nov., 1963).

BARTEL, Roland. "Byron's Respect for Language," PLL 1
    (Aut., 1965).

BARTLETT, Phyllis. "The Old Chartist," Expl 18 (June,
    1960).

BARTON, Cynthia. "Memorabilia," Expl 22 (Dec., 1963).

BASS, Eben [1]. "The Fourth Element in 'Ode to the West
    Wind'," PLL 3 (Fall, 1967).

_____ [2]. "Swinburne, Greene, and 'The Triumph of
    Time'," VP 4 (Wint., 1966).

BATTENHOUSE, Henry Martin. Poets of Christian Thought;
    Evaluations from Dante to T. S. Eliot. New York:
    Ronald Press, 1947.

BAUERLE, Richard F. "Throwing the Apple," Expl 27
    (Nov., 1968).

BAUERLE, Ruth H. "Fish in the Unruffled Lakes," Expl
    26 (Mar., 1968).

BAUM, Paull F. "The Beowulf Poet," PQ 39 (Oct., 1960).

BAUMANN, Walter. "Pound and Layamon's Brut," JEGP
    68 (Apr., 1969).

BAXTER, Ralph C. "Shakespeare's Dauphin and Hopkins'
    Windhover," VP 7 (Spr., 1969).

BAYBAK, Michael, Paul DELANY and A. Kent HIEATT.
    "Placement 'In the Middest' in The Faerie Queene,"
    PLL 5 (Sum., 1969).

BEARDSLEY, Monroe C. and Sam HYNES. "Misunderstand-
    ing Poetry: Notes on Some Readings of Dylan Thomas,"
    CE 21 (Mar., 1960).

BEAURLINE, L. A. " 'Why So Pale and Wan': An Essay
    in Critical Method," TSLL 4 (Wint., 1963).

BECK, Ronald. "I Heard a Fly Buzz When I Died," Expl
    26 (Dec., 1967).

BECK, Rosalie. "A Precedent for Donne's Imagery in
    'Goodfriday, 1613. Riding Westward'," RES 19 (May,
    1968).

BELL, Vereen M. "A Reading of 'Prufrock'," ES 50
    (Anglo-American Suppl., 1969).

BENDER, Todd K. "God's Grandeur," Expl 21 (Mar.,
    1963).

BENNETT, James R. "Lazarus in Browning's 'Karshish',"
    VP 3 (Sum., 1965).

BENOIT, Raymond. "Shelley's Flying Saucer," UR 35 (Dec.,
    1968).

BENSON, Donald R. [1]. "Theology and Politics in Dryden's
    Conversion," SEL 4 (Sum., 1964).

_____ [2]. "Who 'Bred' Religio Laici?" JEGP 65 (Apr.,
    1966).

BENTON, Richard P. "Don't Look Now But Mary Is Every-
    body," Expl 20 (Dec., 1961).

BENTON, Robert M. "Edward Taylor's Use of His Text,"
    AL 39 (Mar., 1967).

BERCOVITCH, Sacvan [1]. "Romance and Anti-Romance in
    Sir Gawain and the Green Knight," PQ 44 (Jan., 1965).

_____ [2]. "Sonnet CXXIV," Expl 27 (Nov., 1968).

BERGER, Harry, Jr. [1]. "The Discarding of Malbecco:
    Conspicuous Allusion and Cultural Exhaustion in The
    Faerie Queene III, ix-x," SP 66(Apr., 1969).

_____ [2]. " 'Faerie Queene' Book III: A General

Description," Criticism 11 (Sum., 1969).

_____ [3]. "Poetry as Revision: Interpreting Robert
Frost," Criticism 10 (Wint., 1968).

_____ [4]. "The Prospect of Imagination: Spenser and
the Limits of Poetry," SEL 1 (Wint., 1961).

_____ [5]. "The Spenserian Dynamics," SEL 8 (Wint.,
1968).

_____ [6]. "The Structure of Merlin's Chronicle in The
Faerie Queene III (iii)," SEL 9 (Wint., 1969).

BERGONZI, Bernard [1]. Heroes' Twilight; A Study of the
Literature of the Great War. New York: Coward-
McCann, 1965.

_____ [2]. "A Poem About the History of Love," CritQ
4 (Sum., 1962).

_____ [3]. "The Poetry of Donald Davie," CritQ 4 (Wint.,
1962).

BERKELMAN, Robert. "The Poet, the Swan, and the
Woman," UR 28 (Mar., 1962).

BERMAN, Ronald. "Rochester and the Defeat of the Senses,"
KR 26 (Spr., 1964).

BERNHARDT-KABISCH, Ernest. "Elegiac Stanzas," Expl
23 (May, 1965).

BERRY, Francis. Poetry and the Physical Voice. New
York: Oxford University Press, 1962.

BERRY, J. Wilkes. "Sonnet XII," Expl 27 (Oct., 1968).

BERTHOFF, Ann Evans [1]. "The Allegorical Metaphor:
Marvell's 'The Definition of Love'," RES 17 (Feb.,
1966).

_____ [2]. "The Falconer's Dream of Trust: Wyatt's
'They Fle From Me'," SR 71 (Sum., 1963).

BERTONASCO, Marc. "A New Look at Crashaw and 'The
Weeper'," TSLL 10 (Sum., 1968).

BETAR, George. "Earthy Anecdote," Expl 22 (Feb., 1964).

BEUM, Robert [1]. "Yeats the Rhymer," PLL 1 (Aut., 1965).

_____ [2]. "Yeats's Octaves," TSLL 3 (Spr., 1961).

BEWLEY, Marius. "The Poetry of Longfellow," HudR 16 (Sum., 1963).

BIEMAN, Elizabeth. "An Eros Manque: Browning's 'Andrea del Sarto'," SEL 10 (Aut., 1970).

BIERMAN, Robert. "The Gyres," Expl 19 (Apr., 1961).

BIGSBY, C. W. E. (ed.) The Black American Writer. Deland, Florida: Everett Edwards, 1969. Vol. 2.

*BIRD, G. Leonard. "Gwendolyn Brooks: Educator Extraordinaire," Discourse 12 (1969).

BISHOP, Ferman. "The Wood-Pile," Expl 18 (June, 1960).

BLAIR, Joe. "Dryden's Ceremonial Hero," SEL 9 (Sum., 1969).

BLAKE, N. F. "The Heremod Digressions in Beowulf," JEGP 61 (Apr., 1962).

BLAKESLEE, Richard C. "Three Ways Past Edinburgh: Stephen Spender's 'The Express'," CE 26 (Apr., 1965).

BLISSETT, William. "Florimell and Marinell," SEL 5 (Wint., 1965).

BLOOM, Edward A. "The Eve of St. Agnes," Expl 20 (Sept., 1961).

BLOOM, Harold. "The Central Man: Emerson, Whitman, Wallace Stevens," MR 7 (Wint., 1966).

BLUESTONE, Max [1]. "Dunciad, IV," Expl 20 (Jan., 1962).

_____ [2]. "The Iconographic Sources of Auden's 'Musee des Beaux Arts'," MLN 76 (Apr., 1961).

BLUM, Margaret M. "Robert Frost's 'Directive': A

Theological Reading," MLN 76 (June, 1961).

BOCK, Frederick. "And a Variable Compass," Poetry 106 (June, 1965).

BOGAN, Louise. Selected Criticism: Prose, Poetry. New York: Noonday Press, 1955.

BOGNER, Delmar. "The Sexual Side of Meredith's Poetry," VP 8 (Sum., 1970).

BOLIN, Donald W. "A Clock Stopped," Expl 22 (Dec., 1963).

BOLLIER, E. P. "A Broken Coriolanus: A Note on T. S. Eliot's 'Coriolan'," SoR 3 (Sum., 1967).

BOLTON, W. F. " 'Variation' in The Battle of Brunan-burh," RES 19 (Nov., 1968).

BONNER, Francis W. "The Bishop Order his Tomb at Saint Praxed's Church," Expl 22 (Mar., 1964).

*BONTEMPS, Arna. "Langston Hughes: He Spoke of Rivers," Freedomways 8 (Spr., 1968).

BOO, Sister Mary Richard [1]. "The Ordeal of Giuseppe Caponsacchi," VP 3 (Sum., 1965).

_____ [2]. "Stanzas from the Grande Chartreuse," Expl 23 (May, 1965).

BOOTH, Philip. "Off Hawthorne's Salem," Poetry 97 (Oct., 1960).

BOSTETTER, Edward E. "Shelley and the Mutinous Flesh," TSLL 1 (Sum., 1959).

BOSWELL, Jackson Campbell. "Milton and Prevenient Grace," SEL 7 (Wint., 1967).

BOULGER, James D. "Imagination and Speculation in Coleridge's Conversation Poems," JEGP 64 (Oct., 1965).

BOWEN, James K. "Propositional and Emotional Knowledge in Robert Frost's 'The Death of the Hired Man, ' 'The

Fear,' and 'Home Burial'," CLAJ 12 (Dec., 1968).

BOWERS, Frederick. "Arthur Hugh Clough: The Modern
Mind," SEL 6 (Aut., 1966).

BOWERS, Fredson [1]. "Adam, Eve and the Fall in Paradise Lost," PMLA 84 (Mar., 1969).

_____ [2]. "Herbert's Sequential Imagery: 'The Temper',"
MP 59 (Feb., 1962).

BOWMAN, Elizabeth. "The Soul Selects Her Own Society,"
Expl 29 (Oct., 1970).

BOYERS, Robert. "A Sovereign Voice: The Poetry of
Robinson Jeffers," SR 77 (Sum., 1969).

BOYETTE, Purvis E. "Epilogue to the Satires," Expl 24
(Jan., 1966).

BRACKER, Jon. "The Love Song of J. Alfred Prufrock,"
Expl 25 (Nov., 1966).

BRADFORD, M. E. "Meaning and Metaphor in Donald
Davidson's 'A Touch of Snow'," SoR 2 (Sum., 1966).

BRADHAM, Jo Allen [1]. "Epistle to Dr. Arbuthnot,"
Expl 26 (Feb., 1968).

_____ [2]. "The Fury of Aerial Bombardment," Expl 22
(May, 1964).

BRANDY, W. T. "An Enigma," Expl 20 (Dec., 1961).

BRASHEAR, William R. [1]. "Tennyson's Third Voice:
A Note," VP 2 (Aut., 1964).

_____ [2]. "Tennyson's Tragic Vitalism: Idylls of the
King," VP 6 (Spr., 1968).

_____ [3]. "The Trouble with Housman," VP 7 (Sum.,
1969).

BRAVERMAN, Albert and Bernard EINBOND. "Two Tramps
in Mud Time," Expl 29 (Nov., 1970).

BREMER, R. "Hopkins' Use of the Word 'Combs' in 'To

R. B.'," ES 51 (Apr., 1970).

BRENNAN, Joseph X. "The Symbolic Framework of Blake's 'The Tyger'," CE 22 (Mar., 1961).

BRENNER, Rica. Ten Modern Poets. Freeport, New York: Books for Libraries Press, 1968.

BRETT, R. L. Reason and Imagination; a Study of Form and Meaning in Four Poems. London: Published for the University of Hull by Oxford University Press, 1960.

BRIDGMAN, Richard [1]. "Melville's Roses," TSLL 8 (Sum., 1966).

_____ [2]. "Whitman's Calendar Leaves," CE 25 (Mar., 1964).

BRIGGS, Pearlanna. "Directive," Expl 21 (May, 1963).

BRISTOL, Michael D. "Structural Patterns in Two Elizabethan Pastorals," SEL 10 (Wint., 1970).

BRITTON, John. "The Palace of Art," Expl 20 (Oct., 1961).

BRODERICK, John C. "Poe's Revisions of 'Lenore'," AL 35 (Jan., 1964).

BRODWIN, Leonora Leet [1]. "Miltonic Allusion in Absalom and Achitophel: Its Function in the Political Satire," JEGP 68 (Jan., 1969).

_____ [2]. "The Structure of Sidney's 'Astrophel and Stella'," MP 67 (Aug., 1969).

*BRONZ, Stephen A. Roots of Racial Consciousness; the 1920's: Three Harlem Renaissance Authors. New York: Libra, 1964.

BROOKS, Cleanth. "Poetry Since 'The Waste Land'," SoR 1 (Sum., 1965).

BROPHY, James [1]. "The Noble Brute: Medieval Nuance in 'The Windhover'," MLN 76 (Dec., 1961).

_____ [2]. "Still Falls the Rain," Expl 29 (Dec., 1970).

BROWN, Bernadine. "Robert Browning's 'The Italian in England'," VP 6 (Sum., 1968).

BROWN, Clarence A. "Walt Whitman and the 'New Poetry'," AL 33 (Mar., 1961).

BROWN, Merle E. "Concordia Discors in the Poetry of Wallace Stevens," AL 34 (May, 1962).

BROWN, Terence. "Robert Frost's In the Clearing: An Attempt to Reestablish the Persona of the "Kindly Grey Poet'," PLL 5 (Suppl., Sum., 1969).

BRUFFEE, Kenneth A. "The Synthetic Hero and the Narrative Structure of Childe Harold III," SEL 6 (Aut., 1966).

BRUMLEVE, Sister Eric Marie, S.S.N.D. "Permanence and Change in the Poetry of Robert Lowell," TSLL 10 (Spr., 1968).

BRYAN, Robert A. [1]. "Adam's Tragic Vision in Paradise Lost," SP 62 (Apr., 1965).

_____ [2]. "John Donne's Use of the Anathema," JEGP 61 (Apr., 1962).

BUCHAN, A. M. "The Sad Wisdom of the Mariner," SP 61 (Oct., 1964).

BUCHEN, Irving H. "Source-Hunting Versus Tradition: Thompson's 'The Hound of Heaven'," VP 2 (Spr., 1964).

BUFKIN, E. C. "Imagery in 'Locksley Hall'," VP 2 (Wint., 1964).

BURCH, Francis F. "Clement Mansfield Ingleby on Poe's 'The Raven': An unpublished British Criticism," AL 35 (Mar., 1963).

BURGESS, C. F. [1]. "Ode on a Grecian Urn," Expl 23 (Dec., 1964).

_____ [2]. "The Oven Bird," Expl 20 (Mar., 1962).

_____ [3]. "William Jay Smith's 'American Primitive':

Toward a Reading, " ArQ 26 (Spr. , 1970).

BURHANS, Clinton S. , Jr.   "With How Sad Steps, O Moon, "
Expl 18 (Jan. , 1960).

BURKHART, Charles.   "Richard Cory, " Expl 19 (Nov. ,
1960).

BURRELL, Paul.   "The Draft Horse, " Expl 25 (Mar. , 1967).

BUSH, Douglas.   "Ironic and Ambiguous Allusion in Paradise Lost, " JEGP 60 (Oct. , 1961).

BUTTEL, Helen [1].   "Bridal Birth, " Expl 23 (Nov. ,1964).

_____ [2].   "I Knew a Woman, " Expl 24 (May, 1966).

BUTTER, P. H.   "Sun and Shape in Shelley's The Triumph
of Life, " RES 13 (Feb. , 1962).

BYERS, John R. , Jr.   "Time, Real and Imaginary, " Expl
19 (Apr. , 1961).

CADBURY, William [1].   "Coming to Terms with 'Dover
Beach', " Criticism 8 (Spr. , 1966).

_____ [2].   "The Structure of Feeling in a Poem by
Patmore: Meter, Phonology, Form, " VP 4 (Aut. , 1966).

_____ [3].   "Tennyson's 'The Palace of Art' and the
Rhetoric of Structures, " Criticism 7 (Wint. , 1965).

CAIN, Thomas H.   "The Strategy of Praise in Spenser's
'Aprill', " SEL 8 (Wint. , 1968).

CALLAN, Edward.   "W. H. Auden: The Farming of a
Verse, " SoR 3 (Spr. , 1967).

CAMBON, Glauco [1].   Recent American Poetry.   Minneapolis: University of Minnesota Press, 1962.

_____ [2].   "William Carlos Williams and Ezra Pound:
Two Examples of Open Poetry, " CE 22 (Mar. , 1961).

CANNON, Charles Kendrick.   "Chapman on the Unity of
Style and Meaning, " JEGP 68 (Apr. , 1969).

CANNON, Garland. " 'The Lady of Shalott' and 'The
    Arabian Nights' Tales," VP 8 (Wint., 1970).

CANUTESON, John. "The Crucifixion and the Second Com-
    ing in 'The Dream of the Rood'," MP 66 (May, 1969).

CAREY, John [1]. "Milton's Ad Patrem, 35-37," RES 15
    (May, 1964).

_____ [2]. "Notes on Two of Donne's Songs and Sonets,"
    RES 16 (Feb., 1965).

CARGILL, Oscar. "Death in a Handful of Dust," Criticism
    11 (Sum., 1969).

CARLISLE, E. F. "Walt Whitman: The Drama of Identity,"
    Criticism 10 (Fall, 1968).

CARLSON, Eric W. [1]. "Poe's 'Eldorado'," MLN 76
    (Mar., 1961).

_____ [2]. "I Started Early, Took My Dog," Expl 20
    (May, 1962).

_____ [3]. "Symbol and Sense in Poe's 'Ulalume',"
    AL 35 (Mar., 1963).

CARPENTER, Margaret Ann [1]. "From Herbert to Mar-
    vell: Poetics in 'A Wreath' and 'The Coronet',"
    JEGP 69 (Jan.,1970).

_____ [2]. "Marvell's 'Garden'," SEL 10 (Wint., 1970).

CARROLL, Paul. "A Note on Isabella Gardner," Poetry
    101 (Dec., 1962).

CARRUTH, Hayden. "A Meaning of Robert Lowell,"
    HudR 20 (Aut., 1967).

CARSON, J. Angela. "The Metaphor of Struggle in 'Carrion
    Comfort'," PQ 49 (Oct., 1970).

CARSON, Mother Angela, O.S.U. "Aspects of Elegy in the
    Middle English 'Pearl'," SP 62 (Jan., 1965).

*CARTEY, Wilfred. "Four Shadows of Harlem," NegroD 18,
    no. 10.

CASWELL, Robert W. [1]. "Lay Your Sleeping Head, My
    Love, " Expl 26 (Jan. , 1968).

_____ [2]. "The Stolen Child, " Expl 25 (Apr. , 1967).

CAVITCH, David. "The Man with the Blue Guitar, " Expl
    27 (Dec., 1968).

CHALLIS, Lorna. "The Use of Oratory in Sidney's
    'Arcadia', " SP 62 (July, 1965).

CHAMBERLAIN, Robert L. "George Crabbe and Darwin's
    Amorous Plants, " JEGP 61 (Oct., 1962).

CHAMBERS, A. B. [1]. "The Fly in Donne's 'Canoniza-
    tion', " JEGP 65 (Apr., 1966).

_____ [2]. "The Meaning of the 'Temple' in Donne's
    La Corona, " JEGP 59 (Apr., 1960).

_____ [3]. "Milton's Proteus and Satan's Visit to the
    Sun, " JEGP 62 (Apr., 1963).

_____ [4]. "The Sea of Matter in Paradise Lost, " MLN
    76 (Dec., 1961).

_____ [5]. "Three Notes on Eve's Dream in Paradise
    Lost, " PQ 46 (Apr., 1967).

CHAMBERS, Jessie Rhodes. "The Episode of Annius and
    Mummius: Dunciad IV 347-96, " PQ 43 (Apr., 1964).

CHAMBERS, Leland H. [1]. "In Defense of 'The Weeper', "
    PLL 3 (Spr., 1967).

_____ [2]. "Vaughan's 'The World': The Limits of Ex-
    trinsic Criticism, " SEL 8 (Wint., 1968).

CHAMBERS, Marlene [1]. "In the White Giant's Thigh, "
    Expl 19 (Oct., 1960).

_____ [2]. "In the White Giant's Thigh, " Expl 19 (Mar.,
    1961).

CHAMPION, Larry S. "The Conclusion of Paradise Lost--
    A Reconsideration, " CE 27 (Feb., 1966).

CHANDLER, Alice [1].   "Cousin Clara Vere de Vere," VP
5 (Spr., 1967).

_____ [2].   " 'The Eve of St. Agnes' and 'Porphyria's
Lover'," VP 3 (Aut., 1965).

_____ [3].   "Tennyson's Maud and the Song of Songs,"
VP 7 (Sum., 1969).

CHATMAN, Seymour.   "The Questioner Who Sits So Sly,"
Expl 28 (Nov., 1969).

CHAYES, Irene H.   "Dreamer, Poet and Poem in The Fall
of Hyperion," PQ 46 (Oct., 1967).

CHERNAIK, Warren L.   "Waller's 'Panegyric to My Lord
Protector' and the Poetry of Praise," SEL 4 (Wint.,
1964).

CHERNISS, Michael D. [1].   "The Meaning of 'The Seafarer',"
Lines 97-102," MP 66 (Nov.,1968).

_____ [2].   "The Progress of the Hoard in Beowulf,"
PQ 47 (Oct., 1968).

CHEVIGNY, Bell Gale.   "Instress and Devotion in the Poetry
of Gerard Manley Hopkins," VS 9 (Dec., 1965).

CHIARENZA, Frank J.   "The Bishop Orders his Tomb at
Saint Praxed's Church," Expl 19 (Jan., 1961).

CHRISTENSEN, Allan C.   "Liturgical Order in Smart's
Jubilate Agno: A Study of Fragment C," PLL 6 (Fall,
1970).

CHRISTENSEN, Francis.   "Intellectual Love: The Second
Theme of The Prelude," PMLA 80 (Mar., 1965).

CHURCH, Margaret.   "Journey of the Magi," Expl 18 (June,
1960).

CINQUEMANI, A. M.   "The Mower Against Gardens," Expl
20 (May, 1962).

CIRILLO, A. R. [1].   "The Fair Hermaphrodite: Love-
Union in the Poetry of Donne and Spenser," SEL 9
(Wint., 1969).

_____ [2]. " 'Hail Holy Light' and Divine Time in Paradise Lost," JEGP 68 (Jan., 1969).

_____ [3]. "Spenser's Epithalamion: The Harmonious
Universe of Love," SEL 8 (Wint., 1968).

CLAGGETT, M. F. " 'Glory, Jest and Riddle'," EJ 55
(Mar., 1966).

CLAIR, John A. "Donne's 'The Canonization'," PMLA 80
(June, 1965).

CLAIRE, William F. "That Rare, Random Descent: The
Poetry and Pathos of Sylvia Plath," AR 26 (Wint.,
1966-67).

CLARE, Sister M. Theresa, O.S.F. "Meditation Sixty-
Two," Expl 19 (Dec., 1960).

CLARK, David R. [1]. "Cummings' 'anyone' and 'noone',"
ArQ 25 (Spr., 1969).

_____ [2]. "Hart Crane's Technique," TSLL 5 (Aut.,
1963).

_____ [3]. "Poem," Expl 22 (Feb., 1964).

CLARK, George. "The Traveler Recognizes His Goal: A
Theme in Anglo-Saxon Poetry," JEGP 64 (Oct., 1965).

CLARK, Ira. "Milton and the Image of God," JEGP 68
(July, 1969).

CLARK, Paul O. "The Hock-Cart, or Harvest Home,"
Expl 24 (Apr., 1966).

CLEMENTS, Arthur L. [1]. "Donne's Holy Sonnet XIV,"
MLN 76 (June, 1961).

_____ [2]. "On the Mode and Meaning of Traherne's
Mystical Poetry: 'The Preparative'," SP 61 (July, 1964).

CLOUGH, Wilson O. "Notes Toward a Supreme Fiction,"
Expl 28 (Nov., 1969).

CLUBB, Merrel D., Jr. "The Heraclitean Element in
Eliot's Four Quartets," PQ 40 (Jan., 1961).

CLUBB, Roger L.   "The Paradox of Ben Jonson's 'A Fit
     of Rime Against Rime," CLAJ 5 (Dec., 1961).

COHEN, Ralph.   " 'Spring': The Love Song of James
     Thomson," TSLL 11 (Fall, 1969).

COLEMAN, Alice.   " 'Doors Leap Open'," EJ 53 (Nov.,
     1964).

COLEMAN, Philip Y.   "Walt Whitman's Ambiguities of
     'I'," PLL 5 (Suppl, Sum., 1969).

COLIE, R. L.   "The Rhetoric of Transcendence," PQ 43
     (Apr., 1964).

COLLETT, Jonathan H.   "Milton's Use of Classical
     Mythology in Paradise Lost," PMLA 85 (Jan., 1970).

COLLIER, Eugenia W. [1].   "I Do Not Marvel Countee
     Cullen," CLAJ 11 (Sept., 1967).

_____ [2].   "James Weldon Johnson: Mirror of Change,"
     Phylon 21 (Wint., 1960).

COLLINS, Dan S.   "Vertue," Expl 27 (Mar., 1969).

*COLLINS, Douglas.   "LeRoi Jones as Poet," LanM 60
     (May-June, 1966).

COLLINS, Thomas J. [1].   "Browning's Essay on Shelley:
     In Context," VP 2 (Spr., 1964).

_____ [2].   "Shelley and God in Browning's Pauline:
     Unresolved Problems," VP 3 (Sum., 1965).

COLUMBUS, Robert R. and Claudette KEMPER.   "Sordello
     and the Speaker: A Problem in Identity," VP 2 (Aut.,
     1964).

COLUSSI, D. L.   "The Gentle," Expl 27 (May, 1969).

COMBELLACK, C. R. B. [1].   "The Oven Bird," Expl
     22 (Nov., 1963).

_____ [2].   "Sonnet XXXIV," Expl 29 (Dec., 1970).

_____ [3].   "Upon Wedlock, and Death of Children,"

Expl 29 (Oct., 1970).

CONARROE, Joel Osborne [1]. "A Local Pride: The
    Poetry of Paterson," PMLA 84 (May, 1969).

_____ [2]. "Without Invention Nothing Is Well Spaced,"
    Expl 27 (Dec., 1968).

CONDEE, Ralph W. "The Structure of Milton's 'Epitaphium
    Damonis'," SP 62 (July, 1965).

CONNELLY, James T. [1] "I Heard a Fly Buzz When I
    Died," Expl 25 (Dec., 1966).

_____ [2]. "Wild Nights," Expl 25 (Jan., 1967).

CONNOLLY, Thomas E. "Ulalume," Expl 22 (Sept., 1963).

CONRAN, Anthony E. M. "The Dialectic of Experience:
    A Study of Wordsworth's Resolution and Independence,"
    PMLA 75 (Mar., 1960).

CONTOSKI, Victor. "Time and Money: The Poetry of
    David Ignatow," UR 34 (Mar., 1968).

COOK, Richard I. "Garth's 'Dispensary' and Pope's 'Rape
    of the Lock'," CLAJ 6 (Dec., 1962).

COOK, Robert G. [1]. "Chaucer's Pandarus and the
    Medieval Ideal of Friendship," JEGP 69 (July, 1970).

_____ [2]. "Emerson's 'Self-Reliance,' Sweeney, and
    Prufrock," AL 42 (May, 1970).

COOLIDGE, John S. "Marvell and Horace," MP 63 (Nov.,
    1965).

COOPER, Wayne. "Claude McKay and the New Negro of
    the 1920's," Phylon 25 (Fall, 1964).

COPE, Jackson I. "Fortunate Falls as Form in Milton's
    'Fair Infant'," JEGP 63 (Oct., 1964).

COPE, John I. "Perseus," Expl 26 (Feb., 1968).

CORDER, Jim W. "Rhetoric and Meaning in 'Religio
    Laici'," PMLA 82 (May, 1967).

CORIN, Fernand. "A Note on Donne's 'Canonization',"
ES 50 (Feb., 1969).

CORNELIUS, David K. [1]. "Batter My Heart, Three
Person'd God," Expl 24 (Nov., 1965).

_____ [2]. "Ode on a Grecian Urn," Expl 20 (Mar.,
1962).

COSMAN, Madeleine Pelner. "Spenser's Ark of Animals:
Animal Imagery in the 'Faery Queen'," SEL 3 (Wint.,
1963).

COTTER, James Finn [1]. " 'Altar and Hour' in The Wreck
of the Deutschland," PLL 5 (Wint., 1969).

_____ [2]. "Astrophel and Stella, Sonnet 40," Expl 27
(Mar., 1969).

_____ [3]. "Astrophel and Stella, Sonnet 75," Expl 27
(May, 1969).

_____ [4]. "The 'Baiser' Group in Sidney's Astrophil and
Stella," TSLL 12 (Fall, 1970).

COURSEN, Herbert R., Jr. [1]. "The Ghost of Christmas
Past: 'Stopping by Woods on a Snowy Evening,' "
CE 24 (Dec., 1962).

_____ [2]. " 'The Moon Lies Fair': The Poetry of
Matthew Arnold," SEL 4 (Aut., 1964).

COURT, Franklin E. "The Theme and Structure of Spenser's
Muiopotmos," SEL 10 (Wint., 1970).

COWAN, Michael H. "Give All to Love," Expl 18 (May,
1960).

COWAN, S. A. [1]. "He Will Watch the Hawk with an
Indifferent Eye," Expl 28 (Apr., 1970).

_____ [2]. "The Legacie," Expl 19 (May, 1961).

_____ [3]. "Lost Anchors," Expl 24 (Apr., 1966).

COWAN, Stanley A. and Fred A. DUDLEY. "Astrophel and
Stella," Expl 20 (May, 1962).

COX, C. B. [1]. "Dylan Thomas's 'Fern Hill'," CritQ 1 (Sum., 1959).

_____ [2]. "The Poetry of Louis Simpson," CritQ 8 (Spr., 1966).

_____ [3]. "T. S. Eliot at the Crossroads," CritQ 12 (Wint., 1970).

_____, and A. R. JONES. "After the Tranquilized Fifties; Notes on Sylvia Plath and James Baldwin," CritQ 6 (Sum., 1964).

COX, James M. [1]. "Walt Whitman, Mark Twain, and the Civil War," SR 69 (Spr., 1961).

_____ [2]. "Longfellow and his Cross of Snow," PMLA 75 (Mar., 1960).

COX, Ollie. "The 'Spot of Joy' in 'My Last Duchess'," CLAJ 12 (Sept., 1968).

COX, Roger L. "Ode: Intimations of Immortality," Expl 19 (Mar., 1961).

CRAIG, David. "The Defeatism of The Waste Land," CritQ 2 (Aut., 1960).

CRAWFORD, John W. "A Unifying Element in Tennyson's Maud," VP 7 (Spr., 1969).

CREED, Howard. " 'The Rime of the Ancient Mariner': A Rereading," EJ 49 (Apr., 1960).

CRIDER, J. R. "Absalom and Achitophel," Expl 23 (Apr., 1965).

CRIDER, John R. "Structure and Effect in Collins' Progress Poems," SP 60 (Jan., 1963).

CRUNDEN, Patricia. " 'The Woods of Westermain'," VP 5 (Wint., 1967).

CRUPI, Charles. "Conrad in Twilight," Expl 29 (Nov., 1970).

CRUTTWELL, Patrick. "Pope and His Church," HudR 13 (Aut., 1960).

CUBETA, Paul M. [1]. "Ben Jonson's Religious Lyrics,"
    JEGP 62 (Jan., 1963).

_____ [2]. "A Jonsonian Ideal: 'To Penshurst'," PQ
    42 (Jan., 1963).

_____ [3]. "Marlowe's Poet in Hero and Leander," CE
    26 (Apr., 1965).

CULBERT, Taylor. "The Narrative Functions of Beowulf's
    Swords," JEGP 59 (Jan., 1960).

_____ and John M. VOILETTE. "Wallace Stevens'
    Emperor," Criticism 2 (Wint., 1960).

CULLEN, Patrick. "Imitation and Metamorphosis: The
    Golden-Age Eclogue in Spenser, Milton and Marvell,"
    PMLA 84 (Oct., 1969).

CUMMINGS, Peter M. "Spenser's Amoretti as an Allegory
    of Love," TSLL 12 (Sum., 1970).

CUMMINGS, R. M. "The Difficulty of Marvell's 'Bermudas',"
    MP 67 (May, 1970).

CUNNINGHAM, J. V. "Sorting Out: The Case of Dickin-
    son," SoR 5 (Spr., 1969).

CUTLER, B. "Long Reach, Strong Speech," Poetry 103
    (Mar., 1964).

DAICHES, David. "1954: The Poetry of Dylan Thomas,"
    CE 22 (Nov., 1960).

DALLETT, Joseph B. " 'The Faerie Queene', IV. i-v: A
    Synopsis of Discord," MLN 75 (Dec., 1960).

DANBY, John F. "Edward Thomas," CritQ 1 (Wint., 1959).

DANIELS, Edgar F. [1]. "Lycidas," Expl 21 (Jan., 1963).

_____ [2]. "The Quip," Expl 23 (Sept., 1964).

_____ [3]. "Satyre III," Expl 28 (Feb., 1970).

_____ [4]. "The World," Expl 22 (May, 1964).

DANIELS, Edgar F. and Wanda J. DEAN. "Elegie," Expl
24 (Dec., 1965).

DANZIG, Allan. "Tennyson's The Princess: A Definition of
Love," VP 4 (Spr., 1966).

D'AVANZO, Mario L. [1]. "King Francis, Lucrezia, and
the Figurative Language of 'Andrea del Sarto,' " TSLL
9 (Wint., 1968).

_____ [2]. "A Pact," Expl 24 (Feb., 1966).

DAVID, Alfred. "Literary Satire in The House of Fame,"
PMLA 75 (Sept., 1960).

DAVIDOW, Mary C. "Journey from Apple Orchard to
Swallow Thronged Loft: 'Fern Hill'," EJ 58 (Jan.,
1969).

DAVIDSON, Clifford. "Jonathan Edwards and Mysticism,"
CLAJ 11 (Dec., 1967).

DAVIDSON, James. "The End of Sweeney," CE 27 (Feb.,
1966).

DAVIS, Arthur P. [1]. "The Black-and-Tan Motif in the
Poetry of Gwendolyn Brooks," CLAJ 6 (Dec., 1962).

_____ [2]. "Gwendolyn Brooks: Poet of the Unheroic,"
CLAJ 7 (Dec., 1963).

_____ [3]. "Langston Hughes: Cool Poet," CLAJ 11
(1967). [Special number on Langston Hughes.]

DAVIS, Charles G. "An Old Man's Winter Night," Expl 27
(Nov., 1968).

DAVIS, Charles T. [1]. "Image Patterns in the Poetry of
Edwin Arlington Robinson," CE 22 (Mar., 1961).

_____ [2]. "Walt Whitman and the Problem of an American Tradition," CLAJ 5 (Sept., 1961).

DAVIS, Jack M. and J. E. GRANT. "A Critical Dialogue
on Shakespeare's Sonnet 71," TSLL 1 (Sum., 1959).

DAVIS, Lloyd M. "I Taste a Liquor Never Brewed," Expl
23 (Mar., 1965).

DAVIS, Thomas M. "Another View of 'The Wife's Lament',"
    PLL 1 (Aut., 1965).

DAWSON, R. MacGregor. "The Structure of the Old
    English Gnomic Poems," JEGP 61 (Jan., 1962).

DAY, Douglas. "Adam and Eve in Paradise Lost, IV,"
    TSLL 3 (Aut., 1961).

DAY, Robert A. [1]. "The 'City Man' in 'The Waste Land':
    The Geography of Reminiscence," PMLA 80 (June,
    1965).

            [2]. "Image and Idea in 'Voyages II'," Criticism
    7 (Sum., 1965).

            [3]. "Soliloquy of the Spanish Cloister," Expl 24
    (Dec., 1965).

DEAN, Christopher. "Weal Wundrum Heah, Wyrmlicum Fah
    and the Narrative Background of 'The Wanderer',"
    MP 63 (Nov., 1965).

DEEN, Leonard W. "Liberty and License in Byron's Don
    Juan," TSLL 8 (Fall, 1966).

DELASANTA, Rodney. "Shelley's 'Sometimes Embarrassing
    Declarations': A Defence," TSLL 7 (Sum., 1965).

DELAURA, David J. [1]. "Arnold, Clough, Dr. Arnold, and
    'Thyrsis'," VP 7 (Aut., 1969).

            [2]. "A Robert Browning Letter: The Occasion of
    Mrs. Browning's 'A Curse for a Nation'," VP 4 (Sum.,
    1966).

DEMBO, L. S. [1]. "Hart Crane and Samuel Greenbery:
    What Is Plagiarism?" AL 32 (Nov., 1960).

            [2]. "Hart Crane's Early Poetry," UR 27 (Mar.,
    1961).

            [3]. "Hart Crane's 'Verticalist' Poem," AL 40
    (Mar., 1968).

DEMING, Robert H. "Herrick's Funereal Poems," SEL 9
    (Wint., 1969).

DEMPSEY, Paul K.   "And Have I Heard Her Say?   O
    Cruel Paine!"   Expl 25 (Feb., 1967).

DENDINGER, Lloyd N.   "The Irrational Appeal of Frost's
    Dark Deep Woods," SoR 2 (Aut., 1966).

DENHAM, Robert D.   "A Bronze Head," Expl 29 (Oct.,
    1970).

DE SELINCOURT, E.   Oxford Lectures on Poetry.   Free-
    port, New York: Books for Libraries Press, 1967.

DEUTSCH, R. H.   "Poetry and Belief in Delmore Schwartz,"
    SR 74 (Aut., 1966).

DEVEREUX, James A., S. J.   "A Note on Troilus and
    Criseyde, Book III, Line 1309," PQ 44 (Oct., 1965).

DIPASQUALE, Pasquale, Jr.   " 'Sikernesse' and Fortune in
    Troilus and Criseyde," PQ 49 (Apr., 1970).

DIXON, Peter [1].   "An Essay on Man, II," Expl 23 (Nov.,
    1964).

_____ [2].   "The Theme of Friendship in the Epistle to
    Dr. Arbuthnot," ES 44 (June, 1963).

DODD, Betty Coshow.   "Epistle to Dr. Arbuthnot," Expl 19
    (Dec., 1960).

DOGGETT, Frank [1].   "Abstraction and Wallace Stevens,"
    Criticism 2 (Wint., 1960).

_____ [2].   "The Poet of Earth: Wallace Stevens," CE
    22 (Mar., 1961).

_____ [3].   "Woman Looking at a Vase of Flowers,"
    Expl 19 (Nov., 1960).

DOHERTY, Paul C.   "Hopkins' 'Spring and Fall: To a
    Young Child'," VP 5 (Sum., 1967).

DONALDSON, Scott.   "The Alien Pity: A Study of Character
    in Edwin Arlington Robinson's Poetry," AL 38 (May,
    1966).

DONNER, Morton.   "Tact as a Criterion of Reality in Sir

Gawain and the Green Knight," PLL 1 (Aut., 1965).

DONOGHUE, Dennis.   "In the Scene of Being," HudR 14
(Sum., 1961).

DORRILL, James F.   "The Riddle," Expl 29 (Sept., 1970).

DORSEY, David F., Jr.   "Countee Cullen's Use of Greek
Mythology," CLAJ 13 (Sept, 1969).

DRAGLAND, S. L.   "Mending Wall," Expl 25 (Jan., 1967).

DRAKE, Constance M.   "An Approach to Blake," CE 29
(Apr., 1968).

DREW, E. A.   Discovering Modern Poetry.   New York:
Holt, Rinehart and Winston, 1961.

DREW, Philip.   "A Note on the Lawyers," VP 6 (Aut.-
Wint., 1968).

DREW-BEAR, Thomas.   "Ezra Pound's 'Homage to Sextus
Propertius'," AL 37 (May, 1965).

DUDDY, Thomas A.   "To Celebrate: A Reading of Denise
Levertov," Criticism 10 (Spr., 1968).

DUNCAN-JONES, Katherine.   "The Date of Raleigh's 21th:
And Last Booke of the Ocean to Scinthia'," RES 21
(May, 1970).

DUNDAS, Judith.   "The Rhetorical Basis of Spenser's
Imagery," SEL 8 (Wint., 1968).

DUNN, Ian S.   "The Love Song of J. Alfred Prufrock,"
Expl 22 (Sept., 1963).

DUNN, John J.   "Love and Eroticism: Coventry Patmore's
Mystical Imagery," VP 7 (Aut., 1969).

DURR, R. A. [1].   "Donne's 'The Primrose'," JEGP 59
(Apr., 1960).

_____ [2].   "Vaughan's 'The Night'," JEGP 59 (Jan.,
1960).

DYE, F.   "Gerontion," Expl 18 (Apr., 1960).

DYSON, A. E. [1]. "The Meaning of Paradise Regained, "
      TSLL 3 (Sum., 1961).

_____ [2]. "Walter de la Mare's 'The Listeners', "
      CritQ 2 (Sum., 1960).

EAGLETON, Terry. Exiles and Emigres; Studies in
      Modern Literature. New York: Schocken Books, 1970.

EBERHART, Richard. "Robert Frost: His Personality, "
      SoR 2 (Aut., 1966).

EBY, Cecil D. " 'I Taste a Liquor Never Brewed': A
      Variant Reading, " AL 36 (Jan., 1965).

ECKLEY, Wilton. "A Noiseless Patient Spider, " Expl 22
      (Nov., 1963).

EDWARDS, Robert R. "Narrative Technique and Distance
      in the Dream of the Rood, " PLL 6 (Sum., 1970).

EDWARDS, Thomas R., Jr. "Light and Nature: A Reading
      of the Dunciad, " PQ 39 (Oct., 1960).

EGGENSCHWILER, David L. [1]. "Arnold's Passive
      Questers " VP 5 (Spr., 1967).

_____ [2]. "Psychological Complexity in 'Porphyria's
      Lover', " VP 8 (Spr., 1970).

ELDREDGE, Harrison. "On an Error in a Sonnet of Ros-
      setti's, " VP 5 (Wint., 1967).

ELEANOR, Mother Mary, S.H.C.J. "Anne Killegrew and
      MacFlecknoe, " PQ 43 (Jan., 1964).

EL-GABALAWY, Saad. "The Pilgrimage: George Herbert's
      Favourite Allegorical Technique, " CLAJ 13 (June,
      1970).

ELLEDGE, W. Paul. "Byron's Hungry Sinner: The Quest
      Motif in Don Juan, " JEGP 69 (Jan., 1970).

ELLIOTT, Philip L. "In Memoriam, XLI, " Expl 28 (Apr.,
      1970).

ELLIS, Frank H. "Gray's Eton College Ode: The Problem

of Tone," PLL 5 (Spr., 1969).

ELLMANN, Richard.   "Yeats Without Analogue," KR 26
(Wint., 1964).

EMANUEL, James A. [1].   "The Literary Experiments of
Langston Hughes," CLAJ 11 (June, 1968).

*   [2].   "A Note on the Future of Negro Poetry,"
NALF 1 (Fall, 1967).

*   [3].   " 'Soul' in the Works of Langston Hughes,"
NegroD 16 (Sept., 1967).

EMIG, Janet A.   "The Poem as Puzzle," EJ 52 (Mar.,
1963).

EMPSON, William [1].   "The Ancient Mariner," CritQ 6
(Wint., 1964).

            [2].   "Donne in the New Edition," CritQ 8 (Aut.,
1966).

EMSLIE, McD.   "Dryden's Couplets: Imagery Vowed to
Poverty," CritQ 2 (Spr., 1960).

ENGLISH, H. M., Jr.   "Spenser's Accommodation of Allegory to History in the Story of Timias and Belphoebe,"
JEGP 59 (July, 1960).

ENSCOE, Gerald E.   "The Content of Vision: Blake's
'Mental Traveller'," PLL 4 (Fall, 1968).

ESSIG, Erhardt H. [1].   "One Dignity Delays for All,"
Expl 23 (Oct., 1964).

            [2].   "With How Sad Steps, O Moon," Expl 20
(Nov., 1961).

EVANS, Arthur and Catherine EVANS.   "Pieter Bruegal and
John Berryman: Two Winter Landscapes," TSLL 5
(Aut., 1963).

EVANS, Maurice.   "Platonic Allegory in The Faerie Queene,"
RES 12 (May, 1961).

EVERETT, Barbara [1].   "Marvell's 'The Mower's Song',"

CritQ 4 (Aut., 1962).

_____ [2]. "The Prelude," CritQ 1 (Wint., 1959).

EVETT, David. " 'Paradice's Only Map': The Topos of
the Locus Amoenus and the Structure of Marvell's
'Upon Appleton House'," PMLA 85 (May, 1970).

*FABRE, Michel. "The Poetry of Richard Wright," SBL 1,
no. 3.

FARIS, Paul. "The Soul Selects Her Own Society," Expl
25 (Apr., 1967).

FARMER, Norman, Jr. "Fulke Greville and the Poetic of
the Plain Style," TSLL 11 (Spr., 1969).

FARRELL, John P. "Matthew Arnold and the Middle Ages:
The Uses of the Past," VS 13 (Mar., 1970).

FARRELL, Robert T. [1]. "A Reading of O. E. Exodus,"
RES 20 (Nov., 1969).

_____ [2]. "The Unity of Old English Daniel," RES 18
(May, 1967).

FARRISON, W. Edward. "Coleridge's 'Christabel,' 'The
Conclusion to Part II'," CLAJ 5 (Dec., 1961).

FASEL, Ida. "The World Below the Brine," Expl 25
(Sept.,1966).

FAULKNER, Virginia. "More Frosting on the Woods,"
CE 24 (Apr., 1963).

FEIN, Richard. "Mary and Bellona: The War Poetry of
Robert Lowell," SoR 1 (Aut., 1965).

FENDERSON, Lewis H. "The Onomato-Musical Element in
Paradise Lost," CLAJ 9 (Mar., 1966).

FENNER, Arthur, Jr. "The Unity of Pope's Essay on
Criticism," PQ 39 (Oct., 1960).

FERGUSON, A. R. "Frost, Sill, and 'A-Wishing Well',"
AL 33 (Nov., 1961).

FERGUSON, Joe M., Jr.   "After Apple-Picking," Expl 22
    (Mar., 1964).

FERGUSON, Mary Heyward.   "The Structure of the Soul's
    Address to the Body in Old English," JEGP 69 (Jan.,
    1970).

FESHBACH, Sidney.   "Empedocles at Dover Beach," VP 4
    (Aut., 1966).

FIELDS, Albert W.   "Milton and Self-Knowledge," PMLA
    83 (May, 1968).

FIELDS, Kenneth [1].   "Past Masters: Walter Conrad Arens-
    berg and Donald Evans," SoR 6 (Spr., 1970).

_____ [2].   "The Poetry of Mina Loy," SoR 3 (Sum.,
    1967).

FIKE, Francis.   "Gerard Manley Hopkins' Interest in
    Painting After 1868: Two Notes," VP 8 (Wint., 1970).

FILLER, Louis.   "Edwin Markham, Poetry, and What Have
    You," AR 23 (Wint., 1963-64).

FINCH, John A.   " 'The Ruined Cottage' Restored: Three
    Stages of Composition, 1795-1798," JEGP 66 (Apr.,
    1967).

FISCHER, John Irwin.   "How to Die: Verses on the Death
    of Dr. Swift," RES 21 (Nov., 1970).

FISH, Stanley [1].   "The Harassed Reader in Paradise Lost,"
    CritQ 7 (Sum., 1965).

_____ [2].   "Standing Only: Christian Heroism in Para-
    dise Lost," CritQ 9 (Sum., 1967).

FISHER, Peter F.   "Blake's Attacks on the Classical Tra-
    dition," PQ 40 (Jan., 1961).

FITZGERALD, Sister Ellen.   "The Tint I Cannot Take is
    Best," Expl 28 (Nov., 1969).

FITZGERALD, Robert P. [1].   "The Form of Christopher
    Smart's Jubilate Agno," SEL 8 (Sum., 1968).

_____ [2]. " 'The Wife's Lament' and 'The Search for
the Lost Husband'," JEGP 62 (Oct., 1963).

FLECK, Richard. "Browning's 'Up at a Villa--Down in the
City' as Satire," VP 7 (Wint., 1969).

FLEISHER, David. " 'Rabbi Ben Ezra,' 49-72: A New Key
to an Old Crux," VP 1 (Jan., 1963).

FLEISSNER, Robert F. [1]. "Browning's Last Lost Duchess:
A Purview," VP 5 (Aut., 1967).

_____ [2]. "The Mystical Meaning of Five: a Notelet
on 'Kubla Khan'," ES 46 (Feb., 1965).

_____ [3]. "Percute Hic: Morris' Terrestrial Paradise,"
VP 3 (Sum., 1965).

FLETCHER, Harris. "Milton's 'Old Damoetas'," JEGP 60
(Apr., 1961).

FOGLE, Richard Harter. "1951: The Romantic Unity of
'Kubla Khan'," CE 22 (Nov., 1960).

FOLTINEK, H. "The Primitive Element in the Poetry of
Kathleen Raine," ES 42 (Feb., 1961).

FORD, Newell F. "The Wit in Shelley's Poetry," SEL 1
(Aut., 1961).

FORD, Thomas W. "Emily Dickinson and the Civil War,"
UR 31 (Mar., 1965).

FORDE, Sister Victoria Marie. "No Brigadier Throughout
the Year," Expl 27 (Feb., 1969).

FORSYTH, R. A. "Herbert, Clough, and Their Church-
Windows," VP 7 (Spr., 1969).

FORTIN, Rene E. "The Waste Land," Expl 21 (Dec., 1962).

FOSTER, Steven [1]. "Bergson's 'Intuition' and Whitman's
'Song of Myself'," TSLL 6 (Aut., 1964).

_____ [2]. "Relativity and The Waste Land: A Postulate,"
TSLL 7 (Spr., 1965).

FOWLER, A. D. S. "Emblems of Temperance in The

Faerie Queene, Book II, " RES 11 (May, 1960).

FOX, Robert C. [1]. "The Character of Mammon in
    Paradise Lost, " RES 13 (Feb. , 1962).

_____ [2]. "Temperance and the Seven Deadly Sins in
    The Faerie Queene, Book II, " RES 12 (Feb. , 1961).

FOXELL, Nigel. Ten Poems Analyzed. Oxford: Perga-
    mon, 1966.

FRANCIS, Robert, Charles W. COLE, and Reginald L.
    COOK. "On Robert Frost, " MR 4 (Wint. , 1963).

FRASER, G. S. [1]. "The Poetry of Thom Gunn, " CritQ
    3 (Wint. , 1961).

_____ [2]. "Yeats's Byzantium, " CritQ 2 (Aut. , 1960).

FREEDMAN, William A. "The World Below the Brine, "
    Expl 23 (Jan. , 1965).

FRENCH, A. L. "Dryden, Marvell and Political Poetry, "
    SEL 8 (Sum. , 1968).

FRENCH, David P. "Mac Flecknoe, " Expl 21 (Jan. , 1963).

FRENCH, J. Milton. "Milton and the Barbarous Disso-
    nance, " TSLL 4 (Aut. , 1962).

FRENCH, Roberts W. [1]. "Adonais, ·36, " Expl 29 (Oct. ,
    1970).

_____ [2]. "Vertue, " Expl 26 (Sept. , 1967).

_____ [3]. "Voice and Structure in Lycidas, " TSLL 12
    (Spr. , 1970).

FRENCH, Warren G. "The Glass of Water, " Expl 19 (Jan. ,
    1961).

FREY, Leonard H. "Exile and Elegy in Anglo-Saxon
    Christian Epic Poetry, " JEGP 62 (Apr. , 1963).

FRIEDMAN, Alan Warren. " 'Beeny Cliff' and 'Under the
    Waterfall': An Approach to Hardy's Love Poetry, "
    VP 5 (Aut. , 1967).

FRIEDMAN, Barton R. "To Tell the Sun from the Druid
Fire: Imagery of Good and Evil in The Ring and the
Book, " SEL 6 (Aut., 1966).

FRIEDMAN, Donald M. [1]. "The Mind in the Poem: Wyatt's
'They Fle From Me', " SEL 7 (Wint., 1967).

_____ [2]. "Wyatt and the Ambiguities of Fancy, " JEGP
67 (Jan., 1968).

FRIEDMAN, Judith S. and Ruth PERLMUTTER. "Voyages
II, " Expl 19 (Oct., 1960).

FRIEDMAN, Norman. "E. E. Cummings and His Critics, "
Criticism 6 (Spr., 1964).

FRIEND, Joseph H. [1]. "Euripides Browningized: The
Meaning of Ballaustion's Adventure, " VP 2 (Sum.,
1964).

_____ [2]. "Teaching the 'Grammar of Poetry', " CE 27
(Feb., 1966).

FRIERSON, J. W. "The Strayed Reveller of Fox How, "
VP 5 (Sum., 1967).

FRYXWELL, Lucy Dickinson and Virginia H. ADAIR.
"Soliloquy of the Spanish Cloister, " Expl 22 (Dec.,
1963).

FUJIMURA, Thomas H. "Dryden's Religio Laici: An
Anglican Poem, " PMLA 76 (June, 1961).

FULMER, O. Bryan. "The Ancient Mariner and the
Wandering Jew, " SP 66 (Oct., 1969).

FULWEILER, Howard W. [1]. "Matthew Arnold: The
Metamorphosis of a Merman, " VP 1 (Aug., 1963).

_____ [2]. "Tennyson and the 'Summons from the Sea', "
VP 3 (Wint., 1965).

GABBARD, G. N. "Browning's Metamorphoses, " VP 4
(Wint., 1966).

GAFFORD, Charlotte K. "God's Grandeur, " Expl 29 (Nov.,
1970).

GAINER, Patrick W.   "Hy, Zy, Hine," VP 1 (Apr., 1963).

GALLAGHER, Edward J.   "Tenzone," Expl 27 (Dec., 1968).

GALLAGHER, Michael P.   "Yeats, Syntax and the Self,"
     ArQ 26 (Spr., 1970).

GALLER, D.   "Three Recent Volumes," Poetry 110 (July,
     1967). [Review of Selected Poems.]

GARAB, Arra M. [1].   "Fabulous Artifice: Yeats's 'Three
     Bushes' Sequence," Criticism 7 (Sum., 1965).

_____ [2].   "Times of Glory: Yeats's 'The Municipal
     Gallery Revisited'," ArQ 21 (Aut., 1965).

GARDNER, Helen.   "The Landscapes of Eliot's Poetry,"
     CritQ 10 (Wint., 1968).

GARDNER, John [1].   "Fulgentius's Expositio Vergiliana
     Continentia and the Plan of Beowulf: Another Approach
     to the Poem's Style and Structure," PLL 6 (Sum.,
     1970).

_____ [2].   "The Owl and the Nightingale: A Burlesque,"
     PLL 2 (Wint., 1966).

GARGANO, James W. [1].   "Pity This Busy Monster,
     Manunkind," Expl 20 (Nov., 1961).

_____ [2].   "Poe's 'To Helen'," MLN 75 (Dec., 1960).

_____ [3].   "Technique in 'Crossing Brooklyn Ferry':
     The Everlasting Moment," JEGP 62 (Apr., 1963).

GARLITZ, Barbara [1].   "The Immortality Ode: Its Cultural
     Progeny," SEL 6 (Aut., 1966).

_____ [2].   "Uprooting 'Trees'," CE 23 (Jan., 1962).

GARMON, Gerald M.   "Open House," Expl 28 (Nov., 1969).

GARRISON, Joseph M., Jr.   "Teaching Early American
     Literature: Some Suggestions," CE 31 (Feb., 1970).

GARROW, A. Scott.   "A Note on Manzanilla," AL 35 (Nov.,
     1963).

GASKELL, Ronald. "The Poetry of Robert Graves," CritQ
3 (Aut., 1961).

GAVIN, Sister Rosemarie Julie, S.N.D. "The Candle Indoors," Expl 20 (Feb., 1962).

GECKLE, George L. "Miltonic Idealism: 'L'Allegro' and
'Il Penseroso'," TSLL 9 (Wint., 1968).

GERARD, Albert [1]. "Counterfeiting Infinity: The Eolian
Harp and the Growth of Coleridge's Mind," JEGP 60
(July, 1961).

_____ [2]. "An Horatian Ode Upon Cromwell's Return
from Ireland," Expl 20 (Nov., 1961).

_____ [3]. "Iconic Organization in Shakespeare's Sonnet
CXLVI," ES 42 (June, 1961).

GERBER, Richard. "Keys to Kubla Khan," ES 44 (Oct.,
1963).

GIANNONE, Richard. "The Quest Motif in 'Thyrsis'," VP
3 (Spr., 1965).

GIBB, Carson. "Mending Wall," Expl 20 (Feb., 1962).

GIBBONS, Edward E. "Point of View and Moral: 'The
Ancient Mariner'," UR 35 (June, 1969).

GILBERT, Allan. "Form and Matter in Paradise Lost,
Book III," JEGP 60 (Oct., 1961).

GILLIS, Everett A. "Religion in a Sweeney World,"
ArQ 20 (Spr., 1964).

GIOVANNINI, Margaret. "God's Grandeur," Expl 24 (Dec.,
1965).

GLADISH, Robert W. "Mrs. Browning's 'A Curse for a
Nation': Some Further Comments," VP 7 (Aut., 1969).

GLECKNER, Robert F. "Blake's Seasons," SEL 5 (Sum.,
1965).

GODSHALK, William Leigh [1]. "Marvell's 'Garden' and
the Theologians," SP 66 (July, 1969).

GODSHALK, William Leigh [2]. "The Mower to the Glo-
     Worms," Expl 25 (Oct., 1966).

GOHDES, Clarence [1]. "Section 50 of Whitman's 'Song of
     Myself'," MLN 75 (Dec., 1960).

_____[2]. "Whitman and the 'Good Old Cause'," AL 34
     (Nov., 1962).

GOING, William T. [1]. "John Addington Symonds and the
     Victorian Sonnet Sequence," VP 8 (Spr., 1970).

_____[2]. "Marianne Moore's 'Dream': Academic By-
     Path to Xanadu," PLL 5 (Suppl., Sum., 1969).

_____[3]. "Matthew Arnold's Sonnets," PLL 6 (Fall,
     1970).

_____[4]. "Wilfrid Scawen Blunt, Victorian Sonneteer,"
     VP 2 (Spr., 1964).

GOLDEN, Morris. "Sterility and Eminence in the Poetry
     of Charles Churchill," JEGP 66 (July, 1967).

GOLDEN, Samuel A. "To My Honored Friend, Dr.
     Charleton," Expl 24 (Feb., 1966).

GOLDFARB, Russell M. "Sexual Meaning in 'The Last Ride
     Together'," VP 3 (Aut., 1965).

GOLDGAR, Bertrand A. "Pope's Theory of the Passions:
     The Background of Epistle II of the Essay on Man,"
     PQ 41 (Oct., 1962).

GOLDKNOPF, David. "The Disintegration of Symbol in a
     Meditative Poet," CE 30 (Oct., 1968).

GOLDMAN, Lloyd. "Samuel Daniel's Delia and the Emblem
     Tradition," JEGP 67 (Jan., 1968).

GOLDMAN, Michael. "The Prelude," Expl 18 (Apr., 1960).

GOLFFING, Francis. "Tennyson's Last Phase: The Poet
     as Seer," SoR 2 (Spr., 1966).

GOODWIN, K. L. "The Toy Horse," Expl 23 (Sept., 1964).

GORDON, Jan B. "Disenchantment with Intimations: A Reading of Arnold's 'In Utrumque Paratus'," VP 3 (Sum., 1965).

GOSE, Elliott B., Jr. [1]. "Coleridge and the Luminous Gloom: An Analysis of the 'Symbological Language' in 'The Rime of the Ancient Mariner'," PMLA 75 (June, 1960).

_____ [2]. "Digging In: An Interpretation of Wilfred Owen's 'Strange Meeting'," CE 22 (Mar., 1961).

GOSSMAN, Ann. "Paradise Lost, II, 1013," Expl 19 (Apr., 1961).

_____, and George W. WHITING. "Milton's First Sonnet on His Blindness," RES 12 (Nov., 1961).

GOTTESMAN, Lillian. "The Hamlet of A. MacLeish," CLAJ 11 (Dec., 1967).

GOTTFRIED, Leon A. "Matthew Arnold's 'The Strayed Reveller'," RES 11 (Nov., 1960).

GOTTFRIED, Rudolf. "Our New Poet: Archetypal Criticism and The Faerie Queene," PMLA 83 (Oct., 1968).

GOTTSCHALK, Jane. "The Owl and the Nightingale: Lay Preachers to a Lay Audience," PQ 45 (Oct., 1966).

GRABO, Norman S. [1]. "Edward Taylor's Spiritual 'Huswifery'," PMLA 79 (Dec., 1964).

_____ [2]. "Sacramental Meditation Six," Expl 18 (Apr., 1960).

GRANT, Damian. "Emerging Image: The Poetry of Edward Brathwaite," CritQ 12 (Sum., 1970).

GRANT, John E. [1]. "Apocalypse in Blake's 'Auguries of Innocence'," TSLL 5 (Wint., 1964).

_____ [2]. "The Art and Argument of 'The Tyger'," TSLL 2 (Spr., 1960).

GRANT, Stephen Allen. "The Mystical Implications of 'In Memoriam'," SEL 2 (Aut., 1962).

GRAY, J. M. [1]. "The Creation of Excalibur: An Appar-
ent Inconsistency in the Idylls," VP 6 (Spr., 1968).

_____ [2]. "The Purpose of an Epic List in 'The Coming
of Arthur'," VP 8 (Wint., 1970).

_____ [3]. "Source and Symbol in 'Geraint and Enid':
Tennyson's Doorm and Limours," VP 4 (Spr., 1966).

GRAZIANI, Rene. "John Donne's 'The Extasie' and Ecstacy,"
RES 19 (May, 1968).

GREENBERG, Robert A. [1]. "Matthew Arnold's Mournful
Rhymes: A Study of 'The World and the Quietist',"
VP 1 (Nov., 1963).

_____ [2]. "Patterns of Imagery: Arnold's 'Shakespeare',"
SEL 5 (Aut., 1965).

GREENBERGER, Evelyn Barish [1]. "Clough's 'The Judgment of Brutus': A Newly Found Poem," VP 8 (Sum.,
1970).

_____ [2]. " 'Salsette and Elephanta': An Unpublished
Poem by Clough," RES 20 (Aug., 1969).

GREENE, Donald. "On Swift's 'Scatological' Poems,"
SR 75 (Aut., 1967).

GREENE, Richard Leighton. "Elegy Written in a Country
Church-Yard," Expl 24 (Jan., 1966).

GREENFIELD, Stanley B. [1]. "Paradise Lost, XII,
629-632," Expl 19 (May, 1961).

_____ [2]. "Min, Sylf, and 'Dramatic Voices' in The
Wanderer and The Seafarer," JEGP 68 (Apr., 1969).

GREGORY, E. R., Jr. "The Balance of Parts: Imagistic
Unity in Donne's 'Elegie XIX'," UR 35 (Oct., 1968).

GREINER, Francis J., S. M. "The Habit of Perfection,"
Expl 21 (Nov., 1962).

GRELLNER, Mary Adelaide, S.C.L. "Britomart's Quest
for Maturity," SEL 8 (Wint., 1968).

GRIDLEY, Roy E. [1]. "Browning's Caponsacchi: 'How the Priest Caponsacchi Said His Say'," VP 6 (Aut.-Wint., 1968).

_____ [2]. "Browning's Pompilia," JEGP 67 (Jan., 1968).

GRIFFIN, Robert J. [1]. "The Castle of Indolence," Expl 21 (Dec., 1962).

_____ [2]. "Song of Myself," Expl 21 (Oct., 1962).

_____ [3]. " 'These Contraries Such Unity Do Hold': Patterned Imagery in Shakespeare's Narrative Poems," SEL 4 (Wint., 1964).

_____ [4] "This Compost," Expl 21 (Apr., 1963).

GRIFFITH, Clark [1]. "Emily Dickinson's Love Poetry," UR 27 (Dec., 1960).

_____ [2]. "Gerontion," Expl 21 (Feb., 1963).

_____ [3]. "The Men That Are Falling," Expl 23 (Jan., 1965).

_____ [4]. "Sex and Death: The Significance of Whitman's Calamus Themes," PQ 39 (Jan., 1960).

GRIGSBY, Gordon K. [1]. "The Genesis of Paterson," CE 23 (Jan., 1962).

_____ [2]. "Hart Crane's Doubtful Vision, A Note on the 'Intention' of The Bridge," CE 24 (Apr., 1963).

GROB, Alan. "Wordsworth's Nutting," JEGP 61 (Oct., 1962).

GROSS, Barry Edward. "Free Love and Free Will in Paradise Lost," SEL 7 (Wint., 1967).

GROSS, Seymour Lee and John Edward HARD. Images of the Negro in American Literature. Chicago: University of Chicago Press, 1966.

GRUBE, John. "Theory," Expl 25 (Nov., 1966).

GUERARD, Albert J. "The Illusion of Simplicity: The

Shorter Poems of Thomas Hardy," SR 72 (Sum., 1964).

GUERIN, Wilfred L. "Irony and Tension in Browning's "Karshish'," VP 1 (Apr., 1963).

GUILHAMET, Leon M. "Dryden's Debasement of Scripture in Absalom and Achitophel," SEL 9 (Sum., 1969).

GUSKIN, Phyllis J. "Ambiguities in the Structure and Meaning of Browning's Christmas-Eve," VP 4 (Wint., 1966).

GUSS, Donald L. "Donne's Petrarchism," JEGP 64 (Jan., 1965).

GUSTAFSON, Richard. "William Carlos Williams' Paterson," CE 26 (Apr., 1965).

GUTH, Hans P. "Allegorical Implications of Artifice in Spenser's Faerie Queene," PMLA 76 (Dec., 1961).

GUTHRIE, Ramon. "Lions in Sweden," Expl 20 (Dec., 1961).

GUTTMANN, Allen. "Walter Lowenfels' Poetic Politics," MR 6 (Aut., 1965).

GWYNN, Frederick L. "Analysis and Synthesis of Frost's 'The Draft Horse'," CE 26 (Dec., 1964).

HABER, Tom Burns. "M. Maurice Pollet's Essay on A. E. Housman," ArQ 25 (Spr., 1969).

HAFLEY, James. "Hopkins: 'A Little Sickness in the Air'," ArQ 20 (Aut., 1964).

HAGOPIAN, John V. "The Mask of Browning's Countess Gismond," PQ 40 (Jan., 1961).

HAHN, Sister M. Norma. "Yeats's 'The Wild Swans at Coole': Meaning and Structure," CE 22 (Mar., 1961).

HALBERT, Cecelia L. "Tree of Life Imagery in the Poetry of Edward Taylor," AL 38 (Mar., 1966).

HALIO, Jay L. [1]. "Delmore Schwartz's Felt Abstractions,"

SoR 1 (Aut., 1965).

_____ [2]. " 'Prothalamion,' 'Ulysses,' and Intention in Poetry," CE 22 (Mar., 1961).

HALL, Mary S. "On Light in Young's Night Thoughts," PQ 48 (Oct., 1969).

HALL, Vernon. "Captain Carpenter," Expl 26 (Nov., 1967).

HALLGARTH, Susan A. "A Study of Hopkins' Use of Nature," VP 5 (Sum., 1967).

HALPEREN, Max [1]. "How Soon the Harvest Sun," Expl 23 (Apr., 1965).

_____ [2]. "If I Were Tickled by the Rub of Love," Expl 21 (Nov., 1962).

HALPERN, Martin. "Keats's Grecian Urn and the Singular 'Ye'," CE 24 (Jan., 1963).

HALVERSON, John [1]. "Prufrock, Freud, and Others," SR 76 (Aut., 1968).

_____ [2]. "Template Criticism: 'Sir Gawain and the Green Knight,'" MP 67 (Nov., 1969).

HAMILTON, A. C. "Venus and Adonis," SEL 1 (Wint., 1961).

HAMM, Victor M. [1]. "Dryden's The Hind and the Panther and Roman Catholic Apologetics," PMLA 83 (May, 1968).

_____ [2]. "Dryden's Religio Laici and Roman Catholic Apologetics," PMLA 80 (June, 1965).

HANLEY, Sara Williams [1]. "Frailtie," Expl 25 (Oct., 1966).

_____ [2]. "Temples in The Temple: George Herbert's Study of the Church," SEL 8 (Wint., 1968).

HANSEN, Erik Arne. "T. S. Eliot's 'Landscapes'," ES 50 (Aug., 1969).

HARDING, Davis P. "Milton's Bee-Simile," JEGP 60

(Oct., 1961).

HARDISON, O. B., Jr. "Milton's 'On Time' and Its
Scholastic Background," TSLL 3 (Apr., 1961).

HARDY, Barbara. "W. H. Auden, Thirties to Sixties: A
Face and a Map," SoR 5 (Sum., 1969).

HARDY, John Edward. The Curious Frame; Seven Poems
in Text and Context. Notre Dame, Ind.: University
of Notre Dame Press, 1962.

HARFST, B. P. "Astrophil and Stella: Precept and Example," PLL 5 (Fall, 1969).

HARRINGTON, David V. [1]. "Manerly Margery Milk and
Ale," Expl 25 (Jan., 1967).

_____ [2]. "The 'Metamorphosis' of Edith Sitwell,"
Criticism 9 (Wint., 1967).

_____ [3]. "The Relique," Expl 25 (Nov., 1966).

HARRINGTON, David V. and Carole SCHNEIDER. "Death
of Little Boys," Expl 26 (Oct., 1967).

HARRIS, Wendell V. "A Reading of Rossetti's Lyrics,"
VP 7 (Wint., 1969).

HARRIS, William O. [1]. " 'Love That Doth Raine': Sur-
reys' Creative Imitation," MP 66 (May, 1969).

_____ [2]. "Upon Julia's Clothes," Expl 21 (Dec., 1962).

HARRISON, Robert [1]. "Symbolism of the Cyclical Myth
in Endymion," TSLL 1 (Wint., 1960).

_____ [2]. "To the Contesse of Huntingdon," Expl 25
(Dec., 1966).

HARRISON, Thomas P. "Keats and a Nightingale," ES 41
(Dec., 1960).

HART, Jeffrey. "Paradise Lost and Order; 'I Know Each
Lane and Every Valley Green'," CE 25 (May, 1964).

HARTMAN, Geoffrey H. [1]. "A Poet's Progress:

Wordsworth and the Via Naturaliter Negativa, " MP 59 (Feb., 1962).

_____ [2]. "Wordsworth's Descriptive Sketches and the Growth of a Poet's Mind, " PMLA 76 (Dec., 1961).

HARTSOCK, Mildred E.   "Bantams in Pine-Woods, " Expl 18 (Mar., 1960).

HARTWIG, Joan.   "The Principle of Measure in 'To His Coy Mistress', " CE 25 (May, 1964).

HARVEY, Nancy Lenz.   "What Soft Cherubic Creatures, " Expl 28 (Oct., 1969).

HARVILL, Olga DeHart.   "O Make Me a Mask, " Expl 26 (Oct., 1967).

HASKELL, Ann Sullivan.   "An Image of 'The Windhover', " VP 6 (Spr., 1968).

HAUSER, David R. [1].   "Medea's Strain and Hermes' Wand: Pope's Use of Mythology, " MLN 76 (Mar., 1961).

_____ [2].   "Pope's Lodona and the Uses of Mythology, " SEL 6 (Sum., 1966).

HAWKINS, Richard H.   "Structure Through Irony in The Tunning of Elinour Rumming, " UR 34 (Spr., 1968).

HAWORTH, Helen E. [1].   "Keats and the Metaphor of Vision, " JEGP 67 (July, 1968).

_____ [2].   "The Titans, Apollo, and the Fortunate Fall in Keats's Poetry, " SEL 10 (Aut., 1970).

HECHT, Anthony.   "Shades of Keats and Marvell, " HudR 15 (Spr., 1962).

HEFFERNAN, James A. W.   "Wordsworth on the Sublime: The Quest for Interfusion, " SEL 7 (Aut., 1967).

HEINEN, Hubert.   "Interwoven Time in Keats's Poetry, " TSLL 3 (Aut., 1961).

HEINRICHS, Vincent L.   "(IM)C-A-T(MO), " Expl 27 (Apr., 1969).

HELD, Leonard E., Jr. "To the Honourable Charles Montague, Esq.," Expl 28 (May, 1970).

HELGERSON, Richard. "Sonnet CXXXVIII," Expl 28 (Feb., 1970).

HENN, T. R. "Yeats and the Picture Galleries," SoR 1 (Wint., 1965).

HENRY, Nat [1]. "I Knew a Woman," Expl 27 (Jan., 1969).

_____ [2]. "262," Expl 21 (May, 1963).

_____ [3]. "275," Expl 20 (Apr., 1962).

_____ [4]. "303 (Nor Woman)," Expl 22 (Sept., 1963).

_____ [5]. "305," Expl 20 (Feb., 1962).

_____ [6]. "Pity This Busy Monster, Manunkind," Expl 27 (May, 1969).

_____ [7]. "Lecture Upon the Shadow," Expl 20 (Mar., 1962).

HEPBURN, James G. "E. A. Robinson's System of Opposites," PMLA 80 (June, 1965).

HERMAN, George. "Space and Dread and the Dark," Expl 22 (Oct., 1963).

HERNDON, Jerry A. "The Oven Bird," Expl 28 (Apr., 1970).

HEYEN, William. "The Divine Abyss: Theodore Roethke's Mysticism," TSLL 11 (Sum., 1969).

HIATT, David [1]. " 'Design' and 'In White'," Expl 28 (Jan., 1970).

_____ [2]. "Of Bronze and Blaze," Expl 21 (Sept., 1962).

HIEATT, A. Kent. "Sir Gawain: Pentangle, Luf-Lace, Numerical Structure," PLL 4 (Fall, 1968).

HIEATT, A. Kent and Constance HIEATT. " 'The Bird with Four Feathers': Numerical Analysis of a Fourteenth-

Century Poem," PLL 6 (Wint., 1970).

HILL, Archibald A. [1]. "Imagery and Meaning: A Passage from Milton, and from Blake," TSLL 11 (Fall, 1969).

_____ [2]. " 'The Windhover' Revisited: Linguistic Analysis of Poetry Reassessed," TSLL 7 (Wint., 1966).

HILL, H. Russell. "Poetry and Experience," EJ 55 (Feb., 1966).

HILL, Thomas D. "Apocryphal Cosmography and the 'Stream Uton Sae': A Note on Christ and Satan, Lines 4-12," PQ 48 (Oct., 1969).

HILLER, Geoffrey G. "Drayton's Muses Elizium: 'A New Way Over Parnassus'," RES 21 (Feb., 1970).

HIRSCH, David H. "T. S. Eliot and the Vexation of Time," SoR 3 (Sum., 1967).

HIRSCH, E. D., Jr. [1]. "Further Comment on 'Music, When Soft Voices Die'," JEGP 60 (Apr., 1961).

_____ [2]. "The Two Blakes," RES 12 (Nov., 1961).

HIRSCH, Gordon D. "Tennyson's Commedia," VP 8 (Sum., 1970).

HOETKER, James. "Frost's 'The Draft Horse'," CE 26 (Mar., 1965).

HOFFMAN, Arthur W. "Spenser and The Rape of the Lock," PQ 49 (Oct., 1970).

HOFFMAN, Richard L. "Gudrinc Astah: Beowulf 1118b," JEGP 64 (Oct., 1965).

HOFFMAN, Stanton de Voren. "The Pearl: Notes for an Interpretation," MP 58 (Nov., 1960).

HOGAN, Patrick G., Jr. "Marvell's 'Vegetable Love'," SP 60 (Jan., 1963).

HOGUE, Caroline. "I Heard a Fly Buzz When I Died," Expl 20 (Nov., 1961).

HOGUE, L. Lynn. "The Complaint of Henry, Duke of
    Buckingham, " Expl 28 (Sept. , 1969).

HOLBERG, Stanley M. "Rossetti and the Trance, " VP 8
    (Wint. , 1970).

HOLDITCH, Kenneth. "The Garden, " Expl 23 (Sept. , 1964).

HOLLAHAN, Eugene [1]. "I Heard a Fly Buzz When I
    Died, " Expl 25 (Sept. , 1966).

_____ [2]. "A Structural Dantean Parallel in Eliot's
    'The Love Song of J. Alfred Prufrock', " AL 42 (Mar. ,
    1970).

HOLLOW, John. "William Morris' 'The Haystack in the
    Floods', " VP 7 (Wint. , 1969).

HOLLOWAY, John [1]. "The Critical Theory of Yvor Win-
    ters, " CritQ 7 (Spr. , 1965).

_____ [2]. "The Poetry of Edwin Muir, " HudR 13 (Wint. ,
    1960-61).

_____ [3]. "Yeats and the Penal Age, " CritQ 8 (Spr. ,
    1966).

HOLMES, Charles M. "The Early Poetry of Aldous Hux-
    ley, " TSLL 8 (Fall, 1966).

HOLMES, Doris. "Herself, " Expl 28 (May, 1970).

*HOLMES, Eugene C. "Langston Hughes: Philosopher-Poet, "
    Freedomways 8 (Spr. , 1968).

HOLMES, Theodore [1]. "Thomas Hardy's City of the
    Mind, " SR 75 (Spr. , 1967).

_____ [2]. " ' ... The Wine-Transfiguring World', "
    Poetry 96 (May, 1960).

HOLTON, Milne. " 'A Baudelairesque Thing': The Direc-
    tions of Hart Crane's 'Black Tambourine', " Criticism
    9 (Sum. , 1967).

HONAN, Park. "The Murder Poem for Elizabeth, " VP 6
    (Aut. -Wint. , 1968).

HOOPLE, Robin P. " 'Chants Democratic and Native
American': A Neglected Sequence in the Growth of
Leaves of Grass, " AL 42 (May, 1970).

HOPKINS, R. H. "Coleridge's Parody of Melancholy
Poetry in 'The Nightingale: A Conversation Poem,
April, 1798', " ES 49 (Oct., 1968).

HOUGH, Graham [1]. "John Crowe Ransom: The Poet and
the Critic, " SoR 1 (Wint., 1965).

_____ [2]. "The Poetry of Wallace Stevens, " CritQ 2
(Aut., 1960).

HOUGH, Ingeborg. "Song for St. Cecilia's Day, " Expl 18
(Mar., 1960).

HOUGHTON, Donald E. "The Butterfly Obtains " Expl 27
(Sept., 1968).

HOUGHTON, Walter E. "Arthur Hugh Clough: A Hundred
Years of Disparagement, " SEL 1 (Aut., 1961).

HOVEY, Richard B. "Sonnet 73, " CE 23 (May, 1962).

HOWARD, H. Wendell. "L'Allegro, " Expl 24 (Sept.,
1965).

HOWARD, John [1]. "Caliban's Mind, " VP 1 (Nov., 1963).

_____ [2]. "Swedenborg's Heaven and Hell and Blake's
Songs of Innocence, " PLL 4 (Fall, 1968).

HOWARD, Richard [1]. Alone with America; Essays on
the Art of Poetry in the United States since 1950.
New York: Atheneum, 1969.

_____ [2]. "Fuel on the Fire, " Poetry 110 (Sept., 1967).

_____ [3]. "Illusion Wedded to Simple Need, " Poetry
108 (Aug., 1966).

_____ [4]. "Second Nature, " Poetry 114 (Aug., 1969).

HOWARD, Ronnalie Roper. "Rossetti's A Last Confession:
A Dramatic Monologue, " VP 5 (Spr., 1967).

HOWARD, William. "I Never Saw a Moor, " Expl 21 (Oct.,
1962).

HOWARD, William J.   "The Mystery of the Cibberian
    Dunciad," SEL 8 (Sum., 1968).

HUDSON, Theodore R.   "Langston Hughes' Last Volume of
    Verse," CLAJ 11 (June, 1968).   (Review of The Panther
    and the Lash.]

HUGHES, Merritt Y.   "Milton and the Symbol of Light,"
    SEL 4 (Wint., 1964).

HUGHES, R. E. [1].   "George Herbert's Rhetorical World,"
    Criticism 3 (Spr., 1961).

_____ [2].   "John Dryden's Greatest Compromise," TSLL
    2 (Wint., 1961).

HUGHES, Richard E.   "Herrick's 'Hock Cart,' Companion
    Piece to 'Corinna's Going A-Maying'," CE 27 (Feb.,
    1966).

HUGHES, Ted.   "The Poetry of Keith Douglas," CritQ 5
    (Spr., 1963).

HUME, Anthea.   "Spenser, Puritanism and the 'Maye'
    Eclogue," RES 20 (May, 1969).

HUME, Robert D.   "Inorganic Structure in The House of
    Life," PLL 5 (Sum., 1969).

HUMPHRIES, Rolfe.   "Attack on Barbados at Sandy Point,"
    Expl 18 (Apr., 1960).

HUNT, Jean M. [1].   "Denise Levertov's New Grief-
    Language II, The Sorrow Dance," UR 35 (Mar., 1969).

_____ [2].   "The New Grief-Language of Denise Levertov,
    The Sorrow Dance," UR 35 (Dec., 1968).

HUNT, John Dixon.   "The Symbolist Vision of In Memoriam,"
    VP 8 (Aut., 1970).

HUNTER, J. Paul.   "Satiric Apology as Satiric Instance:
    Pope's Arbuthnot " JEGP 68 (Oct., 1969).

HUNTER, Parks C., Jr.   "Undercurrents of Anacreontics
    in Shelley's 'To a Skylark' and 'The Cloud'," SP 65
    (July, 1968).

HUNT, James R. "First Song," Expl 20 (Nov., 1961).

HUSTON, J. Dennis [1]. " 'Credences of Summer': An
    Analysis," MP 67 (Feb., 1970).

_____ [2]. "The Function of the Mock Hero in Spenser's
    Faerie Queene," MP 66 (Feb., 1969).

HUTTAR, Charles A. "The Carkanet," Expl 24 (Dec.,
    1965).

HUTTON, Virgil. "Ode on a Grecian Urn," Expl 19 (Mar.,
    1961).

HUX, Samuel. "Sonnet CXXXVIII," Expl 25 (Jan., 1967).

HYDE, William J. "Hardy's Spider Webs," VP 8 (Aut.,
    1970).

HYDER, Clyde R. "Rossetti's Rose Mary: A Study in the
    Occult," VP 1 (Aug., 1963).

HYMAN, Lawrence W. [1]. "Marvell's 'Coy Mistress' and
    Desperate Lover," MLN 75 (Jan., 1960).

_____ [2]. "Poetry and Dogma in Paradise Lost (Book
    VIII)," CE 29 (Apr., 1968).

HYMAN, Stanley Edgar. "The Rape of the Lock," HudR 13
    (Aut., 1960).

IGNATOW, David. "Engagements," Poetry 99 (Jan., 1962).

IREDALE, Roger O. "Giants and Tyrants in Book Five of
    The Faerie Queene," RES 17 (Nov., 1966).

IRVINE, William. "Four Monologues in Browning's Men
    and Women," VP 2 (Sum., 1964).

IRWIN, W. R. [1]. "Robert Frost and the Comic Spirit,"
    AL 35 (Nov., 1963).

_____ [2]. "Unity of Frost's Masques," AL 32 (Nov.,
    1960).

ISAACS, Harold R. "Five Writers and Their African

Ancestors," Phylon 21 (Fall, 1960).

ISAACS, Neil D. [1]. "Six Beowulf Cruces," JEGP 62
(Jan., 1963).

_____ [2]. "Still Waters Run Undiop," PQ 44 (Oct.,
1965).

_____ [3]. "Who Says What in 'Advent Lyric VII'?
(Christ, Lines 164-213)," PLL 2 (Spr., 1966).

ISAACS, Neil D. and Richard M. KELLY. "Dramatic
Tension and Irony in Browning's 'The Glove'," VP 8
(Sum., 1970).

ISLER, Alan D. "The Allegory of the Hero and Sidney's
Two 'Arcadias'," SP 65 (Apr.,1968).

JACK, Ronald D. S. "The Lyrics of Alexander Montgomerie," RES 20 (May, 1969).

Jackson, James L. [1]. "Losses," Expl 19 (Apr., 1961).

_____ [2]. "The Love Song of J. Alfred Prufrock,"
Expl 18 (May, 1960).

*JACKSON, Miles, Jr. "James Weldon Johnson," BW 19,
no. 8.

JACOBS, Willis D. [1]. "The Attic Which Is Desire,"
Expl 25 (Mar., 1967).

_____ [2]. "Between Walls," Expl 28 (Apr., 1970).

_____ [3]. "Great Mullen," Expl 28 (Mar., 1970).

_____ [4]. "The Term," Expl 25 (May, 1967).

_____ [5]. "To Waken an Old Lady," Expl 29 (Sept.,
1970).

_____ [6]. "The Young Housewife," Expl 28 (May,
1970).

JENKINS, Ralph E. "Lost Anchors," Expl 23 (Apr.,
1965).

JEROME, Judson [1]. "Debut of a Poet: An Introduction to the Work of Patrick Brantlinger," AR 23 (Sum., 1963).

_____ [2]. "Introduction to the Poems of William Dickey," AR 23 (Spr., 1963).

_____ [3]. "A Moffitt Sampler," AR 24 (Sum., 1964).

_____ [4]. "On Decoding Humor," AR 20 (Wint., 1960-61).

_____ [5]. "A Sampler of the Poetry of E. Hale Chatfield," AR 22 (Wint., 1962-63).

JOHN, Brian [1]. "High Talk," Expl 29 (Nov., 1970).

_____ [2]. "Ted Hughes: Poet at the Master-Fulcrum of Violence," ArQ 23 (Spr., 1967).

_____ [3]. "Tennyson's 'Recollections of the Arabian Nights' and the Individuation Process," VP 4 (Aut., 1966).

JOHNSON, Alan P. "Sordello: Apollo, Bacchus, and the Pattern of Italian History," VP 7 (Wint., 1969).

JOHNSON, Carol. "Pope's Dunciad: Requisitions of Verity," SoR 1 (Wint., 1965).

JOHNSON, Mary Lynn. "Beulah, 'Mne Seraphim,' and Blake's Thel," JEGP 69 (Apr., 1970).

JOHNSON, Wendell Stacy [1]. "Matthew Arnold's Dialogue," UR 27 (Dec., 1960).

_____ [2]. " 'Rugby Chapel': Arnold as a Filial Poet," UR 34 (Dec., 1967).

JONES, A. R. [1]. "Necessity and Freedom: The Poetry of Robert Lowell, Sylvia Plath and Anne Sexton," CritQ 7 (Spr., 1965).

_____ [2]. "Robert Browning and the Dramatic Monologue: The Impersonal Art," CritQ 9 (Wint., 1967).

JONES, Donald. "Kindred Entanglements in Frost's 'A

Servant to Servants'," PLL 2 (Spr., 1966).

JONES, Evan. "The Nymph Complaining for the Death of Her Faun," Expl 26 (May, 1968).

JONES, Florence. "T. S. Eliot Among the Prophets," AL 38 (Nov., 1966).

JONES, Harry L. "A Danish Tribute to Langston Hughes," CLAJ 11 (1967).

JORDAN, Frank, Jr. "The Caged Skylark," Expl 28 (May, 1970).

JORDAN, John E. "The Hewing of Peter Bell," SEL 7 (Aut., 1967).

JORDAN, Raymond J. [1]. "The Bustle in a House," Expl 21 (Feb., 1963).

_____ [2]. "The Ebb and Flow," Expl 20 (Apr., 1962).

JUHNKE, Anna K. "Religion in Robert Frost's Poetry: The Play for Self-Possession," AL 36 (May, 1964).

JUMPER, Will C. [1]. "All in Green Went My Love Riding," Expl 26 (Sept., 1967).

_____ [2]. "The Soul Selects Her Own Society," Expl 29 (Sept., 1970).

KALLICH, Martin [1]. "The Conversation and the Frame of Love: Images of Unity in Pope's Essay on Man," PLL 2 (Wint., 1966).

_____ [2]. "An Essay on Man, II, 175-194," Expl 25 (Oct., 1966).

_____ [3]. "Unity and Dialectic, the Structural Role of Antitheses in Pope's Essay on Man," PLL 1 (Wint., 1965).

KALLSEN, T. J. "Sonnet XXXIV," Expl 27 (Apr., 1969).

KALMEY, Robert P. "Pope's Eloisa to Abelard and 'Those Celebrated Letters'," PQ 47 (Apr., 1968).

KALSTONE, David. "Sir Philip Sidney and 'Poore Petrarchs Long Deceased Woes'," JEGP 63 (Jan., 1964).

KANTROWITZ, Joanne Spencer. "The Anglo-Saxon Phoenix and Tradition," PQ 43 (Jan., 1964).

KAPLAN, Fred [1]. " 'The Tyger' and its Maker: Blake's Vision of Art and the Artist," SEL 7 (Aut., 1967).

_____ [2]. "Woven Paces and Waving Hands: Tennyson's Merlin as Fallen Artist," VP 7 (Wint., 1969).

KAPLAN, Robert B. and Richard J. WALL. "Gerontion," Expl 19 (Mar., 1961).

_____ [2]. "Journey of the Magi," Expl 19 (Nov., 1960).

KASKE, Carol V. "The Dragon's Spark and Sting and the Structure of Red Cross's Dragon-Fight: The Faerie Queene, I, xi-xii," SP 66 (July, 1969).

KASKE, R. E. " 'Ex Vi Transicionis' and Its Passage in Piers Plowman," JEGP 62 (Jan., 1963).

KAULA, David. " 'In War with Time': Temporal Perspectives in Shakespeare's Sonnets," SEL 3 (Wint., 1963).

KEAN, P. M. [1]. "Langland on the Incarnation," RES 16 (Nov., 1965).

_____ [2]. "Love, Law, and Lewte in Piers Plowman," RES 15 (Aug., 1964).

KEEFER, Frederick. " 'The City in the Sea': A Re-examination," CE 25 (Mar., 1964).

KEEFER, Frederick and Deborah VLAHOS. "If You Were Coming in the Fall," Expl 29 (Nov., 1970).

KEITH, W. J. "Yeats's Arthurian Black Tower," MLN 75 (Feb., 1960).

KELLER, Karl [1]. "California, Yankees, and the Death of God: The Allegory in Jeffers' Roan Stallion," TSLL 12 (Spr., 1970).

_____ [2]. "From Christianity to Transcendentalism: A

Note on Emerson's Use of the Conceit," AL 39 (Mar., 1967).

KELLY, Edward Hanford. "Myth as Paradigm in Troilus and Criseyde," PLL 3 (Suppl., Sum., 1967).

KELLY, Richard. "Captain Carpenter," Expl 25 (Mar., 1967).

KELLY, Robert L. "'Dactyls and Curlews: Satire in 'A Grammarian's Funeral'," VP 5 (Sum., 1967).

KENDALL, J. L. "Unity of Arnold's 'Tristram and Iseult'," VP 1 (Apr., 1963).

KENNER, Hugh [1]. "The Drama of Utterance," MR 3 (Wint., 1962).

_____ [2]. "The Experience of the Eye: Marianne Moore's Tradition," SoR 1 (Aut., 1965).

_____ [3]. "Meditation and Enactment," Poetry 102 (May, 1963).

KENNEY, Blair G. [1]. "Ode on a Grecian Urn," Expl 27 (May, 1969).

_____ [2]. "Woodsman, Spare Those 'Trees'," CE 25 (Mar., 1964).

KEOGH, J. G. [1]. "To His Coy Mistress," Expl 28 (Oct., 1969).

_____ [2]. "Sonnet LXXIII," Expl 28 (Sept., 1969).

KERMODE, Frank. "A Babylonish Dialect," SR 74 (Wint., 1966).

KERN, Alexander C. "The Wood-Pile," Expl 28 (Feb., 1970).

KERNAN, Alvin B. " 'The Dunciad' and the Plot of Satire," SEL 2 (Sum., 1962).

KESSLER, Edward. "The Black Tambourine," Expl 29 (Sept., 1970).

KETCHAM, Carl H. "Meredith and the Wilis," VP 1

(Nov., 1963).

KILBURN, Patrick E. [1]. "Evening Star," Expl 28 (May, 1970).

_____ [2]. "My Last Duchess," Expl 19 (Feb., 1961).

KIME, Wayne R. "Ichabod," Expl 28 (Mar., 1970).

KINCAID, James R. [1]. "Tennyson's 'Crossing the Bar': A Poem of Frustration," VP 3 (Wint., 1965).

_____ [2]. "Tennyson's Mariners and Spenser's Despair: The Argument of 'The Lotos-Eaters'," PLL 5 (Sum., 1969).

KING, Bruce [1]. "Absalom and Achitophel," Expl 21 (Dec., 1962).

_____ [2]. "Absalom and Dryden's Earlier Praise of Monmouth," ES 46 (Aug., 1965).

_____ [3]. "Green Ice and a Breast of Proof," CE 26 (Apr., 1965).

_____ [4]. "Irony in Marvell's 'To His Coy Mistress'," SoR 5 (Sum., 1969).

_____ [5]. "Wallace Stevens' 'Metaphors of a Magnifico'," ES 49 (Oct., 1968).

KING, Montgomery W. "The Two Worlds of Wallace Stevens," CLAJ 8 (Dec., 1964).

*KING, Woodie, Jr. "Remembering Langston: A Poet of the Black Theater," NegroD 18, no. 6.

*KINNAMON, Keneth. "Richard Wright: Proletarian Poet," ConP 2, no. 1.

KINNELL, Galway. "Seeing and Being," Poetry 100 (Sept., 1962).

KINNEY, Arthur F. "Auden, Bruegel, and 'Musee des Beaux Arts'," CE 24 (Apr., 1963).

KINTGEN, Eugene R. "Childe Roland and the Perversity

of the Mind," <u>VP</u> 4 (Aut., 1966).

KIRALIS, Karl. "A Guide to the Intellectual Symbolism of William Blake's Later Prophetic Writings," <u>Criticism</u> 1 (Sum., 1959).

KLIGERMAN, Jack. "An Interpretation of T. S. Eliot's 'East Coker'," <u>ArQ</u> 18 (Sum., 1962).

KLINEFELTER, Ralph A. "An ABC," <u>Expl</u> 24 (Sept., 1965).

KLOTZ, Marvin. "The Tree in Pamela's Garden," <u>Expl</u> 20 (Jan., 1962).

KNAPP, Edgar H. "Dust of Snow," <u>Expl</u> 28 (Sept., 1969).

KNAPP, James F. "Delmore Schwartz: Poet of the Orphic Journey," <u>SR</u> 78 (Sum., 1970).

KNIEGER, Bernard [1]. "Dylan Thomas, the Christianity of the "Altarwise by Owl-Light' Sequence," <u>CE</u> 23 (May, 1962).

_____ [2]. "Love in the Asylum," <u>Expl</u> 20 (Oct., 1961).

_____ [3]. "On the Marriage of a Virgin," <u>Expl</u> 19 (May, 1961).

_____ [4]. "Poetry Imitation," <u>CE</u> 21 (Mar., 1960).

_____ [5]. "The Purchase-Sale: Patterns of Business Imagery in the Poetry of George Herbert," <u>SEL</u> 6 (Wint., 1966).

_____ [6]. "Sonnet III," <u>Expl</u> 18 (Jan., 1960).

_____ [7]. "The Religious Verse of George Herbert," <u>CLAJ</u> 4 (Dec., 1960).

_____ [8]. "Twenty-Four Years," <u>Expl</u> 20 (Sept., 1961).

KNIGHT, W. Nicholas. "The Narrative Unity of Book V of The Faerie Queene: 'That Part of Justice Which Is Equity'," <u>RES</u> 21 (Aug., 1970).

KNIGHTLEY, William J. " 'Pearl': The 'hy3 seysoun',"

MLN 76 (Feb., 1961).

KNOEPFLMACHER, U. C. "Dover Revisited: The Words-
worthian Matrix in the Poetry of Matthew Arnold,"
VP 1 (Jan., 1963).

KNOTT, John R., Jr. [1]. "Milton's Heaven," PMLA 85
(May, 1970).

_____ [2]. "The Visit of Raphael: Paradise Lost, Book
V," PQ 47 (Jan., 1968).

KNUST, Herbert. "The Waste Land," Expl 23 (May, 1965).

KOLLER, Katherine. "Art, Rhetoric and Holy Dying in the
'Faerie Queene' with Special Reference to the Despair
Canto," SP 61 (Apr., 1964).

KORG, Jacob. "A Reading of 'Pippa Passes'," VP 6
(Spr., 1968).

KORSHIN, Paul J. "The Theoretical Bases of Cowley's
Later Poetry," SP 66 (Oct., 1969).

KORTE, Donald M. "Moral Essays, Epistle IV," Expl 28
(Dec., 1969).

KOSTELANETZ, Richard. "Conversation with Berryman,"
MR 11 (Spr., 1970).

KOWALCZYK, R. L. "Horatian Tradition and Pastoral
Mode in Housman's 'A Shropshire Lad'," VP 4 (Aut.,
1966).

KOZICKI, Henry. "Tennyson's 'Idylls of the King' as
Tragic Drama," VP 4 (Wint., 1966).

*KRAMER, Aaron. "Robert Burns and Langston Hughes,"
Freedomways, 8 (Spr., 1968).

KRAMER, Dale [1]. "Character and Theme in 'Pippa
Passes'," VP 2 (Aut., 1964).

_____ [2]. "The Waste Land," Expl 24 (Apr., 1966).

KRAMER, Maurice. "Six Voyages of a Derelict Seer," SR
73 (Sum., 1965).

KRANIDAS, Thomas. "Adam and Eve in the Garden: A
Study of 'Paradise Lost', Book V," SEL 4 (Wint.,
1964).

KRAUSE, Sydney J. "Hollow Men and False Horses,"
TSLL 2 (Aut., 1960).

KROEBER, Karl. "Touchstones for Browning's Victorian
Complexity," VP 3 (Spr., 1965).

KVAPIL, Charline R. " 'How It Strikes a Contemporary':
A Dramatic Monologue," VP 4 (Aut., 1966).

KWINN, David. "Meredith's Psychological Insight in
Modern Love XXIII," VP 7 (Sum., 1969).

LABRANCHE, Anthony [1]. "Drayton's 'The Barons Warres'
and the Rhetoric of Historical Poetry," JEGP 62
(Jan., 1963).

_____ [2]. "Poetry, History, and Oratory: The Renaissance Historical Poem," SEL 9 (Wint., 1969).

LACERVA, Patricia. "Saint," Expl 29 (Dec., 1970).

LAINOFF, Seymour. "Wordsworth's Final Phase: Glimpses
of Eternity," SEL 1 (Aut., 1961).

LAIR, Robert L. "As By the Dead We Love to Sit," Expl
25 (Mar., 1967).

LAMBA, B. P. and R. Jeet LAMBA [1]. "The Agony,"
Expl 28 (Feb., 1970).

_____ [2]. "Sir Gawain and the Green Knight," Expl 27
(Feb., 1969).

LAMPE, David E. "Tradition and Meaning in 'The Cuckoo
and the Nightingale'," PLL 3 (Suppl., Sum., 1967).

LANGFORD, Richard E. and William E. TAYLOR (eds.).
The Twenties, Poetry and Prose; Twenty Critical
Essays. Deland, Fla.: Everett Edwards Press, 1966.

LANGFORD, Thomas. "The Temptations in Paradise Regained," TSLL 9 (Spr., 1967).

LARSON, Judith Sweitzer. "What Is 'The Bowge of Courte'?" JEGP 61 (Apr., 1962).

LASSER, Michael L. "Sonnet Entitled How to Run the World," Expl 24 (Jan., 1966).

LASSER, Michael L. and Yoshiyuki IWAMOTO. "In a Station of the Metro," Expl 19 (Feb., 1961).

LAUBER, John. " 'Don Juan' as Anti-Epic," SEL 8 (Aut., 1968).

LAUGHLIN, Rosemary M. "Anne Bradstreet: Poet in Search of Form," AL 42 (Mar., 1970).

LAWRY, Jon S. [1]. " 'Eager Thought': Dialectic in 'Lycidas'," PMLA 77 (Mar., 1962).

_____ [2]. "Reading Paradise Lost; 'The Grand Master-piece to Observe'," CE 25 (May, 1964).

LEACH, Elsie. "Dylan Thomas' 'Ballad of the Long-Legged Bait'," MLN 76 (Dec., 1961).

LEAVIS, F. R. "T. S. Eliot and the Life of English Literature," MR 10 (Wint., 1969).

LEBRUN, Philip. "T. S. Eliot and Henri Bergson," RES 18, Pt. I (May, 1967); Pt. II (Aug., 1967).

LEE, Young G. "The Human Condition: Browning's 'Cleon'," VP 7 (Spr., 1969).

LEED, Jacob. "A Difficult Passage in 'Astraea Redux'," ES 47 (Apr., 1966).

LEES, Francis Noel. "Mr. Eliot's Sunday Morning 'Satura': Petronius and 'The Waste Land'," SR 74 (Wint., 1966).

LEGGETT, B. J. "The Recruit," Expl 25 (Nov., 1966).

LEGOUIS, Pierre. "The Cartography of 'The Definition of Love'," RES 12 (Feb., 1961).

LEHMAN, David. "When the Sun Tries to Go On," Poetry, 114 (Sept., 1969).

LEHMANN, Ruth P. M. [1]. "The Metrics and Structure of

'Wulf and Eadwacer'," PQ 48 (Apr., 1969).

LEHMANN, Ruth P. M. [2]. "The Old English 'Riming Poem': Interpretation, Text, and Translation," JEGP 69 (July, 1970).

LEITER, Lewis H. [1]. "Deification Through Love; Marlowe's 'The Passionate Shepherd to his Love'," CE 27 (Mar., 1966).

_____ [2]. "George Herbert's Anagram," CE 26 (Apr., 1965).

_____ [3]. "Sense in Nonsense: Wallace Stevens' 'The Bird with the Coppery, Keen Claws'," CE 26 (Apr., 1965).

_____ [4]. "Upon Julia's Clothes," Expl 25 (Jan., 1967).

LENHART, Charmenz S. Musical Influence on American Poetry. Athens: University of Georgia Press, 1956.

LESLIE, Roy F. "The Integrity of Riddle 60," JEGP 67 (July, 1968).

LESSER, Simon O. " 'Sailing to Byzantium'; Another Voyage, Another Reading," CE 28 (Jan., 1967).

LEVIN, Gerald. "The Imagery of Ruskins 'A Walk in Chamouni'," VP 5 (Wint., 1967).

LEVIN, Richard [1]. "Shelley's 'Indian Serenade': A Re-Revaluation," CE 24 (Jan., 1963).

_____ [2]. "Sonnet LXIV," Expl 24 (Dec., 1965).

_____ [3]. "Sonnet LXVI," Expl 22 (Jan., 1964).

LEVINE, Jay Arnold [1]. "Dryden's 'Song for St. Cecelia's Day, 1687'," PQ 44 (Jan., 1965).

_____ [2]. "Pope's 'Epistle to Augustus', Lines 1-30," SEL 7 (Sum., 1967).

LEVITT, Paul M. and Kenneth G. JOHNSTON. "Herbert's 'The Collar' and the Story of Job," PLL 4 (Sum., 1968).

LEVY, Eugene. "Ragtime and Race Pride: The Career of James Weldon Johnson," JPC 1 (1967).

LEVY, Raphael. "Song of a Man Who Has Come Through," Expl 22 (Feb., 1964).

LEWALSKI, Barbara Kiefer [1]. "Structure and Symbolism of Vision in Michael's Prophecy, 'Paradise Lost', Books XI-XII," PQ 42 (Jan., 1963).

_____ [2]. "Theme and Structure in 'Paradise Regained'," SP 57 (Apr., 1960).

LEWIS, R. W. B. "Crane's Visionary Lyric; The Way to The Bridge," MR 7 (Spr., 1966).

LEWIS, Stuart. "The Lamp Burns Sure Within," Expl 28 (Sept., 1969).

LIDDIE, Alexander S. "Metaphors of a Magnifico," Expl 21 (Oct., 1962).

LIEBER, Todd. "Design and Movement in Cane," CLAJ 13 (Sept., 1969).

LIEBERMAN, Laurence. "The Body of the Dream," Poetry 112 (May, 1968).

LIND, Sidney E. "Emily Dickinson's 'Further in Summer than the Birds' and Nathaniel Hawthorne's 'The Old Manse'," AL 39 (May, 1967).

LINDENBERGER, Herbert. "Keats's 'To Autumn' and Our Knowledge of a Poem," CE 32 (Nov., 1970).

LINDHEIM, Nancy Rothwax. "Sidney's 'Arcadia Book II' Retrospective Narrative," SP 64 (Apr., 1967).

LIPP, Frances Randall. "Contrast and Point of View in 'The Battle of Brunanburh'," PQ 48 (Apr., 1969).

LITTLE, G. L. "Ode on Melancholy," Expl 25 (Feb., 1967).

LITTMANN, Mark. " 'The Ancient Mariner' and Initiation Rites," PLL 4 (Fall, 1968).

LITZINGER, Boyd [1]. "Incident as Microcosm: The
    Prior's Niece in 'Fra Lippo Lippi'," CE 22 (Mar.,
    1961).

_____ [2]. "Once More, 'The Windhover'," VP 5 (Aut.,
    1967).

_____ [3]. "The Pattern of Ascent in Hopkins," VP
    2 (Wint., 1964).

_____ [4]. "The Structure of Tennyson's 'The Last
    Tournament'," VP 1 (Jan., 1963).

_____ [5]. "The Wreck of the Deutschland," Expl 20
    (Sept., 1961).

LIVINGSTON, James L. "Walt Whitman's Epistle to the
    Americans," AL 40 (Jan., 1969).

LOFTUS, Richard J. "Yeats and the Easter Rising: A
    Study in Ritual," ArQ 16 (Sum., 1960).

LOGAN, John. "The Poetry of Isabella Gardner," SR 70
    (Spr., 1962).

LORCH, Thomas M. "The Relationship Between Ulysses
    and The Waste Land," TSLL 6 (Sum., 1964).

LORD, George de F. "From Contemplation to Action:
    Marvell's Poetical Career," PQ 46 (Apr., 1967).

LOSCHKY, Helen M. "Free Will Versus Determinism in
    The Ring and the Book," VP 6 (Aut.-Wint., 1968).

LOUGY, Robert. "The Hock-Cart, or Harvest Home,"
    Expl 23 (Oct., 1964).

LOUISE, Sister Robert, O. P. "Spring and Fall: To a Young
    Child," Expl 21 (Apr., 1963).

LOVE, Glen A. "Frost's 'The Census-Taker' and de la
    Mare's 'The Listeners'," PLL 4 (Spr., 1968).

LOVE, Harold [1]. "The Argument of Donne's First Anni-
    versary," MP 64 (Nov., 1966).

_____ [2]. "To His Mistress Going to Bed," Expl 26

(Dec., 1967).

LOW, Anthony [1]. "The Image of the Tower in 'Paradise Lost'," <u>SEL</u> 10 (Wint., 1970).

_____ [2]. "The Morning-Watch," <u>Expl</u> 26 (Oct., 1967).

_____ [3]. "The Parting in the Garden in 'Paradise Lost'," <u>PQ</u> 47 (Jan., 1968).

LOW, Anthony and Paul J. PIVAL. "Rhetorical Pattern in Marvell's 'To His Coy Mistress'," <u>JEGP</u> 68 (July, 1969).

LOWREY, Robert E. " 'Boanerges': An Encomium for Edward Dickinson," <u>ArQ</u> 26 (Spr., 1970).

LUBBERS, Klaus. "Poe's 'The Conqueror Worm'," <u>AL</u> 39 (Nov., 1967).

LUEDTKE, Luther S. "The Noster Was a Ship of Swank," <u>Expl</u> 26 (Mar., 1968).

LUND, Mary Graham. "In Memoriam," <u>Expl</u> 18 (Jan., 1960).

LYNDE, Richard D. "A Note on the Imagery in Christina Rossetti's 'A Birthday'," <u>VP</u> 3 (Aut., 1965).

LYNEN, John F. "The Poet's Meaning and the Poem's World," <u>SoR</u> 2 (Aut., 1966).

LYNSKEY, Winifred. "Ode on the Poetical Character," <u>Expl</u> 19 (Feb., 1961).

MCALEER, Edward C. "Nationality in Drinks," <u>Expl</u> 20 (Dec., 1961).

MCALEER, John J. "Mary Winslow," <u>Expl</u> 18 (Feb., 1960).

MCALINDON, T. "Magic, Fate, and Providence in Medieval Narrative and <u>Sir Gawain and the Green Knight</u>," <u>RES</u> 16 (May, 1965).

MACBETH, George. "Lee-Hamilton and the Romantic Agony," <u>CritQ</u> 4 (Sum., 1962).

MCCANLES, Michael. "Distinguish in Order to Unite: Donne's 'The Extasie'," SEL 6 (Wint., 1966).

MCCONNELL, Daniel J. " 'The Heart of Darkness' in T. S. Eliot's The Hollow Men," TSLL 4 (Sum., 1962).

MCCUTCHEON, Elizabeth. "To Penshurst," Expl 25 (Feb., 1967).

MCDONALD, Daniel. "Too Much Reality: A Discussion of 'The Rime of the Ancient Mariner'," SEL 4 (Aut., 1964).

MACEACHEN, Dougald B. [1]. "Browning's Use of his Sources in 'Andrea del Sarto'," VP 8 (Spr., 1970).

_____ [2]. "Trial by Water in William Morris' 'The Haystack in the Floods'," VP 6 (Spr., 1968).

MACEY, Samuel L. "Dramatic Elements in Chaucer's Troilus," TSLL 12 (Fall, 1970).

MCFADDEN, George [1]. "Elkanah Settle and the Genesis of Mac Flecknoe," PQ 43 (Jan., 1964).

_____ [2]. "Probings for an Integration: Color Symbolism in Wallace Stevens," MP 58 (Feb., 1961).

MCGANN, Jerome J. [1]. "Poetry and Truth," Poetry 117 (Dec., 1970).

_____ [2]. "Rossetti's Significant Details," VP 7 (Spr., 1969).

MCGHEE, Richard D. [1]. " 'Blank Misgivings': Arthur Hugh Clough's Search for Poetic Form," VP 7 (Sum., 1969).

_____ [2]. " 'Thalassius': Swinburne's Poetic Myth," VP 5 (Sum., 1967).

MCGLYNN, Paul D. "The Chimney Sweeper," Expl 27 (Nov., 1968).

MCGRATH, F. C. "The Bunch of Grapes," Expl 29 (Oct., 1970).

MCGUINNESS, Arthur E. "A Question of Consciousness:

Richard Wilbur's Things of This World," ArQ 23 (Wint., 1967).

MACINTYRE, Jean [1]. "The Faerie Queene, III, xi, 47-48," Expl 24 (Apr., 1966).

_____ [2]. "The Faerie Queene, Book I: Toward Making It More Teachable," CE 31 (Feb., 1970).

MACK, Maynard. "1946: On Reading Pope," CE 22 (Nov., 1960).

MACKAY, F. M. "The Visitation," Expl 27 (Oct., 1968).

MACKIN, Cooper R. "The Satiric Technique of John Oldham's 'Satyrs Upon the Jesuits'," SP 62 (Jan., 1965).

MACLAINE, Allan H. "Burns's Use of Parody in 'Tam O'Shanter'," Criticism 1 (Fall, 1959).

MCLEAN, A. F. "Bryant's 'Thanatopsis': A Sermon in Stone," AL 31 (Jan., 1960).

MCNALLY, James. "Suiting Sight and Sound to Sense in 'Meeting at Night' and 'Parting at Morning'," VP 5 (Aut., 1967).

MCNAMARA, Peter L. "The Multi-Faceted Blackbird and Wallace Stevens' Poetic Vision," CE 25 (Mar., 1964).

MCNAMEE, M. B., S.J. [1]. "Beowulf--An Allegory of Salvation?" JEGP 59 (Apr., 1960).

_____ [2]. "Mastery and Mercy in The Wreck of the Deutschland," CE 23 (Jan., 1962).

MACQUEEN, John. "Tradition and the Interpretation of the Kingis Quair," RES 12 (May, 1961).

MADDOX, Notley Sinclair. "Ichabod," Expl 18 (Mar., 1960).

MADSEN, William G. "The Voice of Michael in 'Lycidas'," SEL 3 (Wint., 1963).

MAHONEY, John L. "Donne and Greville: Two Christian Attitudes Towards the Renaissance Idea of Mutability and Decay," CLAJ 5 (Mar., 1962).

MAHONY, Patrick J. [1]. "An Analysis of Shelley's Crafts-
manship in 'Adonais'," SEL 4 (Aut., 1964).

_____ [2]. "The Anniversaries: Donne's Rhetorical Approach to Evil," JEGP 68 (July, 1969).

*MAJOR, Clarence. "The Poetry of LeRoi Jones," NegroD
14 (Mar., 1965).

MAJOR, John W., Jr. "The Education of a Young Knight,"
UR 29 (June, 1963).

MALARKEY, Stoddard and J. Barre TOELKEN. "Gawain
and the Green Girdle," JEGP 63 (Jan., 1964).

MALBONE, Raymond Gates [1]. "Fra Lippo Lippi," Expl
25 (Nov., 1966).

_____ [2]. "I Taste a Liquor Never Brewed," Expl 26
(Oct., 1967).

_____ [3]. "The Road Not Taken," Expl 24 (Nov., 1965).

_____ [4]. "That Blasted Rose-Acacia: A Note on
Browning's 'Soliloquy of the Spanish Cloister'," VP 4
(Sum., 1966).

MALINS, Edward. "Yeats and the Easter Rising," MR 7
(Spr., 1966).

MANDEL, Barrett John. "Pope's 'Eloisa to Abelard',"
TSLL 9 (Spr., 1967).

MANIERRE, William Reid [1]. "Verbal Patterns in the
Poetry of Edward Taylor," CE 23 (Jan., 1962).

_____ [2]. "Versification and Imagery in The Fall of
Hyperion," TSLL 3 (Sum., 1961).

_____ [3]. "E. D.: Visions and Revisions," TSLL 5
(Spr., 1963).

MANIQUIS, Robert M. "Comparison, Intensity, and Time
in 'Tintern Abbey'," Criticism 11 (Fall, 1969).

MANNING, Stephen. "A Psychological Interpretation of Sir

Gawain and the Green Knight," Criticism 6 (Spr.,
1964).

MANSELL, Darrel, Jr. "Range-Finding," Expl 24 (Mar.,
1966).

MARCUS, Mordecai [1]. "Not with a Club the Heart Is
Broken," Expl 20 (Mar., 1962).

_____ [2]. "Structure and Irony in Stephen Crane's 'War
Is Kind'," CLAJ 9 (Mar., 1966).

MARCUS, Mordecai and Erin MARCUS. "During Wind and
Rain," Expl 19 (Dec., 1960).

MARESCA, Thomas E. "The Latona Myth in Milton's
Sonnet XII," MLN 76 (June, 1961).

MARIANI, Paul L. "The Artistic and Tonal Integrity of
Hopkins' 'The Shepherd's Brow'," VP 6 (Spr., 1968).

MAROTTI, Arthur F. "Animal Symbolism in The Faerie
Queene: Tradition and the Poetic Context," SEL 5
(Wint., 1965).

MARSH, T. N. "Hero and Leander, I, 45-50," Expl 21
(Dec., 1962).

MARSHALL, George O., Jr. "Evelyn Hope's Lover," VP
4 (Wint., 1966).

MARSHALL, William H. [1]. "Paradise Lost: Felix Culpa
and The Problem of Structure," MLN 76 (Jan., 1961).

_____ . [2]. "A Reading of Byron's 'Mazeppa'," MLN 76
(Feb., 1961).

_____ [3]. "The Structure of Coleridge's 'The Eolian
Harp'," MLN 76 (Mar., 1961).

MARTIN, Edward A. "H. L. Mencken's Poetry," TSLL 6
(Aut., 1964).

MARTIN, Jay. "Wil as Fool and Wanderer in Piers Plowman," TSLL 3 (Wint., 1962).

MARTIN, Wallace. "Acquainted with the Night," Expl 26

(Apr., 1968).

MARTZ, Louis Lohr. The Poem of the Mind; Essays on Poetry, English and American. New York: Oxford University Press, 1966.

MASSEY, Irving. "Shelley's 'Music, When Soft Voices Die'," JEGP 59 (July, 1960).

MATCHETT, William H. [1]. "Dickinson's Revision of "Two Butterflies Went Out at Noon'," PMLA 77 (Sept., 1962).

_____ [2]. "Donne's 'Peece of Chronicle'," RES 18 (Aug., 1967).

MATHEW, T. C. "Prisoned in Windsor, He Recounteth His Pleasure There Passed," Expl 27 (Oct., 1968).

MATTFIELD, Mary S. [1]. "Let's, From Some Loud Un-world's Most Rightful Wrong," Expl 26 (Dec., 1967).

_____ [2]. "The Puritans," Expl 28 (Feb., 1970).

MATTHEWS, G. M. "Shelley and Jane Williams," RES 12 (Feb., 1961).

MATTHEY, F. "Interplay of Structure and Meaning in the 'Ode to a Nightingale'," ES 49 (Aug., 1968).

MAURER, A. E. Wallace [1]. "Absalom and Achitophel," Expl 20 (Sept., 1961).

_____ [2]. "The Design of Dryden's The Medall," PLL 2 (Fall, 1966).

_____ [3]. "The Structure of Dryden's Astraea Redux," PLL 2 (Wint., 1966).

MAURER, Oscar. "Bishop Blougram's 'French Book'," VP 6 (Sum., 1968).

MAY, Charles E. "Thomas Hardy and the Poetry of the Absurd," TSLL 12 (Spr., 1970).

MAY, Louis F. "Epitaph on Solomon Pavy," Expl 20 (Oct., 1961).

MAYERSON, Caroline W. "Ode to a Nightingale," Expl 25

(Nov., 1966).

*MAYFIELD, Julian. "Langston," NegroD 16 (Sept., 1967).

MAYNARD, Winifred. "The Lyrics of Wyatt: Poems or Songs?" RES 16, Pt. I (Feb., 1965); Pt. II (Aug., 1965).

MEIER, Hans Heinrich. "Ancient Lights on Kubla's Lines," ES 46 (Feb., 1965).

MEINERS, R. K. [1]. "The Art of Allen Tate," UR 27 (Dec., 1960).

_____ [2]. "The End of History: Allen Tate's Seasons of the Soul," SR 70 (Wint., 1962).

_____ [3]. "The Meaning of Life," Expl 19 (June, 1961).

MELCHIORI, Barbara. "Browning's 'Andrea del Sarto': A French Source in De Musset," VP 4 (Spr., 1966).

MELL, Donald C., Jr. "Form as Meaning in Augustan Elegy: A Reading of Thomas Gray's 'Sonnet on the Death of Richard West'," PLL 4 (Spr., 1968).

MELLOWN, Elgin W. "Hopkins and the Odyssey," VP 8 (Aut., 1970).

MENDEL, Sydney [1]. "Andrea del Sarto," Expl 22 (May, 1964).

_____ [2]. "Lapis Lazuli," Expl 19 (June, 1961).

MERCHANT, W. Moelwyn. "R. S. Thomas," CritQ 2 (Wint., 1960).

MERIDETH, Robert. "I Had Not Minded Walls," Expl 23 (Nov., 1964).

MERIVALE, Patricia. "Wallace Stevens' 'Jar'," CE 26 (Apr., 1965).

MERRITT, James D. "The Waste Land," Expl 23 (Dec., 1964).

METZGER, Deena Posy. "Hart Crane's Bridge: The Myth Active," ArQ 20 (Spr., 1964).

METZGER, Lore. "The Eternal Process: Some Parallels

Between Goethe's Faust and Tennyson's In Memoriam,"
VP 1 (Aug., 1963).

MEYER, Sam. "The Figures of Rhetoric in Spenser's Colin
Clout," PMLA 79 (June, 1964).

MEYERS, Joyce S. " 'Childe Roland to the Dark Tower
Came': A Nightmare Confrontation with Death,"
VP 8 (Wint., 1970).

MEYERS, Robert. "Ode: Intimations of Immortality From
Recollections of Early Childhood," Expl 28 (Sept.,
1969).

MICHEL, Pierre. "The Last Stanza of Emily Dickinson's
'One Dignity Delays for All--'," ES 50 (Feb., 1969).

MIDDLEBROOK, Jonathan. " 'Resignation,' 'Rugby Chapel,'
and Thomas Arnold," VP 8 (Wint., 1970).

MILLER, Bruce E. [1]. "On the Incompleteness of Keats'
'Hyperion'," CLAJ 8 (Mar., 1965).

_____ [2]. "On 'The Windhover'," VP 2 (Spr., 1964).

MILLER, Clarence H. [1]. "Donne's 'A Nocturnall Upon
S. Lucies Day' and the Nocturns of Matins," SEL 6
(Wint., 1966).

_____ . [2]. "The Order of Stanzas in Cowley
and Crashaw's 'On Hope'," SP 61 (Jan., 1964).

_____ [3]. "The Styles of The Hind and the Panther,"
JEGP 61 (July, 1962).

MILLER, Dorothy Durkee. "Eve," JEGP 61 (July, 1962).

MILLER, J. Hillis [1]. " 'Orion' in The Wreck of the
Deutschland," MLN 76 (June, 1961).

_____ [2]. "The Theme of the Disappearance of God in
Victorian Poetry," VS 6 (Mar., 1963).

_____ [3]. " 'Wessex Heights': The Persistence of the
Poet in Hardy's Poetry," CritQ 10 (Wint., 1968).

MILLER, John H. "Pope and the Principle of Reconciliation,"

TSLL 9 (Sum., 1967).

MILLER, Lewis H., Jr. [1]. "Phaedria, Mammon, and Sir Guyon's Education by Error," JEGP 63 (Jan., 1964).

_____ [2]. "Two Poems of Winter," CE 28 (Jan., 1967).

MILLHAUSER, Milton [1]. "Poet and Burgher: A Comic Variation on a Serious Theme," VP 7 (Sum., 1969).

_____ [2]. "Structure and Symbol in 'Crossing the Bar'," VP 4 (Wint., 1966).

MILLS, David. "An Analysis of the Temptation Scenes in Sir Gawain and the Green Knight," JEGP 67 (Oct., 1968).

MILOSEVICH, Vincent M. "The Bishop Orders his Tomb at Saint Praxed's Church," Expl 27 (May, 1969).

MINER, Earl [1]. "Annus Mirabilis," Expl 24 (May, 1966).

_____ [2]. "The Death of Innocence in Marvell's 'Nymph Complaining for the Death of her Faun'," MP 65 (Aug., 1967).

_____ [3]. "Dryden and the Issue of Human Progress," PQ 40 (Jan., 1961).

_____ [4]. "Felix Culpa in the Redemptive Order of Paradise Lost," PQ 47 (Jan., 1968).

_____ [5]. "The 'Poetic Picture, Painted Poetry' of 'The Last Instructions to a Painter'," MP 63 (May, 1966).

_____ [6]. "Some Characteristics of Dryden's Use of Metaphor," SEL 2 (Sum., 1962).

MINER, Paul. " 'The Tyger': Genesis and Evolution in the Poetry of William Blake," Criticism 4 (Wint., 1962).

MITCHELL, Charles [1]. "Donne's 'The Extasie': Love's Sublime Knot," SEL 8 (Wint., 1968).

_____ [2]. "Hardy's 'Afterwards'," VP 1 (Jan., 1963).

MITCHELL, Charles [3]. "Little Boy Blue," Expl 22 (Sept.,
    1963).

_____ [4]. "The Mower to the Glo-Worms," Expl 18 (May,
    1960).

_____ [5]. "The Undying Will of Tennyson's Ulysses,"
    VP 2 (Spr., 1964).

MIYOSHI, Masao. "Mill and 'Pauline': The Myth and Some
    Facts," VS 9 (Dec., 1965).

MOEWS, Daniel D. "The 'Prologue' to In Memoriam: A
    Commentary on Lines 5, 17, and 32," VP 6 (Sum.,
    1968).

MOGAN, Joseph J., Jr. "Further Aspects of Mutability in
    Chaucer's Troilus," PLL 1 (Wint., 1965).

MOLDENHAUER, Joseph J. "The Voices of Seduction in
    'To His Coy Mistress': A Rhetorical Analysis,"
    TSLL 10 (Sum., 1968).

MOLLENKOTT, Virginia R. "The Many and the One in
    George Herbert's 'Providence'," CLAJ 10 (Sept., 1966).

MONTAG, George E. [1]. "Hopkins' 'God's Grandeur'
    and 'The Ooze of Oil Crushed'," VP 1 (Nov., 1963).

_____ [2]. " 'The Windhover': Crucifixion and Redemp-
    tion," VP 3 (Spr., 1965).

MONTAGUE, Gene [1]. "Dylan Thomas and Nightwood,"
    SR 76 (Sum., 1968).

_____ [2]. "To-Day, This Insect," Expl 19 (Dec., 1960).

MONTEIRO, George [1]. "The Apostasy and Death of St.
    Praxed's Bishop," VP 8 (Aut., 1970).

_____ [2]. "Birches in Winter: Notes on Thoreau and
    Frost," CLAJ 12 (Dec., 1968).

_____ [3]. "Browning's 'My Last Duchess'," VP 1 (Aug.,
    1963).

_____ [4]. "Gerontion," Expl 18 (Feb., 1960).

_____ [5]. "On His Blindness," Expl 24 (Apr., 1966).

_____ [6]. "Meditation--Eight," Expl 27 (Feb., 1969).

_____ [7]. "A Proposal for Settling the Grammarian's Estate," VP 3 (Aut., 1965).

_____ [8]. "Traditional Ideas in Dickinson's 'I Felt a Funeral in My Brain'," MLN 75 (Dec., 1960).

MONTGOMERY, Robert L, Jr., "The Province of Allegory in George Herbert's Verse," TSLL 1 (Wint., 1960).

MOODY, Peter R. "A Lecture Upon a Shadow," Expl 20 (Mar., 1962).

MOORE, Carlisle. "Faith, Doubt and Mystical Experience in 'In Memoriam'," VS 7 (Dec., 1963).

MOORE, Rayburn S. "Thomas Dunn English, a Forgotten Contributor to the Development of Negro Dialect Verse in the 1870's," AL 33 (Mar., 1961).

MOORE, S. C. "Ballet," Expl 23 (Oct., 1964).

MOORE, Thomas V. "Donne's Use of Uncertainty as a Vital Force in 'Satyre III'," MP 67 (Aug., 1969).

MORRIS, Charles R. "Richard Cory," Expl 23 (Mar., 1965).

MORRIS, John W. "The Germ of Meredith's 'Lucifer in Starlight'," VP 1 (Jan., 1963).

MORRIS, William E. "The Sunne Rising," Expl 23 (Feb., 1965).

MORSE, Samuel French. "Wallace Stevens: The Poet and the Critics," SoR 1 (Spr., 1965).

MORTON, Richard. "Notes on the Imagery of Dylan Thomas," ES 43 (June, 1962).

MOSKOVIT, Leonard A. "Pope and the Tradition of the Neoclassical Imitation," SEL 8 (Sum., 1968).

MOYNIHAN, William T. "Dylan Thomas' 'Hewn Voice'," TSLL 1 (Aut., 1959).

MUDFORD, P. G.   "The Artistic Consistency of Browning's
    In a Balcony," VP 7 (Spr., 1969).

MUELLER, William R.   "Donne's Adulterous Female Town,"
    MLN 76 (Apr., 1961).

MUENCH, Sister Mary de Lourdes.   "Taking the Duchess
    Off the Wall," EJ 57 (Feb., 1968).

MULDROW, George M. [1].   "The Beginning of Adam's Re-
    pentence," PQ 46 (Apr., 1967).

_____ [2].   "An Irony in Paradise Regained," PLL 3
    (Fall, 1967).

MULLICAN, James S. [1].   "Praise It--'Tis Dead," Expl
    27 (Apr., 1969).

_____ [2].   "Water Makes Many Beds," Expl 27 (Nov., 1968).

MURPHY, Michael W. [1].   "Do Not Go Gentle Into That Good
    Night," Expl 28 (Feb., 1970).

_____ [2].   "Violent Imagery in the Poetry of Gerard Manley
    Hopkins," VP 7 (Spr., 1969).

MURRAY, E. B.   " 'Effective Affinity' in The Revolt of
    Islam," JEGP 67 (Oct., 1968).

MUSACCHIO, George L.   "A Note on the Fire-Rose Synthesis of
    T. S. Eliot's Four Quartets," ES 45 (June, 1964).

MYERS, James Phares, Jr.   " 'This Curious Frame': Chap-
    man's 'Ovid's Banquet of Sense'," SP 65 (Apr., 1968).

MYERS, Neil.   "Williams' Imitation of Nature in 'The
    Desert Music'," Criticism 12 (Wint., 1970).

NABHOLTZ, John R.   "Wordsworth's Interest in Landscape
    Design and an Inscription Poem of 1800," PLL 2
    (Sum., 1966).

NARVESON, Robert.   "On Frost's 'The Wood-Pile'," EJ 57
    (Jan., 1968).

NASSAR, Eugene. "Wallace Stevens: 'Peter Quince at the
    Clavier'," CE 26 (Apr., 1965).

NATHANSON, Leonard. "My Last Duchess," Expl 19 (June, 1961).

NATTERSTAD, J. H. "Cap and Bells, " Expl 25 (May, 1967).

NELSON, Charles Edwin. "Role-Playing in The Ring and the Book," VP 4 (Spr. , 1966).

NELSON, Harland S. "Stephen Crane's Achievement as a Poet," TSLL 4 (Wint. , 1963).

NELSON, James G. "Aesthetic Experience and Rossetti's 'My Sister's Sleep'," VP 7 (Sum. , 1969).

NELSON, Phyllis E. "Peter Quince at the Clavier," Expl 24 (Feb. , 1966).

NEMEROV, Howard. "Poems of Darkness and a Specialized Light," SR 71 (Wint. , 1963).

NEUMEYER, Peter F. "The Transfiguring Vision," VP 3 (Aut. , 1965).

NEVO, Ruth. "Marvell's 'Songs of Innocence and Experience'," SEL 5 (Wint. , 1965).

NEWELL, Kenneth B. [1]. "Aurora Is the Effort," Expl 20 (Sept. , 1961).

_____ [2]. "We Should Not Mind So Small a Flower," Expl 19 (June, 1961).

NICKERSON, Charles C. "W. H. Mallock's Contributions to 'The Miscellany'," VS 6 (Dec. , 1962).

NIEMAN, Lawrence J. "The Nature of the Temptations in Paradise Regained, Books I and II," UR 34 (Dec. , 1967).

NILSON, Helge Normann. "Notes on the Theme of Love in the Later Poetry of William Carlos Williams," ES 50 (June, 1969).

NIMS, John Frederick. "The Greatest English Lyric?-- A New Reading of Joe E. Skilmer's 'Therese'," CE 29 (Jan. , 1968).

NIST, John [1]. "Dylan Thomas: 'Perfection of the Work'," ArQ 17 (Sum. , 1961).

NIST, John [2]. "Gerard Manley Hopkins and Textural In-
    tensity: A Linguistic Analysis," CE 22 (Apr., 1961).

NITCHIE, George W. "Eliot's Borrowing: A Note," MR 6
    (Wint.-Spr., 1965).

NORMAN, Sylva. "Twentieth-Century Theories on Shelley,"
    TSLL 9 (Sum., 1967).

NORTH, J. D. "Kalenderes Enlumyned Ben They, Some
    Astronomical Themes in Chaucer," RES 20, Pt. I
    (May, 1969); Pt. II (Aug., 1969).

O'DEA, Richard J. " 'The Loss of the Eurydice': A Pos-
    sible Key to the Reading of Hopkins," VP 4 (Aut.,
    1966).

OETGEN, John. "A Christmas Carol," Expl 19 (Oct., 1960).

OGGEL, L. T. "A Fable for Critics," Expl 27 (Apr., 1969).

O'HARA, J. D. "Ambiguity and Assertion in Wordsworth's
    'Elegiac Stanzas'," PQ 47 (Jan., 1968).

OHLIN, Peter. " 'Cadenus and Vanessa': Reason and Pas-
    sion," SEL 4 (Sum., 1964).

OMANS, Glen. "Browning's 'Fra Lippo Lippi,' A Trans-
    cendentalist Monk," VP 7 (Sum., 1969).

ORANGE, Linwood E. "Sensual Beauty in Book I of The
    Faerie Queene," JEGP 61 (July, 1962).

ORMEROD, David [1]. "The Central Image in Dylan Thomas'
    'Over Sir John's Hill'," ES 49 (Oct., 1968).

_____ [2]. "Invitation to Juno," Expl 25 (Oct., 1966).

_____ [3]. "Twenty-Four Years," Expl 22 (May, 1964).

OSBORN, Scott C. "Blue Girls," Expl 21 (Nov., 1962).

OSBORNE, William R. [1]. "The Bigness of Cannon (La-
    Guerre, I)," Expl 24 (Nov., 1965).

_____ [2]. "Blue Girls," Expl 19 (May, 1961).

_____ [3]. "The Oven Bird," Expl 26 (Feb., 1968).

OSTROFF, Anthony. (ed.) [1]. The Contemporary Poet as
    Artist and Critic; Eight Symposia. Boston: Little,
    Brown, 1964.

_____ [2]. "A Symposium on W. H. Auden's 'A Change of
    Air'," KR 26 (Wint., 1964).

*OTTEN, Charlotte. "LeRoi Jones: Napalm Poet," ConP 3
    no. 1 (1970).

OWEN, Charles A., Jr. [1]. "The Problem of Free Will
    in Chaucer's Narrative," PQ 46 (Oct., 1967).

_____ [2]. "Structure in The Ancient Mariner," CE 23
    (Jan., 1962).

OWER, John. "News for the Delphic Oracle," Expl 28
    (Sept., 1969).

PAFFARD, M. K. "The Extasie," Expl 22 (Oct., 1963).

PAFFORD, Ward. "Coleridge's Wedding-Guest," SP 60
    (Oct., 1963).

PARFITT, G. A. E. "Ethical Thought and Ben Jonson's
    Poetry," SEL 9 (Wint., 1969).

PARIS, Bernard J. "George Eliot's Unpublished Poetry,"
    SP 56 (July, 1959).

PARISH, John E. [1]. "No. 14 of Donne's 'Holy Sonnets',"
    CE 24 (Jan., 1963).

_____ [2]. "Paradise Lost, VI, 362-368," Expl 24 (Oct.,
    1965).

_____ [3]. "The Rehabilitation of Eben Flood," EJ 55
    (Sept., 1966).

_____ [4]. "What If This Present Were the World's
    Last Night?" Expl 22 (Nov., 1963).

PARKER, John W. "Toward an Appraisal of Benjamin
    Brawley's Poetry," CLAJ 6 (Sept., 1962).

PARKIN, Rebecca Price [1].   "Certain Difficulties in Read-
     ing Marianne Moore: Exemplified in Her 'Apparition
     of Splendor'," PMLA 81 (June, 1966).

_____ [2].   "Christopher Smart's Sacramental Cat,"
     TSLL 11 (Fall, 1969).

_____ [3].   "The Facsimile of Immediacy in W. H.
     Auden's 'In Praise of Limestone'," TSLL 7 (Aut.,
     1965).

_____ [4].   "Some Characteristics of Marianne Moore's
     Humor," CE 27 (Feb., 1966).

PARKINSON, Thomas.   "The Poetry of Gary Snyder,"
     SoR 4 (Sum., 1968).

PARSONS, Coleman O.   "Tygers Before Blake," SEL 8
     (Aut., 1968).

PARSONS, D. S. J.   "Night of Dark Intent," PLL 6 (Spr.,
     1970).

PARSONS, Thornton H. [1].   "The Indefatigable Casuist," UR
     30 (Oct., 1963).

_____ [2].   "Ransom the Revisionist," SoR 2 (Spr.,
     1966).

PATRICK, J. Max.   "The Unfortunate Lover," Expl 20
     (Apr., 1962).

PATRIDES, C. A. [1].   "The Godhead in Paradise Lost:
     Dogma or Drama?" JEGP 64 (Jan., 1965).

_____ [2].   "Paradise Lost and the Theory of Accommo-
     dation," TSLL 5 (Spr., 1963).

PATTERSON, Rebecca.   "Emily Dickinson's Geography:
     Latin America," PLL 5 (Fall, 1969).

PAYNE, Michael.   "William C. Williams Without Livery,"
     UR 32 (Dec., 1965).

PEARCE, Roy Harvey.   "A Small Crux in Allen Tate's
     'Death of Little Boys': Postscript," MLN 75 (Mar.,
     1960).

PEARSALL, Derek. "The Assembly of Ladies and Generydes,"
RES 12 (Aug., 1961).

PEARSALL, Robert Brainard [1]. "Housman Versus Vaughan
Williams: 'Is My Team Plowing'," VP 4 (Wint.,
1966).

_____[2]. "Housman's 'He, Standing Hushed'," VP 7
(Spr., 1969).

PEBWORTH, Ted-Larry. "The Problem of Restagnates in
Henry Vaughan's 'The Water-Fall'," PLL 3 (Sum.,
1967).

PEBWORTH, Ted-Larry and Jay Claude SUMMERS. "The
Feet of People Walking Home," Expl 27 (May, 1969).

PECHEUX, Mother Mary Christopher, O.S.U. [1]. "Abraham, Adam, and the Theme of Exile in Paradise Lost,"
PMLA 80 (Sept., 1965).

_____[2]. "The Conclusion of Book VI of Paradise Lost,"
SEL 3 (Wint., 1963).

PECK, Virginia L. [1]. "I Knew a Woman," Expl 22 (Apr.,
1964).

_____[2]. "Prelude to an Evening," Expl 20 (Jan.,
1962).

PECKHAM, Morse. "Historiography and The Ring and the
Book," VP 6 (Aut.-Wint., 1968).

PENDEXTER, Hugh, III. "God's Grandeur," Expl 23 (Sept.,
1964).

PENNER, Allen Richard. "Edward Taylor's Meditation One,"
AL 39 (May, 1967).

PEQUIGNEY, Joseph. "Milton's Sonnet XIX Reconsidered,"
TSLL 8 (Wint., 1967).

PERKUS, Gerald H. "Toward Disengagement: A Neglected
Early Meredith Manuscript Poem," VP 8 (Aut., 1970).

PERLOFF, Marjorie [1]. " 'Another Emblem There': Theme
and Convention in Yeats's 'Coole Park and Ballylee,
1931'," JEGP 69 (Jan., 1970).

PERLOFF, Marjorie [2].   "Irony in Wallace Stevens's The Rock," AL 36 (Nov., 1964).

_____ [3].   "Yeats and the Occasional Poem: 'Easter 1916'," PLL 4 (Sum., 1968).

PERRINE, Laurence [1].   "Acquainted with the Night," Expl 25 (Feb., 1967).

_____ [2].   "An Acre of Grass," Expl 22 (Apr., 1964).

_____ [3].   "The Bishop Orders His Tomb at Saint Praxed's Church," Expl 24 (Oct., 1965).

_____ [4].   "Browning's 'Caliban Upon Setebos': A Reply," VP 2 (Spr., 1964).

_____ [5].   "Browning's 'Too Late': A Reinterpretation," VP 7 (Wint., 1969).

_____ [6].   "Especially When the October Wind," Expl 21 (Sept., 1962).

_____ [7].   "Go West Young Man," Expl 28 (Mar., 1970).

_____ [8].   "Thomas Hardy's 'God-Forgotten'," VP 6 (Sum., 1968).

_____ [9].   "The Importance of Tone in the Interpretation of Literature," CE 24 (Feb., 1963).

_____ [10].   "A Lecture Upon the Shadow," Expl 21 (Jan., 1963).

_____ [11].   "Morris's Guenevere: An Interpretation," PQ 39 (Apr., 1960).

_____ [12].   "My Life Had Stood--A Loaded Gun," Expl 21 (Nov., 1962).

_____ [13].   " 'Peter Quince at the Clavier': A Protest," CE 27 (Feb., 1966).

_____ [14].   "Poem in October," Expl 27 (Feb., 1969).

_____ [15].   "The Road Not Taken," Expl 19 (Feb., 1961).

_____ [16]. "The Rose Family," Expl 26 (Jan., 1968).

_____ [17]. "Tenzone," Expl 28 (May, 1970).

_____ [18]. "When Does Hope Mean Doubt? The Tone of 'Crossing the Bar'," VP (Spr., 1966).

PERRINE, Laurence and Margaret M. BLUM. "The Draft Horse," Expl 24 (May, 1966).

PETERS, Robert. "The Truth of Frost's 'Directive'," MLN 75 (Jan., 1960).

PETERS, Robert L. [1]. "Algernon Charles Swinburne and the Use of Integral Detail," VS 5 (June, 1962).

_____ [2]. "The Salome of Arthur Symons and Aubrey Beardsley," Criticism 2 (Spr., 1960).

PETERSON, R. G. "Larger Manners and Events: Sallust and Virgil in 'Absalom and Achitophel'," PMLA 82 (May, 1967).

PETRONELLA, Vincent F. "St. Erkenwald: Style as the Vehicle for Meaning," JEGP 66 (Oct, 1967).

PETTIGREW, John. "Tennyson's 'Ulysses': A Reconciliation of Opposites," VP 1 (Jan., 1963).

PETTIT, Henry [1]. "Collins's 'Ode to Evening' and the Critics," SEL 4 (Sum., 1964).

_____ [2]. "The Occasion of Young's 'Night Thoughts'," ES 50 (1969 Anglo-American Suppl.).

PHEIFER, J. D. "The Seafarer, 53-55," RES 16 (Aug., 1965).

PHILLIPS, Linus L. and Mrs. William W. DEATON. "The Locust Tree in Flower," Expl 26 (Nov., 1967).

PHILLIPS, Norma. "Observations on the Derivative Method of Skelton's Realism," JEGP 65 (Jan., 1966).

PHILLIPS, Robert S. "Sailing to Byzantium," Expl 22 (Oct., 1963).

PHIPPS, Charles T., S.J. [1]. "The Bishop as Bishop:
     Clerical Motif and Meaning in 'The Bishop Orders his
     Tomb at St. Praxed's Church'," VP 8 (Aut., 1970).

_____ [2]. "The Monsignor in Pippa Passes: Browning's
     First Clerical Character," VP 7 (Spr., 1969).

PICKARD, John B. "Imagistic and Structural Unity in
     'Snow-Bound'," CE 21 (Mar., 1960).

PIERSON, Robert M. "The Meter of 'The Listeners',"
     ES 45 (Oct., 1964).

PINTO, V. de S. "Poet without a Mask," CritQ 3 (Spr.,
     1961).

PIPER, William Bowman [1]. "The Conversational Poetry
     of Pope," SEL 10 (Sum., 1970).

_____ [2]. "Spenser's 'Lyke as a Huntsman'," CE 22
     (Mar., 1961).

PIPES, B. N., Jr. "A Slight Meteorological Disturbance:
     The Last Two Stanzas of Tennyson's 'The Poet',"
     VP 1 (Jan., 1963).

PITTOCK, Malcolm. "Chaucer: The Complaint Unto Pity,"
     Criticism 1 (Spr., 1959).

PITTS, Arthur W., Jr. [1]. "Channel Firing," Expl 26
     (Nov., 1967).

_____ [2]. "The Wreck of the Deutschland," Expl 24
     (Sept., 1965).

PITTS, Gordon. "Housman's 'Be Still, My Soul'," VP 3
     (Spr., 1965).

PLUNKETT, P. M. [1]. "Abt Vogler," Expl 25 (Oct.,
     1966).

_____ [2]. "Modern Love," Expl 28 (Jan., 1970).

POMEROY, Elizabeth. "The Sun Rising," Expl 27 (Sept.,
     1968).

*POOL, Rosey E. "Robert Hayden: Poet Laureate," NegroD
     15 (June, 1966).

PORTER, David T. "Emily Dickinson: The Formative
    Years," MR 6 (Spr. -Sum., 1965).

PORTER, M. Gilbert. "Narrative Stance in Four Quartets:
    Choreography and Commentary," UR 36 (Oct., 1969).

POSTON, Lawrence, III [1]. "The Argument of the Geraint-
    Enid Books in Idylls of the King," VP 2 (Aut., 1964).

_____ [2]. " 'Pelleas and Ettarre': Tennyson's 'Troilus', "
    VP 4 (Sum., 1966).

_____ [3]. "The Two Provinces of Tennyson's 'Idylls', "
    Criticism 9 (Fall, 1967).

POTTER, James L. "The 'Destined Pattern' of Spender's
    'Express', " CE 27 (Feb., 1966).

POULIN, A., Jr. "Voyages II," Expl 28 (Oct., 1969).

POWELL, G. E. "Robert Lowell and Theodore Roethke:
    Two Kinds of Knowing," SoR 3 (Wint., 1967).

POWERS, Richard Gid. "I Will Be," Expl 28 (Feb., 1970).

PRESLEY, James [1]. "The American Dream of Langston
    Hughes," SouthwestR 48 (Aut., 1963).

_____ [2]. "Langston Hughes: A Personal Farewell, "
    SouthwestR 54 (Wint., 1969).

PRESS, John [1]. "Edward Lowbury," SoR 6 (Spr., 1970).

_____ [2]. "Ted Walker, Seamus Heany and Kenneth
    White: Three New Poets, " SoR 5 (Sum., 1969).

PREVITE-ORTON, Charles Williams. Political Satire in
    English Poetry. New York: Haskell House, 1966.

PREYER, Robert. "Alfred Tennyson: The Poetry and
    Politics of Conservative Vision, " VS 9 (June, 1966).

PROFFITT, Bessie. "Political Satire in Dryden's 'Alex-
    ander's Feast', " TSLL 11 (Wint., 1970).

PROSKY, Murray. "Aire and Angels," Expl 27 (Dec., 1968).

PURDUM, Richard. "Shakespeare's Sonnet 128, " JEGP 63

(Apr., 1964).

PUTZEL, Max.   "Astrophel and Stella, IX," Expl 19 (Jan.,
      1961).

QUINN, Dennis.   "Donne's Anniversaries as Celebration,"
      SEL 9 (Wint., 1969).

RABEN, Joseph [1].   "Coleridge as the Prototype of the
      Poet in Shelley's Alastor," RES 17 (Aug., 1966).

_____ [2].   "Shelley's 'Invocation to Misery': An Ex-
      panded Text," JEGP 65 (Jan., 1966).

_____ [3].   "Shelley's 'The Boat on the Serchio': The
      Evidence of the Manuscript," PQ 46 (Jan., 1967).

RACIN, John.   " 'Dover Beach' and the Structure of
      Meditation," VP 8 (Spr., 1970).

RACKIN, Phyllis [1].   "Poetry without Paradox: Jonson's
      'Hymne' to Cynthia," Criticism 4 (Sum., 1962).

_____ [2].   "Recent Misreadings of 'Break, Break,
      Break' and Their Implications for Poetic Theory,"
      JEGP 65 (Apr., 1966).

RADER, Ralph Wilson.   "The Composition of Tennyson's
      'Maud'," MP 59 (May, 1962).

RADLEY, Virginia L.   " 'Christabel': Directions Old and
      New," SEL 4 (Aut., 1964).

RAINE, Kathleen [1].   "Blake's Debt to Antiquity," SR 71
      (Sum., 1963).

_____ [2].   "David Gascoyne and the Prophetic Role," SR
      75 (Spr., 1967).

_____ [3].   "A Defense of Shelley's Poetry," SoR 3
      (Aut., 1967).

_____ [4].   "Traditional Symbolism in Kubla Khan," SR
      72 (Aut., 1964).

RAJAN, B. [1].   " 'Lycidas': The Shattering of the Leaves,"

SP 64 (Jan., 1967).

_____ [2]. "The Overwhelming Questions," SR 74 (Wint., 1966).

RAMSEY, Paul. "Yvor Winters, Some Abstractions Against Abstractions," SR 73 (Sum., 1965).

RANSOM, John Crowe [1]. "Gerontion," SR 74 (Spr., 1966).

_____ [2]. " 'Prelude to an Evening,' a Poem Revised and Explicated," KR 25 (Wint., 1963).

_____ [3]. "The Rugged Way of Genius," SoR 3 (Spr., 1967).

_____ [4]. "Thomas Hardy's Poems, and the Religious Difficulties of a Naturalist," KR 22 (Spr., 1960).

RAPIN, Rene [1]. "The Nymph Complaining for the Death of her Faun," Expl 28 (Apr., 1970).

_____ [2]. "October, 1803," Expl 24 (Sept., 1965).

RAUBER, D. F. "Milton's Sonnet XI--'I Did But Prompt ...'," PQ 49 (Oct., 1970).

RAY, David. "The Irony of E. E. Cummings," CE 23 (Jan., 1962).

RAY, Linda Lee. "Callicles on Etna: The Other Mask," VP 7 (Wint., 1969).

RAYMOND, Meredith B. [1]. "The Arthurian Group in The Defence of Guenevere and Other Poems," VP 4 (Sum., 1966).

_____ [2]. "Swinburne Among the Nightingales," VP 6 (Sum., 1968).

RAYMOND, William O. "The Pope in The Ring and The Book," VP 6 (Aut.-Wint., 1968).

REA, J. "Persephone in 'Corinna's Going a-Maying'," CE 26 (Apr., 1965).

REAMER, Owen J. "Spenser's Debt to Marot--Re-examined,"
    TSLL 10 (Wint., 1969).

REED, John R. [1]. "Matthew Arnold and the Soul's Hori-
    zons," VP 8 (Spr., 1970).

_____ [2]. "Swinburne's Tristram of Lyonesse: The Poet-
    Lover's Song of Love," VP 4 (Spr., 1966).

REED, Mark L. "More on the Wordsworth Poem," CE 28
    (Oct., 1966).

REED, Victor. "High Talk," Expl 26 (Feb., 1968).

REEDY, Gerard, S.J. "Housman's Use of Classical Con-
    vention," VP 6 (Spr., 1968).

REES, Joan. " 'But for Such Faith': A Shelley Crux," RES
    15 (May, 1964).

REESE, Jack E. "Sound and Sense: The Teaching of Pro-
    sody," CE 27 (Feb., 1966).

REICHERT, John F. " 'Grongar Hill': Its Origin and De-
    velopment," PLL 5 (Spr., 1969).

REICHERTZ, Ronald. "Where Knock Is Wide Open," Expl
    26 (Dec., 1967).

REID, B. L. [1]. "The House of Yeats," HudR 18 (Aut.,
    1965).

_____ [2]. "Keats and the Heart's Hornbook," MR 2
    (Spr., 1961).

REIMAN, Donald H. [1]. "Hopkins' 'Ooze of Oil' Rises
    Again," VP 4 (Wint., 1966).

_____ [2]. "Structure, Symbol and Theme in 'Lines Writ-
    ten Among Euganean Hills'," PMLA 77 (Sept., 1962).

_____ [3]. "Shelley's 'The Triumph of Life': The Bio-
    graphical Problem," PMLA 78 (Dec., 1963).

*REIMHERR, Beulah. "Race Consciousness in CC's Poetry,"
    SUS 7 (1963).

REIN, David M. "Introduction," Expl 20 (Sept., 1961).

REISS, Edmund. "A Critical Approach to the Middle English Lyric," CE 27 (Feb., 1966).

REITEN, Sister Paula, O.S.B. "The Snow-Storm," Expl 22 (Jan., 1964).

REITER, Robert E. [1]. "George Herbert's 'Anagram': A Reply to Professor Leiter," CE 28 (Oct., 1966).

_____ [2]. "Paradise Lost, XII," Expl 28 (Sept., 1969).

RENICK, Sue. "The Fish," Expl 21 (Sept., 1962).

REPLOGLE, Justin. "The Gang Myth in Auden's Early Poetry," JEGP 61 (July, 1962).

REVARD, Stella Purce [1]. "The Dramatic Function of the Son in Paradise Lost: A Commentary on Milton's 'Trinitarianism'," JEGP 66 (Jan., 1967).

_____ [2]. "Milton's Critique of Heroic Warfare in Paradise Lost V and VI," SEL 7 (Wint., 1967).

RICH, Adrienne. "Reflections on Lawrence," Poetry 106 (June, 1965).

RICHARDSON, Robert D., Jr. "The Puritan Poetry of Anne Bradstreet," TSLL 9 (Aut., 1967).

RICKEY, Mary Ellen [1]. "Herbert's Technical Development," JEGP 62 (Oct., 1963).

_____ [2]. "The Relique," Expl 22 (Mar., 1964).

RICKS, Christopher. "Over-Emphasis in 'Paradise Regained'," MLN 76 (Dec., 1961).

RIDDEL, Joseph N. [1]. "Cold and Heat in 'Adonais'," MLN 76 (Feb., 1961).

_____ [2]. "Stevens' 'Peter Quince at the Clavier'," CE 23 (Jan., 1962).

_____ [3]. "Wallace Stevens' 'Visibility of Thought'," PMLA 77 (Sept., 1962).

RIDENOUR, George M. "The Mode of Byron's 'Don Juan',"
    PMLA 79 (Sept., 1964).

RIDLON, Harold G. "The Function of the 'Infant-Ey' in
    Traherne's Poetry," SP 61 (Oct., 1964).

RIGGS, Edith. "L'Allegro," Expl 23 (Feb., 1965).

RINGE, Donald A. "Sound Imagery in Whittier's Snow-
    Bound," PLL 5 (Spr., 1969).

ROBERTS, John R. [1]. "Donne's Satyre III Reconsidered,"
    CLAJ 12 (Dec., 1968).

_____ [2]. "The Influence of The Spiritual Exercises of
    St. Ignatius on the Nativity Poems of Robert Southwell,"
    JEGP 59 (July, 1960).

ROBERTS, Philip. "Swift, Queen Anne, and The Windsor
    Prophecy," PQ 49 (Apr., 1970).

ROBERTS, Robert P. [1]. "The Boethian God and the Audi-
    ence of the Troilus," JEGP 69 (July, 1970).

_____ [2]. "The Central Episode in Chaucer's Troilus,"
    PMLA 77 (Sept., 1962).

ROBERTSON, Duncan. "The Wanderer," Expl 28 (Apr.,
    1970).

ROBEY, Cora. "All in Green My Love Went Riding,"
    Expl 27 (Sept., 1968).

ROBINS, H. F. "Satan's Journey: Direction in Paradise
    Lost," JEGP 60 (Oct., 1961).

ROBINSON, Fred C. [1]. " 'Strength Stoops unto the Grave':
    Nashe's Adieu, Farewell Earth's Bliss, L. 22," PLL 6
    (Wint., 1970).

_____ [2]. "Verb Tense in Blake's 'The Tyger'," PMLA
    79 (Dec., 1964).

ROBINSON, William H. "Phillis Wheatley: Colonial
    Quandary," CLAJ 9 (Sept., 1965).

ROBSON, W. W. "The Achievement of Robert Frost," SoR
    2 (Aut., 1966).

ROETHKE, Theodore. "The Poetry of Louise Bogan,"
     CritQ 3 (Sum., 1961).

ROPER, Alan H. "Boethius and the Three Fates of Beowulf,"
     PQ 41 (Apr., 1962).

ROSCELLI, William. "The Metaphysical Milton," TSLL 8
     (Wint., 1967).

ROSE, Edgar Smith. "The Anatomy of Imagination," CE 27
     (Feb., 1966).

ROSE, Edward J. [1]. "Blake's Fourfold Art," PQ 49 (July,
     1970).

_____ [2]. "Blake's Hand: Symbol and Design in Jerusa-
     lem," TSLL 6 (Spr., 1964).

_____ [3]. "The Symbolism of the Opened Center and
     Poetic Theory in Blake's 'Jerusalem'," SEL 5 (Aut.,
     1965).

_____ [4]. "To the Accuser of This World," Expl 22
     (Jan., 1964).

_____ [5]. "Visionary Forms Dramatic: Grammatical and
     Iconographical Movement in Blake's Verse and Designs,"
     Criticism 8 (Spr., 1966).

ROSENBAUM, S. P. "Among School Children, V," Expl 23
     (Oct., 1964).

ROSENBERG, Bruce A. [1]. " 'Annus Mirabilis' Distilled,"
     PMLA 79 (June, 1964).

_____ [2]. "Irish Folklore and 'The Song of Wandering
     Aengus'," PQ 46 (Oct., 1967).

_____ [3]. "To Juan at the Winter Solstice," Expl 21
     (Sept., 1962).

ROSENBERRY, Edward H. "Toward Notes for 'Stopping by
     Woods': Some Classical Analogs," CE 24 (Apr., 1963).

ROSENHEIM, Edward W., Jr. "The Elegiac Act: Auden's 'In
     Memory of W. B. Yeats'," CE 27 (Feb., 1966).

ROSENTHAL, Macha Louis [1]. The New Poets; American

and British Poetry Since World War II.   New York:
Oxford University Press, 1967.

ROSENTHAL, Macha Louis [2]. "Sea Surface Full of Clouds,"
Expl 19 (Mar., 1961).

ROSS, Robert H.   " 'The Marshes of Glynn': A Study in
Symbolic Obscurity," AL 32 (Jan., 1961).

ROSSKY, William.   "A Clock Stopped," Expl 22 (Sept., 1963).

ROSTVIG, Maren-Sofie [1].   "Syncretistic Imagery and the
Unity of Vaughan's 'The World'," PLL 5 (Fall, 1969).

_____ [2].   " 'Upon Appleton House' and the Universal
History of Man," ES 42 (Dec., 1961).

ROTHWELL, Kenneth S.   "Another View of 'The Fredoniad':
A Plea for Method," AL 33 (Nov., 1961).

ROWE, Karen E.   "A Biblical Illumination of Taylorian Art,"
AL 40 (Nov., 1968).

ROWELL, Charles H.   "Coleridge's Symbolic Albatross,"
CLAJ 6 (Dec., 1962).

RUDRUM, Alan.   "The Influence of Alchemy in the Poems of
Henry Vaughan," PQ 49 (Oct., 1970).

RULAND, Richard.   "Longfellow and the Modern Reader,"
EJ 55 (Sept., 1966).

RUOTOLO, Lucio P.   "Three Prelude Events: The Growth
of a Poet's Faith," CE 26 (Apr., 1965).

RUSCHE, Harry.   "Pride, Humility, and Grace in Book I of
The Faerie Queene," SEL 7 (Wint., 1967).

RUSSELL, Gene.   "Upon Wedlock, and Death of Children,"
Expl 27 (May, 1969).

RUSSELL, J. C. "The Patrons of The Owl and the Nightingale," PQ 48 (Apr., 1969).

RUSSELL, Peter.   "Kathleen Raine's New Poems," SoR 2
(Sum., 1966).

RUSSELL, Robert.   "The Leg in the Subway," Expl 19 (Dec.,

1960).

RUTHERFORD, Andrew. "The Influence of Hobhouse on Childe
    Harold's Pilgrimage, Canto IV," RES 12 (Nov., 1961).

RYALS, Clyde de L. [1]. "Arnold's Balder Dead," VP 4
    (Spr., 1966).

_____ [2]. "An Interpretation of Clough's 'Dipsychus',"
    VP 1 (Aug., 1963).

_____ [3]. "The Narrative Unity of The House of Life,"
    JEGP 69 (Jan., 1970).

_____ [4]. "The 'Weird Seizures' in The Princess,"
    TSLL 4 (Sum., 1962).

RYAN, Alvan S. "Frost and Emerson: Voice and Vision,"
    MR 1 (Fall, 1959).

RYKEN, Leland [1]. "The Drama of Choice in Sidney's
    Astrophel and Stella," JEGP 68 (Oct., 1969).

_____ [2]. "Leave Me, O Love Which Reachest But to
    Dust," Expl 26 (Sept., 1967).

SACKTON, Alexander. "Donne and the Privacy of Verse,"
    SEL 7 (Wint., 1967).

ST. GEORGE, Priscilla P. "The Styles of Good and Evil
    in 'The Sensitive Plant'," JEGP 64 (July, 1965).

SALERNO, Nicholas A. [1]. "Andrew Marvell and the Furor
    Hortensis," SEL 8 (Wint., 1968).

_____ [2]. "The Unfortunate Lover," Expl 18 (Apr.,
    1960).

SAMUELS, Charles Thomas. "The Tragic Vision in Para-
    dise Lost," UR 27 (Oct., 1960).

SAN JUAN, E., Jr. [1]. "The Anti-Poetry of Jonathan
    Swift," PQ 44 (July, 1965).

_____ [2]. "Integrity of Composition in the Poems of
    Ernest Hemingway," UR 32 (Oct., 1965).

SANDBANK, S. "Henry Vaughan's Apology for Darkness,"
    SEL 7 (Wint., 1967).

SANDERS, Barry [1]. "All in Green Went My Love Riding,"
    Expl 25 (Nov., 1966).

_____ [2]. "Love's Crack-Up: The House of Fame,"
    PLL 3 (Suppl., Sum., 1967).

SANDERS, Charles. "The Carkanet," Expl 23 (Nov., 1964).

SANDERS, Paul. "The Magi," Expl 25 (Mar., 1967).

SANDSTROM, Glenn. " 'James Lee's Wife'--and Browning's, "
    VP 4 (Aut., 1966).

SANKEY, Benjamin. "Coleridge and the Visible World,"
    TSLL 6 (Spr., 1964).

SATTERFIELD, Leon. "The Prelude," Expl 23 (Oct., 1964).

SATTERWHITE, J. N. "A Healthy Spot," Expl 21 (Mar.,
    1963).

SAUL, George Brandon [1]. "Coda: The Verse of Yeats's
    Last Five Years," ArQ 17 (Spr., 1961).

_____ [2]. "A Frenzy of Concentration: Yeats's Verse
    from Responsibilities to The King of the Great Clock
    Tower," ArQ (Sum., 1964).

SCHAAR, Claes. "An Italian Analogue of Shakespeare's
    Sonnet LXXX, " ES 43 (Aug., 1962).

SCHAKEL, Peter J. "Verses Wrote in a Lady's Ivory
    Tablebook," Expl 28 (May, 1970).

SCHELP, Hanspeter. "Wordsworth's Daffodils Influenced by
    a Wesleyan Hymn?" ES 42 (Oct., 1961).

SCHEUERLE, William H. " 'Magdalen at Michael's Gate':
    A Neglected Lyric," VP 5 (Sum., 1967).

SCHNEIDER, Elisabeth [1]. "The Windhover," Expl 18
    (Jan., 1960).

_____ [2]. " 'The Wreck of the Deutschland': A New
    Reading," PMLA 81 (Mar., 1966).

_____ [3]. "The Yachts," Expl 25 (Jan., 1967).

SCHOLL, Evelyn H. "The Eve of St. Agnes," Expl 20 (Dec., 1961).

SCHOLTEN, Martin. "The Humanism of Edwin Muir," CE 21 (Mar., 1960).

SCHONHORN, Manuel. "The Audacious Contemporaneity of Pope's Epistle to Augustus," SEL 8 (Sum., 1968).

SCHROEDER, Fred E. H. "Obscenity and Its Function in the Poetry of E. E. Cummings," SR 73 (Sum., 1965).

SCHROEDER, Mary C. "Piers Plowman: The Tearing of the Pardon," PQ 49 (Jan., 1970).

SCHROETER, James. "Shakespeare's Not 'To-Be-Pitied Lover'," CE 23 (Jan., 1962).

SCHULZ, Max F. [1]. "Keats's Timeless Order of Things: A Modern Reading of 'Ode to Psyche'," Criticism 2 (Wint., 1960).

_____ [2]. "Point of View in Blake's 'The Clod and the Pebble'," PLL 2 (Sum., 1966).

SCHWARTZ, Elias [1]. "Batter My Heart, Three Person'd God," Expl 26 (Nov., 1967).

_____ [2]. "The Dreame," Expl 19 (June, 1961).

SCHWEIK, Robert C. "The Structure of 'A Grammarian's Funeral'," CE 22 (Mar., 1961).

SCHWEITZER, Edward C. "Lycidas," Expl 28 (Oct., 1969).

SCOTT-CRAIG, T. S. K. [1]. "Paradise Lost, V, 108-109," Expl 24 (Nov., 1965).

_____ [2]. "Toy Horse," Expl 24 (Mar., 1966).

SEAMAN, J. E. "The Chivalric Cast of Milton's Epic Hero," ES 49 (Apr., 1968).

SECOR, Robert. "Upon a Spider Catching a Fly," Expl 26 (Jan., 1968).

SEE, Carolyn. "The Jazz Musician as Patchen's Hero,"
      ArQ 17 (Sum., 1961).

SEIGEL, Jules Paul. "Jenny: The Divided Sensibility of a
      Young and Thoughtful Man of the World," SEL 9 (Aut.,
      1969).

SELLERS, W. H. [1]. "New Light on Auden's 'The Orators',"
      PMLA 82 (Sept., 1967).

_____ [2]. "Wordsworth and Spender: Some Speculations
      on the Use of Rhyme," SEL 5 (Aut., 1965).

SENDRY, Joseph. " 'The Palace of Art' Revisited," VP 4
      (Sum., 1966).

SHAKESHAFT, Mary. "Nicholas Breton's 'The Passion of a
      Discontented Mind': Some New Problems," SEL 5
      (Wint., 1965).

SHAPIRO, Arnold. " 'Participate in Sludgehood': Browning's
      'Mr. Sludge,' the Critics, and the Problem of Morality,"
      PLL 5 (Spr., 1969).

SHARMA, Mohan Lal. "Hamatreya," Expl 26 (Apr., 1968).

SHARMA, Som P. "Self, Soul, and God in 'Passage to
      India'," CE 27 (Feb., 1966).

SHARPLES, Sister Marian. "Conjecturing a Date for Hopkins'
      'St. Thecla'," VP 4 (Sum., 1966).

SHAW, W. David [1]. "The Analogical Argument of Brown-
      ing's 'Saul'," VP 2 (Aut., 1964).

_____ [2]. "Character and Philosophy in 'Fra Lippo
      Lippi'," VP 2 (Spr., 1964).

_____ [3]. "The Idealist's Dilemma in Idylls of the King,"
      VP 5 (Spr., 1967).

_____ [4]. "The Transcendentalist Problem in Tennyson's
      Poetry of Debate," PQ 46 (Jan., 1967).

SHAW, W. David and Carl W. GERTLEIN. "The Aurora:
      A Spiritual Metaphor in Tennyson," VP 3 (Aut., 1965).

SHAWCROSS, John T. [1]. "The Balanced Structure of

Paradise Lost, " SP 62 (Oct., 1965).

_____ [2]. "A Nocturnall Upon S. Lucie's Day, Being
the Shortest Day, " Expl 23 (Mar., 1965).

SHEA, F. X., S.J. "Another Look at 'The Windhover', "
VP 2 (Aut., 1964).

SHEEHAN, Donald. "Wallace Stevens' Theory of Metaphor, "
PLL 2 (Wint., 1966).

SHEFFEY, Ruthe T. "From Delight to Wisdom: Thematic
Progression in the Poetry of Robert Frost, " CLAJ 8
(Sept., 1964).

SHEIDLEY, William E. "George Turberville and the Problem of Passion, " JEGP 69 (Oct., 1970).

SHERMAN, Dean. "Battle After War, " Expl 27 (Apr.,
1969).

SHMIEFSKY, Marvel [1]. " 'In Memoriam': Its Seasonal
Imagery Reconsidered, " SEL 7 (Aut., 1967).

_____ [2]. "Yeats and Browning: The Shock of Recog-
nition, " SEL 10 (Aut., 1970).

SHORT, Clarice. "Childe Roland, Pedestrian, " VP 6
(Sum., 1968).

SHUCHTER, J. D. "Upon Julia's Clothes, " Expl 25 (Nov.,
1966).

SICKELS, Eleanor M. "MacLeish and the Fortunate Fall, "
AL 35 (May, 1963).

SILVER, Carole G. " 'The Defense of Guenevere': A
Further Interpretation, " SEL 9 (Aut., 1969).

SILVERSTEIN, Norman and Arthur L. LEWIS. "Song for
Zarathustra, " Expl 21 (Oct., 1962).

SIMMONDS, James D. [1]. "Henry Vaughan's 'Fellow-
Prisoner', " ES 45 (Dec., 1964).

_____ [2]. "Vaughan's Masterpiece and its Critics: 'The
World' Revaluated, " SEL 2 (Wint., 1962).

SIMMONS, J. L. "The Picture of Little T. C. in a
    Prospect of Flowers," Expl 22 (Apr., 1964).

SIMONS, Joan O. "Teaching Symbolism in Poetry," CE 23
    (Jan., 1962).

SIMPSON, Arthur L., Jr. [1]. "Meredith's Pessimistic
    Humanism: A New Reading of 'Modern Love'," MP 67
    (May, 1970).

_____ [2]. "Why Are We by All Creatures Waited On?"
    Expl 27 (May, 1969).

SIMPSON, Evelyn M. "Two Notes on Donne," RES 16 (May,
    1965).

SINYAVSKY, Andrei. "On Robert Frost's Poems," MR 7
    (Sum., 1966).

SLACK, Robert C. "Victorian Literature as It Appears to
    Contemporary Students," CE 22 (Feb., 1961).

SLAKEY, Roger L. [1]. "The Grandeur in Hopkins' 'God's
    Grandeur'," VP 7 (Sum., 1969).

_____ [2]. "A Note on Browning's 'Rabbi Ben Ezra',"
    VP 5 (Wint., 1967).

_____ [3]. "Soliloquy of the Spanish Cloister," Expl 21
    (Jan., 1963).

SLATE, Joseph Evans. "William Carlos Williams, Hart
    Crane, and 'The Virtue of History'," TSLL 6 (Wint.,
    1965).

SLIGHTS, Camille and William SLIGHTS. "The Witch of
    Coos," Expl 27 (Feb., 1969).

SLOAN, Thomas O. "The Rhetoric in the Poetry of John
    Donne," SEL 3 (Wint., 1963).

SLOTE, Bernice [1]. "La Belle Dame as Naiad," JEGP 60
    (Jan., 1961).

_____ [2]. "Of Chapman's Homer and Other Books,"
    CE 23 (Jan., 1962).

SMAILES, T. A. "Journey of the Magi," Expl 29 (Nov., 1970).

SMITH, A. J. "Ambiguity as Poetic Shift," CritQ 4 (Spr.,
    1962).

SMITH, Barbara Herrnstein. " 'Sorrow's Mysteries':
    Keats's 'Ode on Melancholy'," SEL 6 (Aut., 1966).

SMITH, David J. "The Divine Image," Expl 25 (Apr., 1967).

SMITH, Gerald. "The Love Song of J. Alfred Prufrock,"
    Expl 21 (Oct., 1962).

SMITH, Hammett W. "Karl Jay Shapiro: A Poet of Human
    Relations," CLAJ 1 (Mar., 1958).

SMITH, Hugh L., Jr. [1]. "Earthy Anecdote," Expl 24
    (Dec., 1965).

_____ [2]. "Life Is Motion," Expl 19 (Apr., 1961).

SMITH, Julian. "Spring and Fall: To a Young Child,"
    Expl 27 (Jan., 1969).

SMITH, Richard Eugene. "Ezra Pound and the Haiku,"
    CE 26 (Apr., 1965).

SMITH, T. Henry. "The Day of Judgment," Expl 22 (Sept.,
    1963).

SNIPES, Katherine W. "Two in August," Expl 26 (Oct.,
    1967).

SOLOMON, Stanley J. "Tennyson's Paradoxical King.," VP
    1 (Nov., 1963).

SOLT, Mary Ellen. "William Carlos Williams: Idiom and
    Structure," MR 3 (Wint., 1962).

SONN, Carl Robinson. "Sir Guyon in the Cave of Mammon,"
    SEL 1 (Wint., 1961).

SONSTROEM, David [1]. "Animal and Vegetable in the
    Spanish Cloister," VP 6 (Spr., 1968).

_____ [2]. " 'Crossing the Bar' as Last Word," VP 8
    (Spr., 1970).

SOUTHAM, B. C. "Long-Legged Fly," Expl 22 (May, 1964).

SOUTHWORTH, James G. [1]. "The Poetry of John Ciardi,"
EJ 50 (Dec., 1961).

_____ [2]. "The Poetry of Karl Shapiro," EJ 51 (Mar.,
1962).

_____ [3]. "The Poetry of Richard Wilbur," CE 22
(Oct., 1960).

_____ [4]. "The Poetry of Theodore Roethke," CE 21
(Mar., 1960).

_____ [5]. "Theodore Roethke: The Far Field," CE 27
(Feb., 1966).

SPACKS, Patricia Meyer [1]. "Collins' Imagery," SP 62
(Oct., 1965).

_____ [2]. "Eighteenth-Century Poetry, the Teacher's
Dilemma," CE 23 (May, 1962).

_____ [3]. "Statement and Artifice in Thomas Gray,"
SEL 5 (Sum., 1965).

SPANOS, William V. [1]. "The Real Toad in the Jonsonian
Garden: Resonance in the Nondramatic Poetry," JEGP
68 (Jan., 1969).

_____ [2]. "Sacramental Imagery in the Middle and Late
Poetry of W. B. Yeats," TSLL 4 (Sum., 1962).

SPEARING, A. C. [1]. "The Development of a Theme in
Piers Plowman," RES 11 (Aug., 1960).

_____ [2]. "Symbolic and Dramatic Development in
'Pearl'," MP 60 (Aug., 1962).

_____ [3]. "Verbal Repetition in Piers Plowman B and
C," JEGP 62 (Oct., 1963).

SPENCER, Benjamin T. "Criticism: Centrifugal and
Centripetal," Criticism 8 (Spr., 1966).

SPERRY, Stuart M., Jr. "Keats, Milton and The Fall of
Hyperion," PMLA 77 (Mar., 1962).

SPITZER, Leo. "Herrick's 'Delight in Disorder'," MLN
76 (Mar., 1961).

SPIVAK, Gayatri C. " 'Principles of the Mind': Continuity in Yeats' Poetry, " MLN 83 (Dec., 1968).

SPIVEY, Edward. "The Oracles, " Expl 21 (Jan., 1963).

SQUIER, Charles L. [1]. "Anyone Lived in a Pretty How Town, " Expl 25 (Dec., 1967).

_____ [2]. "Dullness in America: A Study in Epic Badness: The Fredoniad, " AL 32 (Jan., 1961).

SQUIRES, Radcliffe. "Will and Vision: Allen Tate's Terza Rima Poems, " SR 78 (Aut., 1970).

STALLMAN, R. W. "A Recollection, " Expl 19 (Apr., 1961).

STALLWORTHY, Jon [1]. "W. B. Yeats and Wilfred Owen, " CritQ 11 (Aut., 1969).

_____ [2]. "W. B. Yeats's 'Under Ben Bulben', " RES 17 (Feb., 1966).

STANFORD, Ann. "May Swenson: The Art of Perceiving, " SoR 5 (Wint., 1969).

STANFORD, Donald E. "Classicism and the Modern Poet, " SoR 5 (Spr., 1969).

STANWOOD, Paul Grant. "St. Teresa and Joseph Beaumont's Psyche, " JEGP 62 (July, 1963).

STAPLES, Hugh B. "The Rose in the Sea-Wind: A Reading of Theodore Roethke's 'North American Sequence', " AL 36 (May, 1964).

STAPLETON, Laurence. "Perspectives of Time in Paradise Lost, " PQ 45 (Oct., 1966).

STARKMAN, Miriam K. "The Manichee in the Cloister: A Reading of Browning's 'Soliloquy of the Spanish Cloister', " MLN 75 (May, 1960).

STARR, Nathan Comfort. "Coleridge's Sacred River, " PLL 2 (Spr., 1966).

STATON, Walter F., Jr. [1]. "Italian Pastorals and the Conclusion of the Serena Story, " SEL 6 (Wint., 1966).

STATON, Walter F., Jr. [2]. "Ralegh and the Amyas-
Aemylia Episode," SEL 5 (Wint., 1965).

_____[3]. "Spenser's 'April' Lay as a Dramatic Chorus,"
SP 59 (Apr., 1962).

STAVROS, George. "An Interview with Gwendolyn Brooks,"
ConL 11 (Wint., 1970).

STEADMAN, John M. [1]. "Image and Idol: Satan and the
Element of Illusion in Paradise Lost," JEGP 59 (Oct.,
1960).

_____[2]. "Tantalus and the Dead Sea Apples (Paradise
Lost, X, 547-73)," JEGP 64 (Jan., 1965).

_____[3]. "The 'Tree of Life' Symbolism in Paradise
Regained," RES 11 (Nov., 1960).

STEESE, Peter. "A Song," Expl 21 (Dec., 1962).

STEIN, Richard L. "Dante Gabriel Rossetti: Printing and
the Problem of Poetic Form," SEL 10 (Aut., 1970).

STEIN, William Bysshe [1]. " 'After Apple-Picking':
Echoic Parody," UR 35 (June, 1969).

_____[2]. "Emily Dickinson's Parodic Masks," UR 36
(Oct., 1969).

_____[3]. "Time, History, and Religion: A Glimpse of
Melville's Late Poetry," ArQ 22 (Sum., 1966).

STEIN, William Bysshe, et al. "Brahma," Expl 20 (Dec.,
1961).

STEMPEL, Daniel. "A Reading of 'The Windhover'," CE 23
(Jan., 1962).

STEPANCHEV, Stephen. American Poetry Since 1945; a
Critical Survey. 1st ed. New York: Harper and Row,
1965.

STEVENS, L. Robert. "Aestheticism in Browning's Early
Renaissance Monologues," VP 3 (Wint., 1965).

STEVENS, Sister Mary Dominic, O.P. "That Nature Is a
Heraclitean Fire and of the Comfort of the Resurrection," Expl 22 (Nov., 1963).

STEVENSON, Warren. "Artful Irony in Blake's 'The Fly,"
TSLL 10 (Spr., 1968).

STEVICK, Robert D. "Formal Aspects of 'The Wife's Lament'," JEGP 59 (Jan., 1960).

STEWART, Jack F. "Amoretti," Expl 27 (May, 1969).

STEWART, Stanley. "Time and The Temple," SEL 6 (Wint.,
1966).

STILLINGER, Jack [1]. "The Biographical Problem of
Astrophel and Stella," JEGP 59 (Oct., 1960).

_____ [2]. "The Hoodwinking of Madeline: Scepticism in
'The Eve of St. Agnes'," SP 58 (July, 1961).

_____ [3]. "Keats and Romance," SEL 8 (Aut., 1968).

STOEHR, Taylor. "Syntax and Poetic Form in Milton's
Sonnets," ES 45 (Aug., 1964).

STOKES, Edward. "The Metrics of 'Maud'," VP 2 (Spr.,
1964).

STOREY, Mark. "Love and Beauty," Expl 28 (Mar., 1970).

STRANDBERG, Victor. "Warren's Osmosis," Criticism 10
(Wint., 1968).

STRIER, Richard. "Crashaw's Other Voice," SEL 9 (Wint.,
1969).

STRINGER, Gary. "The Unity of 'L'Allegro' and 'Il Penseroso'," TSLL 12 (Sum., 1970).

STROUD, T. A. "Animula," Expl 28 (Oct., 1969).

STUCKEY, William J. "The Love Song of J. Alfred Prufrock," Expl 20 (Sept., 1961).

STURTEVANT, Peter A. "Troilus and Criseyde, III," Expl
28 (Sept., 1969).

SULLIVAN, Harry R. "MacLeish's 'Ars Poetica'," EJ 56
(Dec., 1967).

SULLIVAN, Mary Rose. "The Function of Book I in The

Ring and the Book," VP 6 (Aut.-Wint., 1968).

SULLIVAN, Ruth Elizabeth. "Browning's 'Childe Roland'
    and Dante's 'Inferno'," VP 5 (Wint., 1967).

SUMMERS, Joseph H. [1]. "The Achievement of Edwin
    Muir," MR 2 (Wint., 1961).

_____ [2]. "The Two Great Sexes in Paradise Lost,"
    SEL 2 (Wint., 1962).

SUNDELL, Michael G. [1]. "The Development of The Giaour,"
    SEL 9 (Aut., 1969).

_____ [2]. "The Intellectual Background and Structure of
    Arnold's Tristram and Iseult," VP 1 (Nov., 1963).

_____ [3]. "Story and Context in 'The Strayed Reveller',"
    VP 3 (Sum., 1965).

_____ [4]. " 'Tintern Abbey' and 'Resignation'," VP 5
    (Wint., 1967).

SUTHERLAND, James R. "A Note on the Satirical Poetry
    of Andrew Marvell," PQ 45 (Jan., 1966).

SUTTON, Max Keith. "Language as Defense in 'Porphyria's
    Lover'," CE 31 (Dec., 1969).

SUTTON, Walter. "Dr. Williams' 'Paterson' and the Quest
    for Form," Criticism 2 (Sum., 1960).

SVAGLIC, Martin J. [1]. "Browning's Grammarian: Ap-
    parent Failure or Real?" VP 5 (Sum., 1967).

_____ [2]. "A Framework for Tennyson's In Memoriam,"
    JEGP 61 (Oct., 1962).

SWANSON, Donald R. "The Conqueror Worm," Expl 19 (Apr.,
    1961).

SWANSON, Roy Arthur. "Form and Content in Keats's 'Ode
    on a Grecian Urn'," CE 23 (Jan., 1962).

SWANTON, Michael J. "The Battle of Maldon: a Literary
    Caveat," JEGP 67 (July, 1968).

SWENNES, Robert H. "Man and Wife: The Dialogue of

Contraries in Robert Frost's Poetry," AL 42 (Nov., 1970).

SWETNAM, Ford T., Jr. "Witness to Death," Expl 25 (Mar., 1967).

SWINDEN, Patrick. "Old Lines, New Lines: The Movement Ten Years After," CritQ 9 (Wint., 1967).

SWINGLE, L. J. "Truth and The Ring and the Book: A Negative View," VP 6 (Aut.-Wint., 1968).

SYFRET, R. H. "Marvell's 'Horatian Ode'," RES 12 (May, 1961).

SYLVESTER, Bickford. "Natural Mutability and Human Responsibility: Form in Shakespeare's Lucrece," CE 26 (Apr., 1965).

TAAFFE, James G. "Circle Imagery in Tennyson's 'In Memoriam'," VP 1 (Apr., 1963).

TAGLICHT, Josef. "Beowulf and Old English Verse Rhythm," RES 12 (Nov., 1961).

TALON, Henri A. "The Ring and the Book, Truth and Fiction in Character-Painting," VP 6 (Aut.-Wint., 1968).

TANNENBAUM, Earl. "Pattern in Whitman's 'Song of Myself': A Summary and a Supplement," CLAJ 6 (Sept., 1962).

TANNER, Tony. "Reason and the Grotesque: Pope's 'Dunciad'," CritQ 7 (Sum., 1965).

TANSELLE, G. Thomas. "Serinade," Expl 23 (Feb., 1965).

TARGAN, Barry. "Irony in John Skelton's Philip Sparrow," UR 32 (Oct., 1965).

TATE, Allen [1]. "The Poetry of Edgar Allan Poe," SR 76 (Spr., 1968).

_____ [2]. (ed.) "T. S. Eliot (1888-1965)," SR 74 (Wint., 1966). [Entire issue.]

TATE, Eleanor. "Milton's 'L'Allegro' and 'Il Penseroso'--
    Balance, Progression or Dichotomy?" MLN 76 (Nov.,
    1961).

TAUBE, Myron. "An Acre of Grass," Expl 26 (Jan., 1968).

TAYLOR, Michael. "God's Grandeur," Expl 25 (Apr.,
    1967).

TAYLOR, Paul Beckman. "Heofon Riece Swealq: A Sign of
    Beowulf's State of Grace," PQ 42 (Apr., 1963).

TEICH, Nathaniel. "Criticism and Keats's Grecian Urn,"
    PQ 44 (Oct., 1965).

TEMPLEMAN, William Darby [1]. "A Consideration of the
    Fame of 'Locksley Hall'," VP 1 (Apr., 1963).

_____ [2]. "Ruskin's Ploughshare and Hopkins' 'The
    Windhover'," ES 43 (Apr., 1962).

TENFELDE, Nancy L. "Chaucer," Expl 22 (Mar.,1964).

THATCHER, David S. "The Convergence of the Twain,"
    Expl 29 (Dec., 1970).

THERESE, Sister, S.N.D. "The Glass of Water," Expl 21
    (Mar., 1963).

THOMAS, J. D. "The Windhover," Expl 20 (Dec., 1961).

THOMAS, J. L. "Drama and Doctrine in God's Determina-
    tions," AL 36 (Jan., 1965).

THOMAS, W. K. [1]. "Absalom and Achitophel," Expl 27
    (May, 1969).

_____ [2]. "Leave Me, O Love, Which Reachest But to
    Dust," Expl 28 (Jan., 1970).

_____ [3]. "The Matrix of Absalom and Achitophel," PQ
    49 (Jan., 1970).

_____ [4]. "To Sleep," Expl 26 (Mar., 1968).

_____ [5]. "Tam O'Shanter," Expl 28 (Dec., 1969).

THOMPSON, Gordon W. "Authorial Detachment and Imagery

in The Ring and the Book, " SEL 10 (Aut., 1970).

THOMPSON, Leslie M. [1]. "Biblical Influence in 'Childe Roland to the Dark Tower Came'," PLL 3 (Fall, 1967).

_____ [2]. "Regular and Irregular Deeds in The Ring and the Book," PLL 3 (Wint., 1967).

_____ [3]. "A Ring of Criticism: The Search for Truth in The Ring and the Book," PLL 5 (Sum., 1969).

THOMPSON, William I. "Collapsed Universe and Structured Poem: Essay in Whiteheadian Criticism," CE 28 (Oct., 1966).

THORNBURG, Thomas. "Mundus et Infans," Expl 27 (Jan., 1969).

THORNTON, Weldon. "Out, Out," Expl 25 (May, 1967).

THORPE, James. "Love (III)," Expl 24 (Oct., 1965).

THUMBOO, Edwin. "The Bracelet," Expl 27 (Oct., 1968).

TILLYARD, E. M. W. [1]. "On Annotating Paradise Lost, Books IX and X," JEGP 60 (Oct., 1961).

_____ [2]. Poetry and Its Background; Illustrated by Five Poems, 1470-1870. London: Chatto and Windus, 1970.

TILLOTSON, Geoffrey [1]. "A Word for Browning," SR 72 (Sum., 1964).

_____ [2]. "Wordsworth," SR 74 (Spr., 1966).

TIMKO, Michael [1]. "Ah, Did You Once See Browning Plain?" SEL 6 (Aut., 1966).

_____ [2]. "Browning Upon Butler: or, Natural Theology in the English Isle," Criticism 7 (Spr., 1965).

_____ [3]. "The Satiric Poetry of Arthur Hugh Clough," VP 1 (Apr., 1963).

TODASCO, Ruth. "Dramatic Characterization in Frost, A Masque of Reason," UR 29 (Mar., 1963).

TOLIVER, Harold E. [1]. "Pastoral Form and Idea in Some

Poems of Marvell," TSLL 5 (Spr., 1963).

TOLIVER, Harold E. [2]. "The Strategy of Marvell's Re-
solve Against Created Pleasure," SEL 4 (Wint., 1964).

TOLLEY, A. T. "Rhetoric and the Moderns," SoR 6 (Spr.,
1970).

TOMPKINS, J. M. S. "Meredith's Periander," RES 11
(Aug., 1960).

TOOLE, William B., III. "At the Slackening of the Tide,"
Expl 22 (Dec., 1963).

TOOR, David. "Spring Pools," Expl 28 (Nov., 1969).

TORCHIANA, Donald T. "Brutus: Pope's Last Hero,"
JEGP 61 (Oct., 1962).

TOWERS, Tom H. "The Lineage of Shadwell: An Approach
to 'Mac Flecknoe'," SEL 3 (Sum., 1963).

TREMAINE, Hadley P. "Beowulf Ecg Brun and Other Rusty
Relics," PQ 48 (Apr., 1969).

TRITSCHLER, Donald. "The Metamorphic Stop of Time in
'A Winter's Tale'," PMLA 78 (Sept., 1963).

TRUSS, Tom J., Jr. "Shakespeare," Expl 19 (May, 1961).

TUGWELL, Simon [1]. "The Crickets Sang," Expl 23
(Feb., 1965).

_____ [2]. "The Soul Selects Her Own Society," Expl 27
(Jan., 1969).

TUNG, Mason. "The Abdiel Episode: A Contextual Reading," SP 62 (July, 1965).

TURNER, C. Steven. "In Just," Expl 24 (Oct., 1965).

TURNER, Paul [1]. "The Parable of the Idiot Boy," ES 41
(Dec., 1960).

_____ [2]. "Some Ancient Light on Tennyson's Oenone,"
JEGP 61 (Jan., 1962).

TURNER, Steven. "Richard Cory," Expl 28 (May, 1970).

TWOMBLY, Robert G. [1]. "Beauty and the (Subverted) Beast; Wyatt's 'They Fle From Me'," TSLL 10 (Wint., 1969).

_____ [2]. "Thomas Wyatt's Paraphrase of the Penitential Psalms of David," TSLL 12 (Fall, 1970).

TYNER, R. E. "To M. Denham, on His Prospective Poem," Expl 23 (May, 1965).

UHLMAN, Thompson. "Death of Little Boys," Expl 28 (Mar., 1970).

UNGER, Leonard [1] (ed.). Seven Modern American Poets; an Introduction. Minneapolis: University of Minnesota, 1967.

_____ [2]. "T. S. Eliot's Images of Awareness," SR 74 (Wint., 1966).

_____ [3]. "Yeats and 'Hamlet'," SoR 6 (Sum., 1970).

UNTERECKER, John. "The Bridge Explained," SR 69 (Spr., 1961).

VANDIVER, Edward P. "Tears, Idle Tears," Expl 21 (Mar., 1963).

VAN DUYN, Mona. "Ways to Meaning," Poetry 100 (Sept., 1962).

VASTA, Edward [1]. "Pearl: Immortal Flowers and the Pearl's Decay," JEGP 66 (Oct., 1967).

_____ [2]. "Truth, the Best Treasure, in Piers Plowman," PQ 44 (Jan., 1965).

VENDLER, Helen Hennessy. "Stevens' 'Like Decorations in a Nigger Cemetery'," MR 7 (Wint., 1966).

VIETH, David M. [1]. "The Dunciad, IV," Expl 25 (Dec., 1966).

_____ [2]. "Irony in Dryden's Ode to Anne Killigrew," SP 62 (Jan., 1965).

VIETH, David M. [3]. "Pope's Dunciad, I, 203-4, and Christ Among the Elders," PLL 2 (Wint., 1966).

VISWANATHAN, S. [1]. " 'Ay, Note that Potter's Wheel': Browning and 'That Metaphor'," VP 7 (Wint., 1969).

_____ [2]. "The Faerie Queene, Book I, Canto I, Stanza V," Expl 27 (Feb., 1969).

VOGEL, Joseph F. [1]. "Death's Songsters," Expl 21 (Apr., 1963).

_____ [2]. "Memorial Thresholds," Expl 23 (Dec., 1964).

VOGLER, Thomas A. "A New View of Hart Crane's Bridge," SR 73 (Sum., 1965).

WADDINGTON, Raymond B. "Appearance and Reality in Satan's Disguises," TSLL 4 (Aut., 1962).

WADSWORTH, Randolph, Jr. "Comment and Rebuttal," CE 31 (Mar., 1970).

WAGENER, W. Yeaton. "305," Expl 21 (Oct., 1962).

WAGNER, Linda Welshimer [1]. "The Last Poems of William Carlos Williams," Criticism 6 (Fall, 1964).

_____ [2]. "Metaphor and William Carlos Williams," UR 31 (Oct., 1964).

_____ [3]. "William Carlos Williams: Giant," CE 25 (Mar., 1964).

WAGNER, Selma. "A Fence," Expl 27 (Feb., 1969).

WAIN, John [1]. "Engagement or Withdrawal?: Some Notes on the Work of Philip Larkin," CritQ 6 (Sum., 1964).

_____ [2] (ed.). Interpretations; Essays on Twelve English Poems. London, Routledge and K. Paul, 1965.

_____ [3]. "The Poetry of Thomas Hardy," CritQ 8 (Sum., 1966).

_____ [4]. "Theodore Roethke," CritQ 6 (Wint., 1964).

WAINGROW, Marshall. " 'Verses on the Death of Dr. Swift', "
SEL 5 (Sum., 1965).

WALCUTT, Charles C. [1]. "Among School Children, V, "
Expl 26 (May, 1968).

_____ [2]. "The Garden, " Expl 24 (Jan., 1966).

WALDHORN, Arthur. "Walt Whitman's 'Leaves of Grass', "
CritQ 8 (Wint., 1966).

WALKER, Warren S. "Burnes's Influence on Sohrab and
Rustum: A Closer Look, " VP 8 (Sum., 1970).

WALLACE, John M. "Marvell's Horatian Ode, " PMLA 77
(Mar., 1962).

WALLER, John O. "Doctor Arnold's Sermons and Matthew
Arnold's 'Rugby Chapel', " SEL 9 (Aut., 1969).

WALSH, Robert C. "Anyone Lived in a Pretty How Town, "
Expl 22 (May, 1964).

WALTON, James. "Tennyson's Patrimony: From 'The
Outcast' to 'Maud', " TSLL 11 (Spr., 1969).

WANNIGER, Mary Tenney. "Batter My Heart, Three
Person'd God, " Expl 28 (Dec., 1969).

WARD, J. A. " 'The Wife's Lament': An Interpretation, "
JEGP 59 (Jan., 1960).

WARD, William S. "Lifted Pot Lids and Unmended Walls, "
CE 27 (Feb., 1966).

WARE, Malcolm. "The Rime of the Ancient Mariner: A
Discourse on Prayer?" RES 11 (Aug., 1960).

WARLOW, Francis W. "To a Snail, " Expl 26 (Feb., 1968).

WARNKE, Frank J. "Play and Metamorphosis in Marvell's
Poetry, " SEL 5 (Wint., 1965).

WARREN, Leland E. "Wordsworth's Conception of Man: A
Study in Apocalyptic Vision, " SHR 4 (Spr., 1970).

WARREN, Robert Penn. "Melville's Poems, " SoR 3 (Aut.,
1967).

WASSERMAN, Earl R.   "The Limits of Allusion in The Rape
    of the Lock," JEGP 65 (July, 1966).

WASSERMAN, George R. [1].   "The Hind and the Panther,"
    Expl 24 (Apr., 1966).

_____ [2].   "The Indian Burying Ground," Expl 20 (Jan.,
    1962).

_____ [3].   "Johannes Agricola in Meditation," Expl 24
    (Mar., 1966).

WATERS, D. Douglas [1].   " 'Mistress Missa,' Duessa, and
    the Anagogical Allegory of The Faerie Queene, Book I,"
    PLL 4 (Sum., 1968).

_____ [2].   "Prince Arthur as Christian Magnanimity in
    Book One of The Faerie Queene," SEL 9 (Wint., 1969).

WATERS, Leonard A.   "Stanzas Written in Dejection: Near
    Naples," Expl 18 (June, 1960).

WATKINS, Charlotte Crawford. "Browning's 'Red Cotton
    Night-Cap Country' and Carlyle," VS 7 (June, 1964).

WATKINS, Floyd C.   "T. S. Eliot's Painter of the Umbrian
    School," AL 36 (Mar., 1964).

WATKINS, Vernon.   "W. B. Yeats--The Religious Poet,"
    TSLL 3 (Wint., 1962).

WATSON, J. R.   "Edwin Muir and the Problem of Evil,"
    CritQ 6 (Aut., 1964).

WATSON, Melvin R.   "The Redemption of Peter Bell,"
    SEL 4 (Aut., 1964).

WATSON, Thomas L.   "God's Grandeur," Expl 22 (Feb.,
    1964).

WEATHERBY, H. L. [1].   "Two Medievalists: Lewis and
    Eliot on Christianity and Literature," SR 78 (Spr.,
    1970).

_____ [2].   "The Way of Exchange in James Dickey's
    Poetry," SR 74 (Sum., 1966).

WEATHERHEAD, A. Kingsley.   "Imagination and Fancy:

Robert Lowell and Marianne Moore," TSLL 6 (Sum.,
1964).

WEATHERS, Winston. "Christiana Rossetti: A Sisterhood
of Self," VP 3 (Spr., 1965).

WEBB, Howard. "The Deacon's Masterpiece," Expl 24
(Oct., 1965).

WEBB, Timothy [1]. "Coleridge and Shelley's Alastor: A
Reply," RES 18 (Nov., 1967).

_____[2]. "Shelley's 'Hymn to Venus': A New Text,"
RES 21 (Aug., 1970).

WEGELIN, Christof [1]. "A Man Said to the Universe,"
Expl 20 (Sept., 1961).

_____ [2]. "Wild Nights," Expl 26 (Nov., 1967).

WEINBERG, Gail S. "Upon Julia's Clothes," Expl 27 (Oct.,
1968).

WELCHER, Jeanne K. "The Opening of Religio Laici and
Its Virgilian Associations," SEL 8 (Sum., 1968).

WELLINGTON, James E. "Pope and Charity," PQ 46 (Apr.,
1967).

WENGER, A. Grace. "The Four Zoas; Night the Ninth,"
Expl 27 (Mar., 1969).

WENZEL, Siegfried. "Chaucer's Troilus of Book IV."
PMLA 79 (Dec., 1964).

WERKMEISTER, Lucyle. "Some Whys and Wherefores of
Coleridge's 'Lines Composed in a Concert-Room'," MP
60 (Feb., 1963).

WESLING, Donald. "Eschatology and the Language of Satire
in Piers Plowman," Criticism 10 (Fall, 1968).

WESTON, John C. "The Narrator of Tam O'Shanter,"
SEL 8 (Sum., 1968).

WHEATCROFT, J. S. "Emily Dickinson's White Robes,"
Criticism 5 (Spr., 1963).

WHEELER, Thomas [1].   "Milton's Blank Verse Couplets,"
    JEGP 66 (July, 1967).

_____ [2].   "Milton's Twenty-Third Sonnet," SP 58 (July,
    1961).

WHICHER, Stephen.   "Elysium Is as Far as To," Expl 19
    (Apr., 1961).

WHITBREAD, Thomas.   "Wallace Stevens' 'Highest Candle',"
    TSLL 4 (Wint., 1963).

WHITE, Gertrude M.   "Hopkins' 'God's Grandeur': A
    Poetic Statement of Christian Doctrine," VP 4 (Aut.,
    1966).

WHITE, James E.   "I," Expl 21 (Sept., 1962).

WHITE, Norman E.   " 'Hearse' in Hopkins' 'Spelt from
    Sibyls' Leaves'," ES 49 (Dec., 1968).

WHITE, Robert.   "The Love Song of J. Alfred Prufrock,"
    Expl 20 (Nov., 1961).

WHITE, Robert L. [1].   "Brahma," Expl 21 (Apr., 1963).

_____ [2].   "Sonnet 73 Again: A Rebuttal and New Read-
    ing," CLAJ 6 (Dec., 1962).

WHITTLE, Ambreys R.   "The Dust of Seasons: Time in the
    Poetry of Trumbull Stickney," SR 74 (Aut., 1966).

WIEHE, R. E.   "Summoned by Nostalgia: John Betjeman's
    Poetry," ArQ 19 (Spr., 1963).

WIERSMA, Stanley M.   "To John Donne," Expl 25 (Sept.,
    1966).

WIGHT, John.   "A Source of A. E. Housman's 'The Land of
    Biscay'," VP 8 (Wint., 1970).

WILCOX, Earl.   "Stopping by Woods on a Snowy Evening,"
    Expl 27 (Sept., 1968).

WILD, Paul H.   "Hearing Poetry: W. S. Merwin's 'Levia-
    than'," EJ 56 (Oct., 1967).

WILDI, Max.   "Wordsworth and the Simplon Pass, II," ES

43 (Oct., 1962).

WILKENFELD, Roger B. [1]. "The Argument of 'The Scholar-Gipsy'," VP 7 (Sum., 1969).

_____ [2]. "The Shape of Two Voices," VP 4 (Sum., 1966).

WILKINS, Frederick C. "Ode on a Distant Prospect of Eton College," Expl 25 (Apr., 1967).

WILLARD, Rudolph and Elinor D. CLEMONS. "Bliss's Light Verses in the Beowulf," JEGP 66 (Apr., 1967).

WILLIAMS, Aubrey. "The 'Fall' of China and The Rape of the Lock," PQ 41 (Apr., 1962).

WILLIAMS, David. "The Point of 'Patience'," MP 68 (Nov., 1970).

WILLIAMS, J. M. "A Possible Source for Spenser's Labryde," MLN 76 (June, 1961).

WILLIAMS, Kathleen. "Courtesy and Pastoral in The Faerie Queene, Book VI," RES 13 (Nov., 1962).

WILLIAMS, Paul O. [1]. "Kind)," Expl 23 (Sept., 1964).

_____ [2]. "One Day Is There of the Series," Expl 23 (Dec., 1964).

WILLIAMS, Porter, Jr. "On Sitting Down to Read King Lear Once Again," Expl 29 (Nov., 1970).

WILLIAMS, R. Darby. "Two Baroque Game Poems on Grace: Herbert's 'Paradise' and Milton's 'On Time'," Criticism 12 (Sum., 1970).

WILLIAMSON, C. F. "The Design of Daniel's Delia," RES 19 (Aug., 1968).

WILLIAMSON, George [1]. "The Context of Marvell's 'Hortus' and 'Garden'," MLN 76 (Nov., 1961).

_____ [2]. "The Design of Donne's 'Anniversaries'," MP 60 (Feb., 1963).

WILLOUGHBY, John W. [1]. "Browning's 'Childe Roland to the Dark Tower Came'," VP 1 (Nov., 1963).

_____ [2]. "Johannes Agricola in Meditation," Expl 21 (Sept., 1962).

WILSON, A. J. N. " 'An Horation Ode Upon Cromwell's Return from Ireland': The Thread of the Poem and Its Use of Classical Allusion," CritQ 11 (Wint., 1969).

WILSON, F. A. C. "Parnell's Funeral," Expl 27 (May, 1969).

WILSON, Gayle Edward. "Jonson's Use of the Bible and the Great Chain of Being in 'To Penshurst'," SEL 8 (Wint., 1968).

WILSON, G. R., Jr. "The Interplay of Perception and Reflection: Mirror Imagery in Donne's Poetry," SEL 9 (Wint., 1969).

WILSON, Suzanne M. [1]. "Emily Dickinson and Twentieth-Century Poetry of Sensibility," AL 36 (Nov., 1964).

_____ [2]. "Structural Patterns in the Poetry of Emily Dickinson," AL 35 (Mar., 1963).

WIMSATT, William Kurtz. (ed.). Explication as Criticism: Selected Papers from the English Institute, 1941-1952. New York: Columbia University Press, 1963.

WINE, M. L. "Spenser's 'Sweet Themmes' of Time and the River," SEL 2 (Wint., 1962).

WINTER, J. L. "Notes on 'The Windhover'," VP 4 (Sum., 1966).

WINTERS, Yvor [1]. "The Poetry of Charles Churchill," Poetry 98; Pt. I (Apr., 1961); Pt. II (May, 1961).

_____ [2]. "The Poetry of T. Sturge Moore," SoR 2 (Wint., 1966).

WITEMEYER, Hugh H. " 'Line' and 'Round' in Emerson's 'Uriel'," PMLA 82 (Mar., 1967).

WITHERINGTON, Paul. " 'Faith' Is a Fine Invention," Expl

26 (Apr., 1968).

WITTREICH, Joseph Anthony, Jr. [1]. "The Little Girl
Lost," Expl 27 (Apr., 1969).

_____ [2]. "Milton's Destin'd Urn: The Art of Lycidas,"
PMLA 84 (Jan., 1969).

WOLFE, Jane E. "George Herbert's 'Assurance'," CLAJ 5
(Mar., 1962).

WOLFE, Patricia. "The Paradox of Self: A Study of Hopkins' Spiritual Conflict in the 'Terrible' Sonnets," VP
6 (Sum., 1968).

WOODBERY, Potter. "T. S. Eliot's Metropolitan World,"
ArQ 22 (Spr., 1966).

WOODS, Samuel H., Jr. " 'Philomela': John Crowe Ransom's Ars Poetica," CE 27 (Feb., 1966).

WOODWARD, Daniel H. "Herrick's Oberon Poems," JEGP
64 (Apr., 1965).

WOOTON, Carl [1]. "The Mass: 'Ash-Wednesday's' Objec-
tive Correlative," ArQ 17 (Spr., 1961).

_____ [2]. "The Terrible Fire of Gerard Manley Hopkins," TSLL 4 (Aut., 1962).

WORDSWORTH, Jonathan. "The New Wordsworth Poem," CE
27 (Mar., 1966).

WRIGHT, Elizabeth. "The Tree in Pamela's Garden," Expl
21 (Feb., 1963).

WRIGHT, James. "A Poetry Chronicle," Poetry 95 (Mar.,
1960).

WYANT, Jerome L. "The Legal Episodes in The Ring and
the Book," VP 6 (Aut.-Wint., 1968).

YANNELLA, Philip R. "Toward Apotheosis: Hart Crane's
Visionary Lyrics," Criticism 10 (Fall, 1968).

YEOMANS, W. E. "T. S.Eliot, Ragtime, and the Blues,"
UR 34 (June, 1968).

YOST, George, Jr. "The Poetic Drive in the Early Keats,"
    TSLL 5 (Wint., 1964).

ZIEGELMAIER, Gregory. "The Comedy of Paradise Lost,"
    CE 26 (Apr., 1965).

ZIETLOW, Paul. "The Tentative Mode of Hardy's Poems,"
    VP 5 (Sum., 1967).

ZIGERELL, James [1]. "Dead Leaf in May," Expl 25 (Sept.,
    1966).

_____ [2]. "When All My Five and Country Senses See,"
    Expl 19 (Nov., 1960).

ZIMMERMAN, Michael [1]. "The Pursuit of Pleasure and the
    Uses of Death; Wallace Stevens' 'Sunday Morning',"
    UR 33 (Dec., 1966).

_____ [2]. "War and Peace: Longfellow's 'The Occulta-
    tion of Orion'," AL 38 (Jan., 1967).

ZIVLEY, Sherry. "Imagery in John Donne's Satyres," SEL
    6 (Wint., 1966).

ZWICKY, Laurie. "The Definition of Love," Expl 22 (Mar.,
    1964).

BIBLIOGRAPHY

Books

Allen, Don Cameron. Four Poets on Poetry. Baltimore: Johns Hopkins Press, 1967.

_____. Image and Meaning; Metaphoric Traditions in Renaissance Poetry. New enl. ed. Baltimore: Johns Hopkins Press, 1968.

_____. The Moment of Poetry. Baltimore: Johns Hopkins Press, 1962.

Alpers, Paul J. (comp.). Elizabethan Poetry; Modern Essays in Criticism. New York: Oxford University Press, 1967.

Bader, Arno Lehman. (ed.). To the Young Writer. Hopwood Lectures. Second Series. Ann Arbor: University of Michigan Press, 1965.

Bailey, John Cann. Continuity of Letters. Freeport, New York: Books for Libraries Press, 1967.

Barnes, T. R. English Verse: Voice and Movement from Wyatt to Yeats. Cambridge: Cambridge University Press, 1967.

Battenhouse, Henry Martin. Poets of Christian Thought; Evaluations from Dante to T. S. Eliot. New York: Ronald Press Co., 1947.

Bergonzi, Bernard. Heroes' Twilight; a Study of the Literature of the Great War. New York: Coward-McCann, 1965.

Berry, Francis. Poetry and the Physical Voice. New York: Oxford University Press, 1962.

267

Bigsby, C. W. E. (comp.).   The Black American Writer.
    Deland, Fla.: Everett Edwards, 1969. [Vol. 2,
    Poetry and Drama.]

Bogan, Louise.   Selected Criticism: Prose, Poetry.   New
    York: Noonday Press, 1955.

Brenner, Rica.   Ten Modern Poets.   Freeport, New York:
    Books for Libraries Press, 1968.

Brett, R. L.   Reason and Imagination; a Study of Form and
    Meaning in Four Poems.   London: Published for the
    University of Hull by Oxford University Press, 1960.

Cambon, Glauco.   Recent American Poetry.   Minneapolis:
    University of Minnesota Press, 1962.

DeSelincourt, Ernest.   Oxford Lectures on Poetry.   Freeport,
    New York: Books for Libraries Press, 1967.

Drew, Elizabeth A. and George Connor.   Discovering Modern
    Poetry.   New York: Holt, Rinehart and Winston, 1961.

Eagleton, Terence.   Exiles and Emigres; Studies in Modern
    Literature.   New York: Schocken Books, 1970.

Foxell, Nigel.   Ten Poems Analyzed.   1st ed.   Oxford:
    Pergamon, 1966.

Gross, Seymour Lee and John Edward Hard. (eds.).   Images
    of the Negro in American Literature.   Chicago: Uni-
    versity of Chicago Press, 1966.

Hardy, John Edward.   The Curious Frame; Seven Poems in
    Text and Context.   Notre Dame, Ind.: University of
    Notre Dame Press, 1962.

Howard, Richard.   Alone with America; Essays on the Art
    of Poetry in the United States Since 1950.   New York:
    Atheneum, 1969.

Langford, Richard E. and William E. Taylor. (eds.).   The
    Twenties; Poetry and Prose; 20 Critical Essays.
    Deland, Fla.: Everett Edwards, 1966.

Lenhart, Charmenz S.   Musical Influence on American Poetry.
    Athens: University of Georgia Press, 1956.

Martz, Louis Lohr. The Poem of the Mind; Essays on
    Poetry, English and American. New York: Oxford
    University Press, 1966.

Ostroff, Anthony. The Contemporary Poet as Artist and
    Critic; Eight Symposia. Boston: Little, Brown, 1964.

Previte-Orton, Charles William. Political Satire in English
    Poetry. New York: Haskell House, 1966.

Rosenthal, Macha Louis. The New Poets; American and
    British Poetry Since World War II. New York: Oxford
    University Press, 1967.

Stepanchev, Stephen. American Poetry Since 1945; a Critical
    Survey. 1st ed. New York: Harper and Row, 1965.

Tillyard, Eustace Mandeville Wetenhall. Poetry and Its Back-
    ground, Illustrated by Five Poems, 1470-1870. London:
    Chatto and Windus, 1970.

Unger, Leonard. (ed.). Seven Modern American Poets; an
    Introduction. Minneapolis: University of Minnesota
    Press, 1967.

Wain, John. (ed.). Interpretations: Essays on Twelve
    English Poems. London: Routledge and K. Paul, 1965.

Wimsatt, William Kurtz. (ed.). Explication as Criticism;
    Selected Papers from the English Institute, 1941-1952.
    New York: Columbia University Press, 1963.

                            Periodicals

American Literature; vols. 32-42. 1960-70.

Antioch Review; vols.20-30, 1960-70.

Arizona Quarterly; vols. 16-26, 1960-70.

CLA Journal, vols. 1-14, 1957-70.

College English; vols. 21-32, 1960-70.

Critical Quarterly; vols. 1-12, 1959-70.

Criticism; vols. 1-12, 1959-70.

English Journal; vols. 49-59, 1960-70.

English Studies; vols. 41-51, 1960-70.

Explicator; vols. 18-29, 1960-70.

Hudson Review; vols. 13-23, 1960-70.

Journal of English and Germanic Philology; vols. 59-69, 1960-70.

Kenyon Review; vols. 22-32, 1960-70.

MLN (Modern Language Notes); vols. 75-85, 1960-70.

Massachusetts Review; vols. 1-11, 1959-70.

Modern Philology; vols. 57-68; 1960-70.

PMLA; vols. 75-85, 1960-70.

Papers on Language and Literature; vols. 1-6, 1965-70.

Philological Quarterly; vols. 39-49, 1960-70.

Poetry; vols. 95-117, 1960-70.

Review of English Studies (new series); vols. 11-21, 1960-70.

Sewanee Review; vols. 68-78, 1960-70.

Southern Humanities Review; vols. 1-4, 1967-70.

Southern Review (new series); vols. 1-6, 1965-70.

Studies in English Literature 1500-1900; vols. 1-10, 1961-70.

Studies in Philology; vols. 57-67, 1960-70.

Texas Studies in Literature and Language; vols. 1-12, 1959-70.

University Review; vols. 26-37, 1960-70.

Victorian Poetry; vols. 1-8, 1963-70.

Victorian Studies; vols. 3-14, 1960-70.

AN INDEX TO POEM TITLES